SPECIAL
PURPOSE
ROOMS

TIME
LIFE BOOKS ®

Other Publications:

THE EPIC OF FLIGHT
THE GOOD COOK
THE SEAFARERS
THE ENCYCLOPEDIA OF COLLECTIBLES
THE GREAT CITIES
WORLD WAR II
THE WORLD'S WILD PLACES
THE TIME-LIFE LIBRARY OF BOATING
HUMAN BEHAVIOR
THE ART OF SEWING
THE OLD WEST
THE EMERGENCE OF MAN
THE AMERICAN WILDERNESS
THE TIME-LIFE ENCYCLOPEDIA OF GARDENING
LIFE LIBRARY OF PHOTOGRAPHY
THIS FABULOUS CENTURY
FOODS OF THE WORLD
TIME-LIFE LIBRARY OF AMERICA
TIME-LIFE LIBRARY OF ART
GREAT AGES OF MAN
LIFE SCIENCE LIBRARY
THE LIFE HISTORY OF THE UNITED STATES
TIME READING PROGRAM
LIFE NATURE LIBRARY
LIFE WORLD LIBRARY
FAMILY LIBRARY:
   HOW THINGS WORK IN YOUR HOME
   THE TIME-LIFE BOOK OF THE FAMILY CAR
   THE TIME-LIFE FAMILY LEGAL GUIDE
   THE TIME-LIFE BOOK OF FAMILY FINANCE

HOME REPAIR
AND IMPROVEMENT

SPECIAL PURPOSE ROOMS

BY THE EDITORS OF
TIME-LIFE BOOKS

TIME-LIFE BOOKS
ALEXANDRIA, VIRGINIA

Time-Life Books Inc.
is a wholly owned subsidiary of
TIME INCORPORATED

Founder	Henry R. Luce 1898-1967

Editor-in-Chief	Henry Anatole Grunwald
President	J. Richard Munro
Chairman of the Board	Ralph P. Davidson
Executive Vice President	Clifford J. Grum
Editorial Director	Ralph Graves
Vice Chairman	Arthur Temple

TIME-LIFE BOOKS INC.

Managing Editor	Jerry Korn
Executive Editor	David Maness
Assistant Managing Editors	Dale M. Brown (planning), George Constable, Thomas H. Flaherty Jr. (acting), Martin Mann, John Paul Porter
Art Director	Tom Suzuki
Chief of Research	David L. Harrison
Director of Photography	Robert G. Mason
Assistant Art Director	Arnold C. Holeywell
Assistant Chief of Research	Carolyn L. Sackett
Assistant Director of Photography	Dolores A. Littles

Chairman	Joan D. Manley
President	John D. McSweeney
Executive Vice Presidents	Carl G. Jaeger, John Steven Maxwell, David J. Walsh
Vice Presidents	George Artandi (comptroller); Stephen L. Bair (legal counsel); Peter G. Barnes; Nicholas Benton (public relations); John L. Canova; Beatrice T. Dobie (personnel); Carol Flaumenhaft (consumer affairs); James L. Mercer (Europe/South Pacific); Herbert Sorkin (production); Paul R. Stewart (marketing)

HOME REPAIR AND IMPROVEMENT

Editorial Staff for Special Purpose Rooms

Editor	Robert M. Jones
Assistant Editors	Betsy Frankel, Peter Pocock, Brooke Stoddard
Designer	Edward Frank
Picture Editor	Adrian Allen
Associate Designer	Kenneth E. Hancock
Text Editors	Lynn R. Addison, Robert A. Doyle, Steven J. Forbis, Leslie Marshall
Staff Writers	Patricia C. Bangs, Jan Leslie Cook, Carol J. Corner, Kathleen M. Kiely, Victoria W. Monks, Ania Savage, Mary-Sherman Willis, William Worsley
Researcher	Kimberly K. Lewis
Art Associates	George Bell, Fred Holz, Lorraine D. Rivard
Editorial Assistant	Susan Larson

Editorial Production

Production Editor	Douglas B. Graham
Operations Manager	Gennaro C. Esposito, Gordon E. Buck (assistant)
Assistant Production Editor	Feliciano Madrid
Quality Control	Robert L. Young (director), James J. Cox (assistant), Daniel J. McSweeney, Michael G. Wight (associates)
Art Coordinator	Anne B. Landry
Copy Staff	Susan B. Galloway (chief), Diane Ullius Jarrett, Celia Beattie
Picture Department	Betsy Donahue, Greg Schaler
Traffic	Jeanne Potter

Correspondents: Elisabeth Kraemer (Bonn); Margot Hapgood, Dorothy Bacon, Lesley Coleman (London); Susan Jonas, Lucy T. Voulgaris (New York); Maria Vincenza Aloisi, Josephine du Brusle (Paris); Ann Natanson (Rome). Valuable assistance was also provided by: Karin B. Pearce (London); Carolyn T. Chubet, Miriam Hsia, Christina Lieberman (New York); Mimi Murphy (Rome).

THE CONSULTANTS: Roswell W. Ard is a consulting structural engineer and a professional home inspector in northern Michigan. He has written professionally on the structural uses of wood and on wood-frame construction techniques, and is experienced in finish carpentry.

Harris Mitchell, special consultant for Canada, has worked in the field of home repair and improvement for more than two decades. He is Homes editor of *Today* magazine and author of a syndicated newspaper column, "You Wanted to Know," as well as a number of books on home improvement.

Robert T. Ricketts, a gardening enthusiast, lectures widely on hydroponics and light gardening. He has served as feature editor of *Light Garden*, the national publication of the Indoor Light Gardening Society of America, and as director of the Potomac Valley Chapter of the Indoor Light Gardening Society in Maryland.

Dr. Romeo Segnan, a specialist in sound and acoustics, is Professor of Physics and director of the audio technology program at The American University in Washington, D.C.

David Stiles is an industrial designer who specializes in children's furniture. He has written several books on creating play spaces for children, and his designs for playgrounds for handicapped children have won awards from the New York Planning Commission.

For information about any Time-Life book, please write:
Reader Information
Time-Life Books
541 North Fairbanks Court
Chicago, Illinois 60611

Library of Congress Cataloguing in Publication Data
Time-Life Books.
    Special purpose rooms.
    (Home repair and improvement; 25)
    Includes index.
    1. Dwellings—Remodeling—Amateurs' manuals.
I. Title.
TH4816.T55   1980   643'.7   80-19808
ISBN 0-8094-3460-1
ISBN 0-8094-3459-8 (lib. bdg.)
ISBN 0-8094-3458-X (retail ed.)

Contents

Providing for provender. Wooden crates and bins installed in a basement storeroom afford nearly ideal conditions for long-term storage of vegetables, fruits and wines. The coolness of the brick-walled basement, which varies little during the year, is complemented by humidity from the dampened straw on the floor. Raised duckboards have been included, to provide sure footing around the storage bins.

In times past, homes in Europe and America abounded in rooms with special purposes, sometimes to satisfy an owner's whims, sometimes to help the household run smoothly. In Adare Manor, a relatively modest Irish manor house begun in the 15th Century and now open to the public, visitors are shown a minstrel's gallery, two billiard rooms, several halls, drawing rooms and libraries, a wine cellar, and a game room for displaying the results of the hunt—subdivisions of domestic architecture so varied that it is hard to equate them with our conventional kitchen, bedroom and bath.

Today's homeowners have interests and needs no less special than those of their forebears, but the luxuries of space and scale are diminished. Yet it is not necessary to live in a castle to have a room tailored to a particular purpose. Usually, all it takes is a few elementary changes. By rearranging the furniture you can often convert an ordinary living room into a room acoustically tuned for listening to high-fidelity sound. A basement becomes a room for family entertaining with the addition of some games and a wet bar. An unused clothes closet can house a handy sewing center—with a fold-down worktable and with shelves, drawers and pegboard for storage.

Planning such a conversion usually begins with the need rather than with the room. The antics of a growing child, a newfound interest in photography, the physical limitations of a disabled family member stimulate you to think of building a playroom, a darkroom or an invalid's room. Or the conversion could be prompted simply by a desire to put extra space to better use. A well-equipped utility room in a basement or pantry is not only an added convenience to you but an attractive feature to prospective buyers.

With a bit of ingenuity, many of these specialized areas can be fitted into corners or sections of rooms already used for other purposes. A child's playroom can be part of a bedroom. A bathroom can double as a darkroom with the addition of lightproof blinds and a foldaway wet bench. By lining a living-room wall with floor-to-ceiling bookcases you acquire, in effect, a library. Look for ways to pair special purposes—the sewing and laundry rooms, for example—so that each shares the appliances and utilities of the other.

Although some of these conversions will require extra plumbing or wiring, and occasionally you may have to soundproof a wall or cut a new window, in most cases permanent structural changes are to be avoided. If a playroom or darkroom is demountable, it can move when you move or be altered as your needs change. And the future value of the house must be considered: What benefits your family may not interest later owners. Consequently, most of the conversions in this book are designed for rapid and simple reconversion.

The Utility Room, Where Messes Can Be Mastered

A utility room exists for one purpose: to consolidate the messy jobs of a household. It is the room where you can rinse the mop, clean the paintbrushes, leave muddy boots, do the laundry and ironing. It can be in the basement, in a spare room, even in a rear entryway—but wherever it is located, it must be outfitted with simple plumbing, a few special storage units, and electrical wiring that will handle a washer and dryer.

Getting electricity to the washer and dryer is described on pages 130-131, and extending the water-supply and drainage systems for a washer and a utility tub is explained on pages 124-128. Special connections are needed for the washer (page 129), and a licensed plumber should make connections for a gas dryer; but hooking up a utility tub, illustrated on page 9, is a relatively simple matter of tapping into existing hot- and cold-water lines. Disposing of waste water is simple too: A utility tub drains into a standard tailpipe and trap connected to a branch drain line leading to the main drain.

Actually, the same drain system will serve the washing machine if you run the washer's rubber drain hose into the tub. However, if you want to be able to use the tub and the washer at one time, you will need to install a separate standpipe for draining the washer, preferably in a plumbing connection station (page 129).

All of the plumbing outside the wall can be done with rigid plastic pipe and fittings; use ½-inch CPVC (chlorinated polyvinyl chloride) pipe for supply lines and 1½-inch PVC (polyvinyl chloride) pipe for drain lines. The pipe can be cut with a hacksaw and joined with a plumber's cement made for plastic.

Once the plumbing and electricity are installed, the job of equipping the utility room is half-finished. The other half consists of creating a work surface for folding sheets and towels and storage units to hold such space-consuming items as an ironing board and laundry baskets.

The storage units shown on the following pages are built from ½-inch plywood and standard framing lumber. They have butt joints, held with yellow glue and wood screws. Sand each completed unit smooth and coat it with enamel to eliminate splinters that could snag fabrics and to protect the wood from moisture.

Moisture, ever present in a utility room, can sometimes be turned to good account. With a special fitting called an air director (page 10), the exhaust pipe of a clothes dryer can be regulated to route the dryer's warm, moist air back into the house instead of outdoors. Useful in the cold months of the year, when additional warmth and humidity are welcome, the air director also saves fuel. It has been estimated that a family of four uses a dryer about 40 hours a month, and that a dryer draws in about 150 cubic feet of warm air a minute—air already warmed by the furnace. When this air is vented outdoors, fresh air must be drawn in and warmed to replace it. Reusing the dryer's warm air avoids wasting heat.

A well-equipped utility room. In this typical utility-room arrangement, the washing machine stands beside a lightweight fiberglass utility tub so that the additional plumbing needed for the room can be confined to one area. Hot and cold water flow into the tub through a swiveling mixing faucet mounted on the tub rim; the washer gets water through a valve assembly that is part of a plumbing connection station (page 129), mounted between two wall studs.

The washer drains into a standpipe in the same plumbing station; the tub drains through a standard trap underneath it. Inside the wall, the standpipe and the drainpipe from the tub join the main house drain at the same place, a four-armed cross fitting. Since the standpipe is 2 inches in diameter and the tub drain is only 1½ inches, an adapter reduces one end of the 2-inch cross fitting.

Storage and work areas are located where space permits. A 2-by-5-foot plywood counter, convenient for folding laundry, tops a frame that supports two sliding trays sized to hold four plastic laundry baskets. A shelf unit with a clothes rod beneath provides space for storing laundry supplies and for hanging drip-dry clothing. A fold-up plywood ironing board fits in the space between two studs. Shelves mounted on metal wall standards fit almost anywhere.

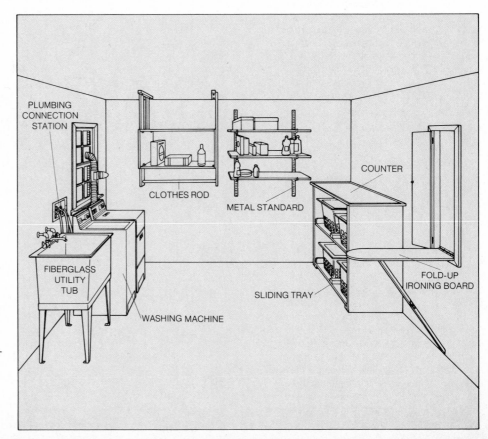

PLUMBING CONNECTION STATION

CLOTHES ROD

METAL STANDARD

COUNTER

SLIDING TRAY

FOLD-UP IRONING BOARD

FIBERGLASS UTILITY TUB

WASHING MACHINE

Adding a Light Utility Tub

1 Connecting supply lines and faucet. Mount the swiveling-faucet assembly on the tub by slipping the braces over the tub's rear rim and tightening the installation bolt against the tub back. Then screw a plastic pipe adapter into the slip nut for each supply line, push a 2-inch length of ½-inch plastic pipe over the adapter and add a 90° elbow *(inset, top)*. Place the tub against the wall, keeping the strainer hole lined up with the previously installed drainpipe *(pages 124-127)*, and level the tub by adjusting the leveling bolts at the ends of the legs. Mark the positions for the supply pipes on the wall, matched with the open ends of the elbows; then remove the tub and install the pipes *(page 128)*.

If the tub has a built-in strainer at the drain opening, fasten a tailpipe to its threaded end, using the strainer sleeve and slip nut that come with the tailpipe. If the tub has no strainer, insert one, cementing it in place. Then, as above, fasten the tailpipe to the strainer.

Prepare the trap assembly by pushing a slip fitting and slip nut into one end of the trap and a 90° elbow into the other end *(inset, bottom)*.

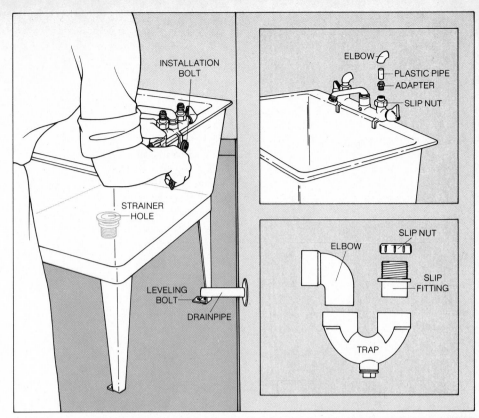

2 Measuring and cutting the drainpipe. Position the tub so that the tailpipe is slightly to the side of the installed drainpipe, then hold the trap assembly so that the elbow points toward the wall, push the slip nut up onto the tailpipe and tighten the nut. Mark a line on the drainpipe where it meets the flange on the elbow, and cut the pipe at the mark with a hacksaw. Remove the trap assembly from the tailpipe, and push the elbow onto the cut drainpipe.

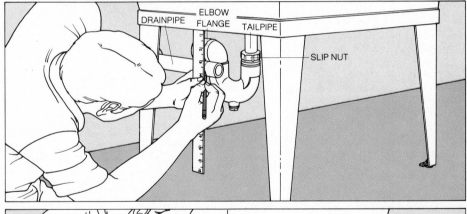

3 Measuring and cutting the tailpipe. Move the tub until the tailpipe rests against the slip nut on the trap, and mark a line on the tailpipe at the bottom of the slip nut. Cut the tailpipe there.

Remove the trap assembly from the drainpipe, and reposition the tub so that the tailpipe and the drainpipe are directly in line. Connect the elbows on the faucet assembly to the supply pipes, cementing the joints as on page 125. Next, cement the trap-assembly elbow onto the drainpipe; complete the drain connection by cementing the joint between the trap assembly and the elbow and then tightening the slip nut around the end of the tailpipe. Readjust the leveling bolts if necessary; fasten the tub to the floor by drilling pilot holes and driving screws or anchor fasteners through the anchor clips at the bottoms of the tub legs.

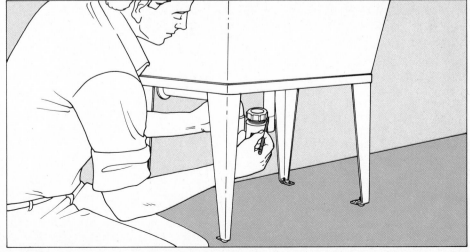

A Device for Recycling Warm Air from a Dryer

Hooking up an air director. For maximum efficiency, locate the air director 12 to 25 inches above the top of the dryer. If the dryer exhaust is vented through a window above the dryer, cut the plastic vent hose with a utility knife, and clip the reinforcing wire with wire cutters. Then slip the two hose ends over the openings of the director and fasten them with the clamps provided with the director.

If the dryer is vented to the outside through an opening at floor level, reroute the existing hose to extend 12 to 25 inches above the dryer, cut the hose as above, and clamp the cut end to the bottom of the director. Then fasten the director to the wall, using plumber's strapping, and clamp an 8-foot extension hose to the top of the director. Route the other end of the extension down to the outside opening at floor level.

To control the air flow from the director, move the inside baffle up or down by turning the lever on the side of the director. In the "up" position, the baffle deflects warm air from the dryer into the room through a mesh lint filter that is stretched over the front opening. In the "down" position, the baffle allows the exhaust air to pass through the hose directly to the outside.

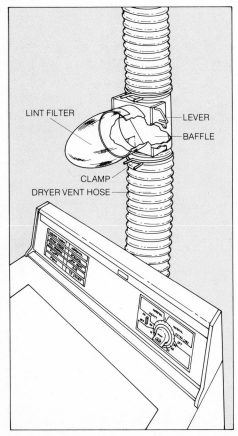

LINT FILTER — LEVER — BAFFLE — CLAMP — DRYER VENT HOSE

An Ironing Board That Folds into a Wall Pocket

1 Cutting a recess in the wall. Draw a horizontal guideline between two studs, 2 feet 10 inches above the floor; draw a second line 3 feet 9 inches above the first. Drill pilot holes at both ends of each line, then cut along the lines with a wallboard or keyhole saw, keeping your strokes short to avoid puncturing the next wall. Cut vertically between the horizontal cuts, using the inside faces of the bordering studs as guides. Remove the cut piece, leaving an opening 3 feet 9 inches high.

Cut four 2-inch pieces of 2-by-4 to use as supporting cleats for the top and bottom of the opening. Predrill nailing holes through the cleats, then nail them to the studs 1½ inches beyond each corner of the opening (inset), making sure that each pair of cleats is level.

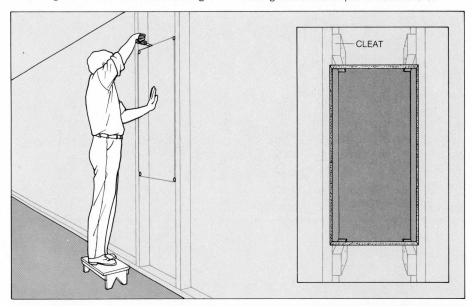

CLEAT

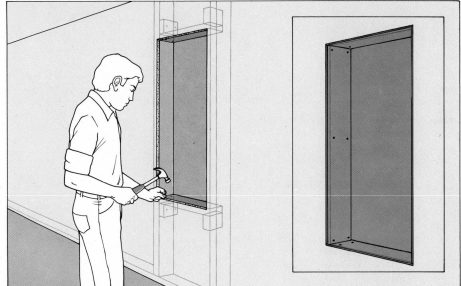

2 Framing the opening. Cut two 2-by-4s to fit between the studs; set them flat in the top and bottom of the opening so that the exposed surfaces are flush with the wallboard edges. Drive two nails into the cleats at each end.

Glue a rectangle of ½-inch plywood to the back of the opening, then cover the cut edges of wallboard around the opening with a frame constructed of ¼-inch plywood. Cut the horizontal strips first, trimmed just wide enough so that they will hide the cut edges; tack them to the top and bottom 2-by-4s, keeping the edges flush with the opening. Measure and cut the vertical strips to fit between the horizontal ones, and tack them to the studs (inset).

3 **Cutting the ironing board.** Center a standard ironing board, top down, on a 15-by-40-inch piece of ½-inch plywood, tapered end of the board touching one end of the plywood. Trace the outline of the board on the plywood, then narrow the side lines, if necessary, to make the board 13 inches wide. Cut out with a saber saw.

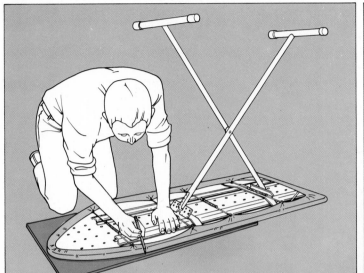

4 **Hinging the board in place.** Center one leaf of a 12-inch piano hinge on the top of the board at the straight end, hinge pin flush with the edge, and screw the leaf down. Have a helper hold the board flat against the lower crosspiece, centered in the opening, while you screw the second hinge leaf to the opening's plywood back.

5 **Measuring for the leg.** Mark a spot on the underside of the board, 1 foot from the curved end and midway between the two sides. Have a helper hold the board level while you measure the diagonal distance from this spot down to the bottom of the wall, directly beneath the midpoint of the opening. Mark off this distance on a strip of 2-by-2 lumber.

Use a T bevel to draw a 48° angle at the mark you have just made, with the angle pointing toward the end of the 2-by-2 where you began the measurement (*inset, top*). Cut the miter. When the board is open, the mitered end of the leg will fit against the wall where it meets the floor.

Cut the leg in half and fasten the halves together with a strap hinge, positioning the hinge on one side so that the leg will fold to fit inside the opening. On the side of the leg opposite the hinge, install a bolt latch to keep the leg rigid when the board is in use (*inset, bottom*).

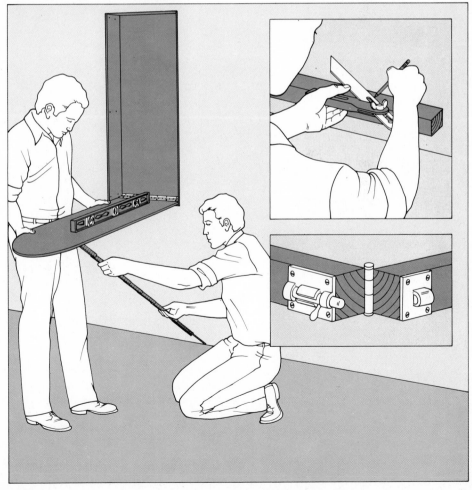

6 **Fastening the leg to the board.** Using a T hinge, fasten the square end of the leg to the underside of the board at the point marked in Step 5, page 11. Screw the strap of the hinge to the end of the leg; then screw the crosspiece of the hinge to the underside of the board, lining up the hinge pin with the mark. Position the strap of the hinge in such a way that the leg will fold to lie flat against the board.

To keep the leg in its folded position when the board is stored, screw a hook to the underside of the board and an eye to the outside of the mitered end of the leg. To keep the board in place, fasten a second hook to the back of the opening, where the board tip meets it, and tack a loop of cord to the underside of the board, at the tip (inset, left).

Frame the opening with four 1-by-2s nailed to the studs and crosspieces, setting the 1-by-2s ½ inch out from the inner edges of the opening. Then cut a door of ½-inch plywood to fit within the frame, and install it with butt hinges (inset, right). Add a catch to keep the door closed and a screw-on knob to pull it open.

An Ironing-Board Cabinet Hung on a Masonry Wall

A plywood box for a fold-up board. This storage cabinet has a back and four sides of ½-inch plywood, glued and screwed together to form an open box 45 inches high, 18 inches wide and 3½ inches deep. The back of the box is fastened to the wall with six masonry anchors. The ironing board is cut and installed as in Steps 3-6, pages 11-12. A 1-by-2 face frame is nailed to the front of the cabinet, outside edges of the frame flush with the outer edges of the box. A ½-inch plywood door, cut to fit in the frame, is installed on two butt hinges, as in Step 6, left, and finished with a catch and a screw-on knob.

Building a Counter with Laundry-Basket Trays

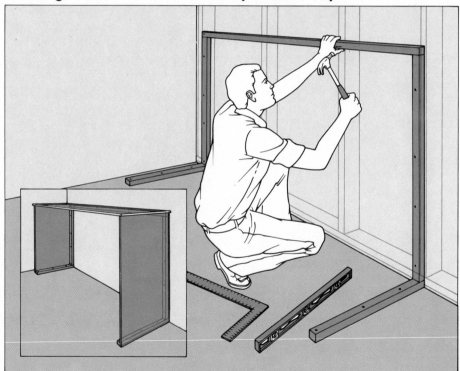

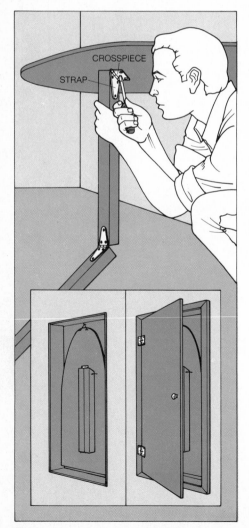

1 **Installing cleats for a counter.** Make a frame of 2-by-2 cleats, nailing two to the floor and three to the wall. Cut the two floor cleats 2 feet long, the two vertical wall cleats 4 feet long and the horizontal wall cleat 5 feet long.

Set the outside edges of the floor cleats 5 feet apart, perpendicular to the wall, and nail them to the floor (use hardened nails for a concrete floor). Set the ends of the vertical wall cleats on top of the floor cleats, use a level to make sure they are plumb and fasten them to the wall. Then set the horizontal cleat across the tops of the vertical cleats, check to be sure it is level and fasten it to the wall. Nail the cleats to studs wherever possible; otherwise use toggle bolts with wallboard or plaster walls, masonry nails with masonry walls.

Use ½-inch plywood to make two side panels, 2 feet by 4 feet 1½ inches, and a top, 2 feet 1 inch by 5 feet 3 inches. Glue and screw the pieces to the cleats and to each other; the top will overhang 1 inch on three sides. Paint the unit and add a C-shaped, snap-on metal molding to the edges (inset).

2 **Making a plywood tray.** Cut the tray bottom from ½-inch plywood, making it 2 feet wide and 4 feet 11 inches long; frame the back and side edges with a rim of 1-by-4 strips, set on edge on the top surface of the plywood. Glue the strips on, then drive 1-inch wood screws into them from the bottom. Round off the front corners.

Cut a 2-by-2 center support to fit between the front and back of the tray, fastening the support in place with 1-inch wood screws driven through the back rim into the end. Drive two additional screws through the tray bottom into the support, about 6 inches in from each end. Construct a second tray in the same way.

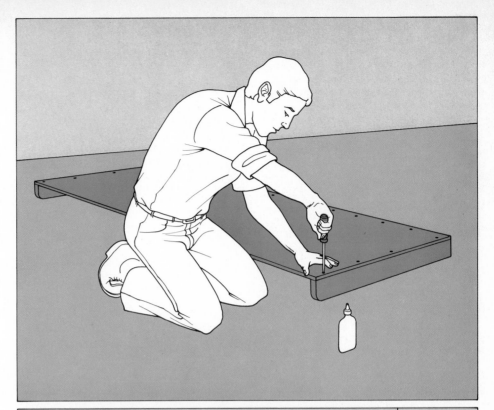

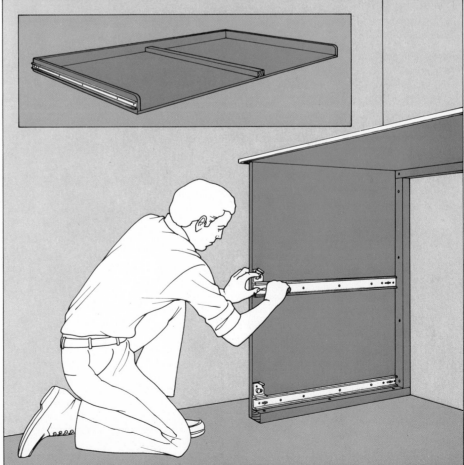

3 **Installing tray glides.** After marking level lines across the inside faces of both of the side panels, 3 inches and 24 inches above the floor, set the lower edge of a metal drawer-glide track flush with each line, and then mark the locations of the oblong screw holes. Drill pilot holes, and fasten the track in place with the screws provided by the manufacturer. Then screw the glides to the outsides of the tray rims at the positions specified in the manufacturer's instructions (inset).

Slide each tray into place, and check to be sure it fits squarely. To adjust the clearances at the sides of the tray, loosen the screws holding the track, and move the track up or down. To adjust the depth of run, loosen the glide screws, and slide the glide forward or back. When the trays fit, drill pilot holes at the remaining screw holes, and drive in the remaining screws.

A Box of Storage Shelves with a Drip-dry Hanging Rod

1 Installing hanging cleats. To construct a shelf unit that will parallel concealed ceiling joists, mark parallel lines on the ceiling at each end of the proposed shelf span, long enough to cross two joists (at least 28 inches). Cut two 2-by-2 cleats 20 inches long, and position the cleats just inside the lines so that their ends cross both joists. Fasten each cleat to a joist, using two 3-inch lag bolts.

To construct a unit perpendicular to concealed joists, cut cleats 10 inches long, position them along the joists, and fasten them 2 inches in from each end with lag bolts (*inset, near right*).

For ceilings with exposed joists, cleats are not needed. If the unit will run parallel to the joists, nail a block between the two joists at each end of the unit span (*inset, far right*). If the unit will run perpendicular to the joists, fasten its side supports directly to the joist faces.

2 Constructing the shelf unit. Cut two 1-by-10s long enough to reach the outside edges of the nailing cleats, blocks or joists. Cut two more 1-by-10s, each 1½ feet long; glue and screw the four 1-by-10s together to form an open box with butt joints, the top and bottom of the box overlapping the sides. Reinforce the joints with eight 2-inch steel corner braces, positioning the braces 2 inches in from the front and back of the box; fasten the braces with 1-inch wood screws.

Cut four 1-by-3 supports, making two of the supports long enough to reach from the ceiling to the proposed height of the bottom shelf, and the two remaining supports 1 foot longer than this measurement. Drill a 1½-inch hole 4 inches from one end of each long support, and round off the corners of that end.

Set the supports 1½ inches in from the front and back of the box. Put the short supports at the back, lower ends flush with the bottom of the box; put the long supports at the front, holes extending below the box. Fasten each support to the box with three 1-inch wood screws driven through the support and into the side of the box.

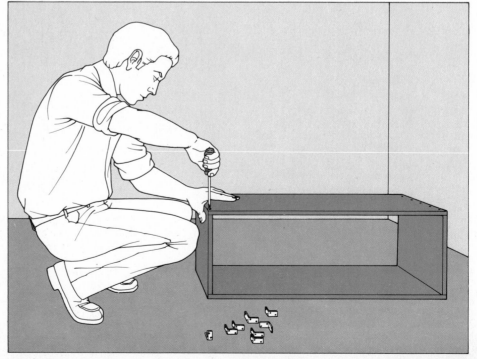

3 **Installing a clothes rod.** Cut a 1½-inch dowel long enough to reach to the outside faces of the front supports, slide the rod through the drilled holes, and nail through the supports and into the rod. Then, while a helper holds the unit in place, mark and drill holes for lag bolts to fasten the top of each support to its overhead cleat, nailing block or joist. Bolt the unit in place.

Shelves on Standards: The Basic Storage Unit

1 **Installing the first standard.** Mark positions for standards in the center of every other stud along the proposed shelf span, or at 32-inch intervals if the standards are to be mounted on a masonry wall. Position the first standard over the mark you have made for it and, using a level to set the standard plumb, mark the locations for the screw holes. Drill pilot holes and fasten the standard to the wall with wood screws (into studs), toggle bolts (into wallboard), or plastic or lead anchors (into masonry).

2 **Installing additional standards.** Insert a bracket at eye level on the first standard and a bracket on the second standard in the corresponding slots; then hold the second standard against the wall over its mark. Set a shelf across the two brackets, and place a level atop the shelf; then slide the second standard up and down against the wall until the shelf is level. Mark the screwhole locations, drill pilot holes and fasten the second standard to the wall. Repeat the procedure for additional standards.

A Place for Sewing, Cutting, Fitting and Pressing

Although the basic piece of equipment for a sewing room is a sewing machine, the range of activities that go on there encompasses everything from cutting fabric to pressing the finished work. Thus it is necessary to find space for such sizable items as a cutting table and an ironing board, as well as systematic storage for the myriad sundries that are part of sewing—needles and pins, thread, buttons and patterns, as well as bolts of fabric and packets of trim.

Ideally, a sewing center should occupy an entire room, so that a project can be interrupted at any time without necessitating a cleanup operation. With some clever corner-cutting and careful planning, however, it is possible to fit a well-equipped and efficient sewing area into a space as small as a little-used closet *(opposite, top)*. Of course, adequate light and at least two accessible electric outlets are essential.

Within a sewing space the central concern is the placement of the sewing machine. It should, if possible, be near a window, preferably oriented so that the light falls across your left shoulder as you sew. If there is no natural light, either incandescent or fluorescent overhead lighting will do. If you are installing the lighting, choose a large shallow, ceiling-mounted fluorescent fixture fitted with a diffuser for soft, shadowless light.

Besides this general illumination, you will need localized light for use when the machine is in operation. It should be placed about a foot to the left of the needle and fitted with a 60- or 75-watt bulb. This can be a wall lamp, a desk lamp or a clamp-on draftsman's lamp with a jointed, spring-mounted arm.

The machine, if it is not already mounted in its own console, will require the support of a desk or a worktable. This should be 28 to 30 inches high, with a kneehole at least 18 inches wide and a top surface that is spacious enough to allow for easy manipulation of fabric as you move it through the machine. There should be a minimum of 1 foot of clearance between the needle and the back of the table, 2 feet of clearance to the left of the needle, and 6 inches of clearance to the right of the machine.

For the cutting table, the sewing center's other main work surface, the dimensions can be much more flexible. The height should be adjusted to your own, since you will be standing up while working at the table; a typical height is 36 inches. Ideally the top surface should be large enough to accommodate several yards of the widest fabric, 60 inches. But this is seldom practicable. More commonly, cutting tables are 36 inches wide (some are as narrow as 28 inches) and between 56 and 72 inches long.

Wishbone or H-style folding legs can be purchased at home-improvement centers, and they make the table easy to store when it is not in use. A 1-inch grid ruled on the cutting surface increases the table's usefulness, making it easy to measure off lengths of fabric without having to mark them first.

Storage space for sewing supplies should be as plentiful and as varied as possible. Even in the limited space of a sewing center built into a closet, you will need shelves for see-through plastic boxes to contain fabrics and patterns, a roll-out chest with at least one shallow drawer for such items as buttons, thread and sewing-machine attachments, and a pegboard panel on the door for keeping scissors, tape measures and other sewing accessories within easy reach.

In more spacious quarters you could hang a corkboard on a nearby wall for pinning up instruction sheets for patterns, add a wall of open shelves or storage cabinets, and mount a full-length mirror to make hemming and fitting easier. The most useful mirror is one with hinged wings that adjust to give you a three-way view. It can be made from stock mirror panels, sold in mirror stores in widths from 16 to 24 inches and a usual height of 68 inches. These can be mounted with special U-shaped channels on a hinged plywood frame, the center section of which is attached to the wall. To avoid the distortion common in thin glass, use mirror that is ¼ inch thick.

A Minimum Closet Center

Converting a closet for sewing. This compact sewing center combines a work surface, shelves and a chest of drawers that all fit inside an average-sized closet when not in use. The fold-down table, 2 inches narrower than the door opening, is as long as the distance between the top and bottom shelves; it hooks against the top shelf when closed. Hinged to the bottom shelf, the table rests on a chest of drawers fitted with ball casters—metal-rimmed for a carpeted floor, rubber-trimmed for a wood or tile floor.

The chest of drawers is ready-made, purchased in a size that clears the door opening by 2 inches and is 2 inches shorter than the distance from the door to the back wall. The combined height of the chest and its added casters is 1½ inches less than the desired height of the table. The shelves are 4 inches shallower than the depth of the closet, to allow clearance for the table in its upright position.

The sewing machine is slid onto the bottom shelf when not in use. Do not attach it to the ta-ble; its weight would make the table difficult and dangerous to operate.

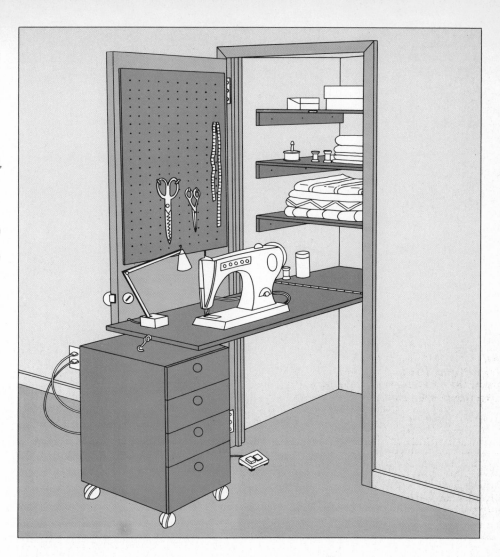

A Foldaway to Save Space

1 **Mounting casters on the chest.** To reinforce the bottom of the chest for mounting casters, glue and screw 1-by-3 braces to the front and the back. Drive the screws into the braces from the side of the chest, or remove the bottom drawer and drive screws through the chest bottom into the braces. If the bottom is recessed, as shown here, cut the braces to fit snugly between the sides, and tap them into position with a mallet; if the bottom is flush with the sides, surface-mount the braces. Use yellow glue and ¾-inch wood screws. When the glue is dry, place platform-type ball casters (inset) at each corner, and mark the positions of screw holes. Drill pilot holes, and attach the casters to the braces with the screws supplied with the casters.

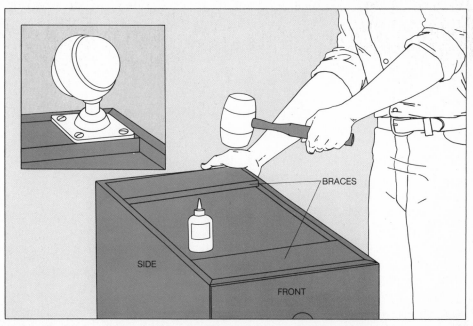

2 **Installing the shelves.** Use a carpenter's level and a pencil to mark a horizontal line on one wall of the closet, ¾ inch lower than the desired height of the bottom shelf and table. Cut a cleat out of 1-by-2 long enough to span the depth of the shelf and, after locating the studs in the wall (*page 112*), drive tenpenny nails through the cleat into each stud, positioning the top of the cleat flush with the marked line. Again using a level, mark lines at the same height on the back wall and the opposite wall. Attach a second cleat to the opposite wall. Then join the two cleats with a third, across the back wall. Install cleats for the other shelves in the same manner. Then cut shelves from ¾-inch plywood and lay them atop the cleats; for convenience in cleaning, do not fasten them in place.

3 **Making the table.** Measure and cut the fold-down tabletop from ¾-inch A-A grade interior plywood. The length should equal the distance from the bottom of the bottom shelf to the bottom of the top shelf; the width should be 2 inches narrower than the door. Then cut a 2-inch-wide spacer board from ¾-inch plywood, 2 inches shorter than the table width, to lift the tabletop above the top of the supporting chest. Screw the spacer board to the underside of the table 6 inches from the outer end, centering it between the sides of the table. Glue a piece of felt or other soft material to the spacer board, to protect the chest top.

Cut a piece of ¾-inch piano hinge as long as the table width. Screw it to one end of the table, keeping the hinge pin flush with the tabletop.

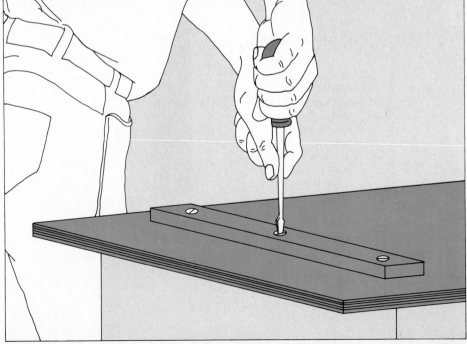

4 **Installing the table.** Have a helper hold the tabletop while you screw the other leaf of the piano hinge to the edge of the bottom shelf. Make sure that the surfaces of the table and shelf are flush when the table is folded down and that the tabletop is centered in the door opening. Complete the installation by screwing a hook to the outer edge of the table and an eye to the corresponding point on the edge of the top shelf. Sand all edges well to avoid snags; fill in imperfections with wood putty or spackling compound; then finish with paint or polyurethane.

A Table for Measured Cutting

1 **Attaching folding legs.** Cut a tabletop from ½-inch plywood, as large as you have space for, and reinforce the bottom with lengthwise 1-by-6 battens to provide support for a pair of lightweight folding legs. Make the battens 8 inches shorter than the table length, and center them between the table ends, positioning them so that the leg assemblies will be centered on the battens. Drill pilot holes; then attach the battens to the plywood with 1-inch wood screws, driven through the tabletop into the battens and countersunk. Then position the legs and screw them to the battens. (If you make the top of ¾-inch plywood, no battens are needed.)

Set the table upright, and fill the screw holes and any imperfections on the top and sides with spackling compound or wood putty. Then apply two coats of flat paint, allowing the paint to dry thoroughly after each coat.

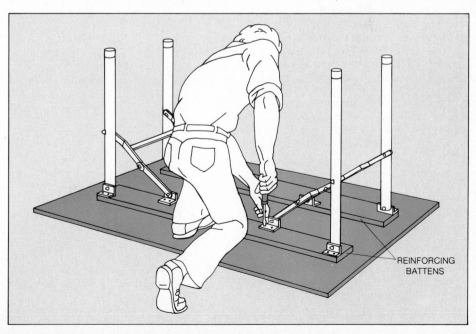

REINFORCING BATTENS

2 Drawing a grid. Use a pencil and a long metal or wooden straightedge—practically any piece of molding will do—to draw parallel lines at 1-inch intervals, running from one end of the table to the other. Clamp the straightedge in place, and check frequently with a ruler to make sure your lines are accurate. Then draw a similar set of parallel lines across the table from one side to the other. Use a square to verify that the lines are crossing at right angles. After all the lines are drawn, use the straightedge and a fine felt-tipped marker with permanent ink to trace over the grid.

Along a short side and a long side of the cutting table, use the felt-tipped marker to number each line of the grid according to its distance from the edge in inches. Apply at least two thin coats of polyurethane over the grid, allowing the finish to dry between coats and before using.

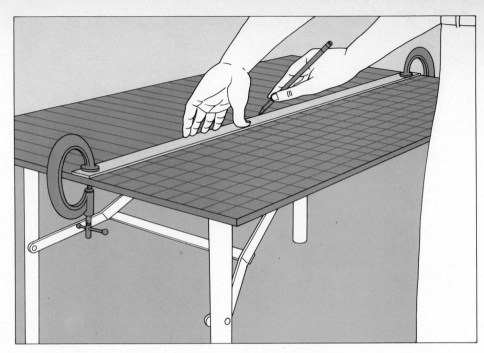

A Mirror That Opens for Viewing All Sides

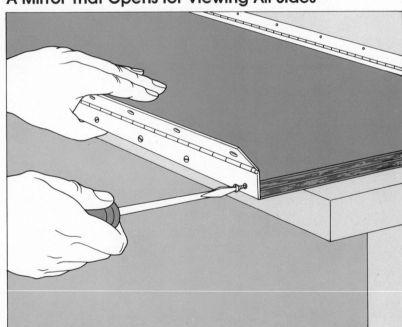

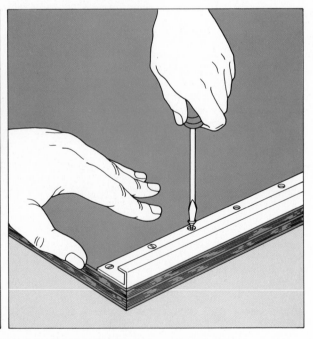

1 Hinging the backing panels. Cut three backing panels from ¾-inch plywood, the same width as the mirror panels and ¼ inch longer. Cut two pieces of 1-inch-wide piano hinge, the same length as the backing panels. Screw one leaf of each hinge to an edge of the center panel, positioning each hinge so that its hinge pin is ⅜ inch above the panel's front face. Drill pilot holes, and use ¾-inch screws to ensure sufficient holding power. Screw the other leaf of each hinge to an edge of one side panel, hinge pins again ⅜ inch above the front of the panel.

2 Attaching mirror channels. Using a hacksaw, cut lengths of U-shaped aluminum mirror channel to fit the top and bottom of each panel; use channel with a wide lip for the top, a narrow lip for the bottom. Secure the channel to the panels with ½-inch screws at 2-inch intervals, placing the bottom of each channel flush with the edge of the panel. Cover the screwheads with masking tape to protect the mirrors.

3 Hanging the unit. Locate the studs in the wall, and have a helper hold the plywood unit against the wall so that the center panel spans two studs; drive two tenpenny nails through the panel into the studs, to hold it in place temporarily. Mark the stud locations on the face of the center panel, and drill pilot holes at 1-foot intervals to accommodate 3-inch wood screws. Drive the screws through the plywood into the studs. Be sure to countersink all screws and nails slightly; then cover the heads with masking tape.

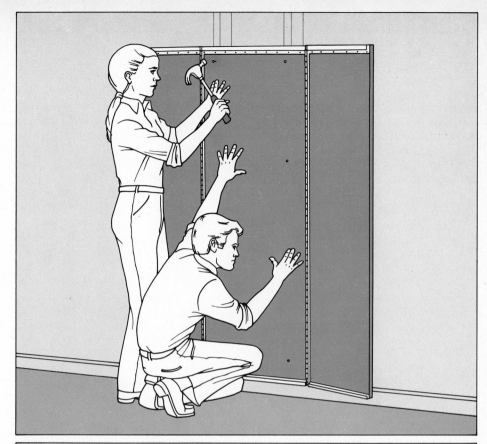

4 Inserting the mirrors. Pad the lower channel of the center panel with ½-by-¼-inch rubber cushioning blocks, placed 2 inches in from each end. With the aid of a helper, slide a mirror into the deep top channel, then gently lower it into the shallow bottom channel. Install mirrors in each of the wings in the same way. Finish the outside edge of each wing with a strip of 1-inch-wide wooden or plastic molding, glued and fastened to the edge with wire brads. Finally, paint the moldings and the backs of the side wings.

Stocking Up: Cool Storage for Food and Wines

Before the advent of supermarkets and freezers, the wintering over of a harvest of fruits and vegetables was a necessity. Root cellars with dirt floors and cool masonry walls were common, and could be found below houses or dug into hillsides. Though few modern homes are equipped with such a specialized space, it is simple enough to create one, provided you have a below-grade basement and winter temperatures that do not average above 50° F. A 10-by-10-foot area will accommodate the surplus from an abundant backyard crop, a winter's supply of staples and a cache of favorite wines.

Though the specific storage conditions and length of storage times vary for different provisions (chart, opposite), most require a fairly cool, dark, moist environment. Locate your simulated root cellar in a northeast or northwest corner of the basement that has at least one window for ventilation and is well away from any sources of heat— the furnace, hot-water heater, heat ducts or hot-water pipes. By building two partition walls at right angles to the corner's foundation walls and insulating the partitions with 3½-inch fiberglass batts, you can create an adequately cool area in the basement of even a centrally heated house. One of the partition walls, of course, will need an access door.

It is also advisable to insulate between the ceiling joists in the storage area. To retain the desired high humidity inside, you should cover the new partition walls, as well as the ceiling joists, with wallboard, taking care to seal all joints. Paint these surfaces with a high-gloss latex paint or a latex vapor-barrier paint to prevent mold from forming on them, and use plastic baseboard moldings to protect the walls from moisture on the floor.

Once the storage area has been partitioned off from the rest of the basement, you must devise a means of monitoring and regulating the temperature and humidity within the enclosed space. Gardening-supply stores have minimum-maximum thermometers that record daily lows and highs, and hygrometers that measure the moisture in the air. Both of these instruments will help you to keep a record of the room's temperature and relative humidity.

Even in dry climates you can maintain the high humidity required for a food storage room if you cover a cement or tile floor with sterilized potting soil or clean straw, and wet it daily with a sprinkling of water. An equally effective but more expensive option is to install a cool-air vaporizer or a humidifier made automatic with a humidistat. In climates that are naturally quite humid, boxes of moist sand alone may do the trick.

A ventilation system also helps to keep temperature constant, and in many cases a simple air-duct box mounted on an open window (pages 24-25) is sufficient. The duct, constructed of 1-by-8s and plywood in a simple open-ended design, fits over the lower part of an open window to direct cool air downward while warm air exits through the portion of the window above the duct. Though the duct can be installed in any type of window, it is most suitable for the outward-opening awning design of many basement windows, because these windows can be left open even when it rains. Regardless of design, the window should be screened to keep out insects, animals and leaves.

Deciding when to open and close the window in a storeroom will depend on the relative inside and outside temperatures on any given day. You may, for instance, close the window to trap coolness inside when the outdoor temperature soars or to keep the inside temperature from dropping too low when the outside temperature is very cold. However, in adjusting the window, keep in mind that increasing ventilation almost always reduces the humidity. In a climate where it is difficult to balance ventilation and humidity, you can install a ventilating fan with louvered shutters, connecting it to a thermostat and a humidistat for automatic control.

Once you have provided a desirable climate, constructing the rest of the storage facilities needed for fruits, vegetables and wines is simple—a matter of making boxes and walkways. Crates with slatted sides that allow air to circulate are ideal for storing fruits or vegetables packed between layers of straw, leaves or paper packing material. The crates should be large enough to hold several bushels of produce but small enough to be manageable—24 inches wide, 24 inches high and 30 inches long is a typical size.

You can stack the crates, but be sure to separate them with scrap lumber so that their solid bottoms do not cut off air from the layer of produce directly beneath. Add rope handles to reinforce the crates and to make lifting easier. Fruits should be stored at some distance from vegetables, since the two tend to pick up odors from each other.

Bottled wines, which are best stored in a constant temperature slightly warmer than the temperature needed for most produce, should be laid on their sides along the warmest wall and away from vibration caused by opening and closing the door. An open-ended 18-inch-square unit of ¾-inch plywood or 1-by-12s, bisected diagonally, will hold as many as 12 bottles of wine—the number in a case. Since a single case of wine weighs about 40 pounds, always secure the stacked units to each other and to the wall.

Taking care of a cold-storage room is more than a matter of venting stale air. You will have to check it regularly for spoiled food, which should be promptly removed, and a floor covering of soil or straw should be periodically changed. During the winter months, keep the window free of accumulated snow, and monitor the temperature and humidity daily. Each summer set all food-storage containers out in the sun to air.

Requirements for Long-Term Storage

Optimum storage conditions. Listed in the left-hand column of this chart are vegetables and fruits that can be stored for one to four months in most home basements. The columns to the right list the temperatures and levels of relative humidity that will keep the quality of the produce high for the longest period of time. Wines, unaffected by humidity, require only cool, constant temperatures and protection from light.

Commodity	Temperature	Humidity	Length of storage
Vegetables			
Beets	32°-40°F.	90-95%	2-4 months
Cabbage	32°-40°F.	90-95%	2 months
Carrots	32°-40°F.	90-95%	2-4 months
Cauliflower	32°-40°F.	90-95%	6-8 weeks
Onions	45°-55°F.	50-60%	2-4 months
Parsnips	32°-40°F.	90-95%	2-4 months
Potatoes	32°-40°F.	90-95%	2-4 months
Pumpkins/squash	55°-60°F.	60-70%	2-4 months
Sweet potatoes	55°-60°F.	80-85%	2-4 months
Tomatoes (green)	55°-70°F.	80-90%	4-6 weeks
Fruits			
Apples	32°-40°F.	80-95%	2-4 months
Grapefruits	32°-40°F.	80-95%	4-6 weeks
Grapes	32°-40°F.	80-95%	1-2 months
Oranges	32°-40°F.	80-95%	4-6 weeks
Pears	32°-40°F.	80-95%	2-4 months
Wines			
All	45°-60°F.	not applicable	indefinitely

Wet Straw and Insulation for a Special Indoor Climate

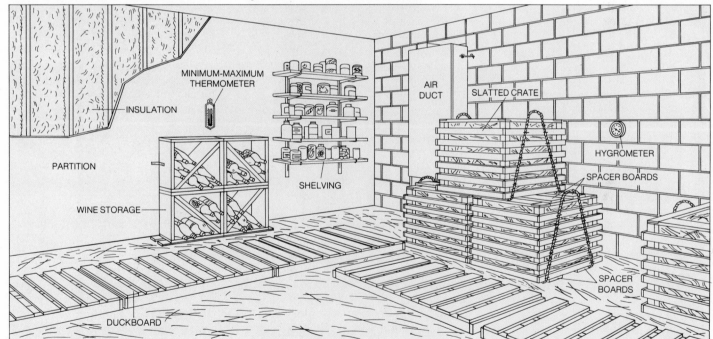

A basement food-storage room. This below-grade corner of a basement has been isolated by partition walls for winter storage of root vegetables, fruits and wines. Insulation in the partition walls and between the ceiling joists helps retain natural coolness provided by the masonry walls in winter, and a homemade air duct, mounted over the lower two-thirds of an open window, channels cool outside air down to the storage-room floor. At the same time, warm air rising in the room exits through the top of the open window. Dampened straw or soil is spread across the floor to keep humidity in the room high, and slat walkways, called duckboards, protect feet from the dampness. The wall and ceiling surfaces of wallboard are covered with a special vapor-barrier paint.

Slatted crates containing fruits and vegetables packed between layers of straw are stored along a masonry wall, where they will be kept cool. To ensure air circulation, the crates are positioned slightly away from the wall and stacked on spacer boards that separate them from the floor and from each other. A hygrometer mounted on the same wall shows the relative humidity. Wine bottles rest on their sides (to keep the corks from drying) in 12-inch deep, stackable, open-ended units along a partition wall, where temperatures are slightly warmer; the units are divided diagonally to help separate different wine types. Since temperature is important for wine storage, a minimum-maximum thermometer is hung near the wines to keep track of daily temperatures. Wall shelves provide open storage for canned goods as well.

Keeping Your Cool while Blocking the Heat

Insulating between studs and joists. Insulate the stud partition walls *(page 112)*; use 3½-inch-thick fiberglass batts with stapling flanges *(below, left)*. Position the batts between studs so that the vapor barrier will be facing the rest of the basement, and staple the flanges to the outside edges of the studs at 6-inch intervals. Finally, install wallboard over both sides of the partition walls *(page 116)*.

If the ceiling joists are exposed, install 6-inch-thick fiberglass batts without stapling flanges. Place the batts between joists, the vapor barrier facing up to confine the high humidity and protect the floor above *(below, right)*. To hold the batts in place, cut lengths of heavy steel wire, like that used for coat hangers, to fit snugly between joists. Push the wires under the batts at 16-inch intervals; do not compress the batts with the wires, as this reduces the insulation's effectiveness. Finish the ceiling with wallboard.

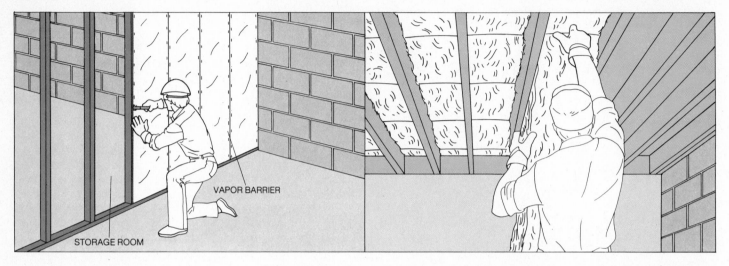

VAPOR BARRIER

STORAGE ROOM

Channeling Air In and Out

1 Measuring for the top board. Measure across the window opening between the outside edges of the window, and cut a 1-by-8 board to this length plus 4 inches. Cut two 1-by-8 sidepieces for the duct, long enough to extend from the floor to a point two thirds of the way up the window. Cut a ¾-inch plywood front for the box, making it the same width as the top board but 2 feet shorter than the sides.

Glue and nail each end of the top board to a sidepiece *(inset)*. Then position the plywood front over the edges of the assembled 1-by-8 frame, flush with the top edge, and fasten the front to the frame with glue and fourpenny nails.

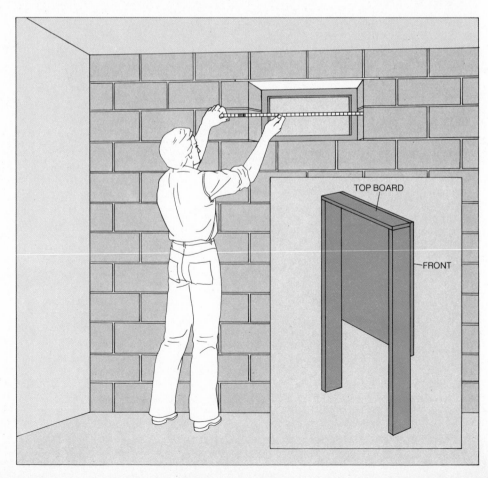

TOP BOARD

FRONT

2 **Installing the duct.** Stand the assembled duct against the window, and mark a location for a 4-inch hook-and-eye latch on each side, about 6 inches from the top. Install the latches, using masonry-wall anchors to hold the eye screws in the masonry wall. The latches will permit you to move the duct to open or close the window; in position, the duct will draw cool air in and discharge it near the floor, while warmer air goes out through the top part of the window (*inset*).

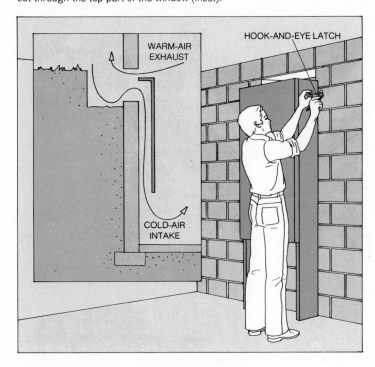

Duckboards for a Dry Walkway

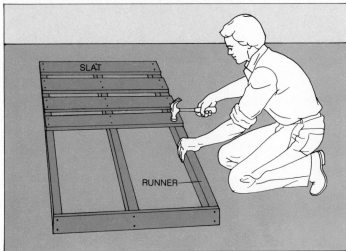

Building duckboards. For each section of the walkway, construct a simple rectangular frame of three evenly spaced 2-by-4 runners, 4 feet long, joined by two 1-by-4 end boards, 2 feet long. Cut eight slats, 2 feet long, from 1-by-4 lumber, and nail them across the top of the frame, leaving about 2 inches between slats.

Building Slat Boxes for Storing Food

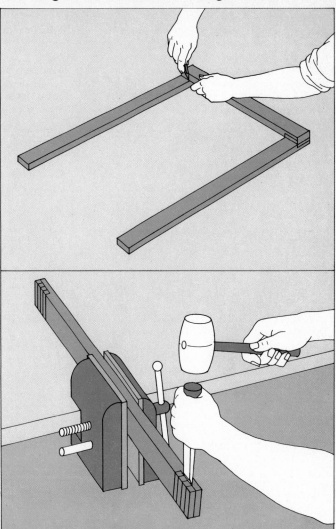

1 **Rabbeting the top frame for end lap joints.** Cut four pieces of 1-by-3 to make a top frame for each crate—two pieces the planned length of the crate, and two the planned width. Lap the end of one long piece over the end of one short piece (*above, top*), with outside edges flush, and draw a line where they overlap. Extend the line ⅜ inch down the edges of the short piece, and connect the extensions at the end of the board, creating a guideline for cutting a rabbet half the thickness of the board. Then turn the two pieces over, putting the short piece on top of the long, and use the same technique to mark a guideline for rabbeting the long piece. Repeat to mark rabbets on the remaining three corners.

Using a miter box and a backsaw, cut a series of parallel kerfs ½ inch apart, to the marked depth of the rabbet. Then place each frame piece in a woodworking vise and, with a mallet and chisel, remove the kerfed wood (*above, bottom*). Sand the rabbets smooth and test-fit the joints to make sure they interlock evenly.

2 **Assembling the top frame.** Apply glue to all the surfaces of one lap joint, fit the pieces together and secure them with a corner clamp. Then reinforce the joint with four 1-inch brads, blunted slightly with a hammer and driven into the joint at a slight angle to prevent the wood from splitting. Secure the joints at the other three corners in the same way.

Cut a bottom of ¾-inch exterior-grade plywood for the box, the same width and length as the assembled top frame. Then cut four 2-by-2s for the corner posts, making them 1½ inches shorter than the height you have planned for the box.

3 **Finishing the box.** As a helper steadies the pieces, glue and nail the plywood bottom to each corner post. Turn the assembly over, and glue and nail the top frame to the other ends of the posts. Cut 1-by-2 slats for the box sides, trimming the side slats exactly to size, but adding 1½ inches to the end slats so that they will overlap the side slats. Nail the slats in place, starting at the bottom and nailing the first slat onto the edge of the plywood base. Leave 1- to 2-inch gaps between slats (*inset*). Add a reinforcing rope handle by stapling a loop of rope across the bottom and up the sides, knotting it between slats.

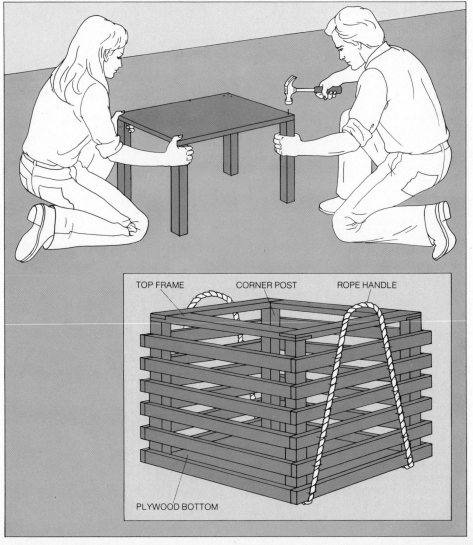

TOP FRAME   CORNER POST   ROPE HANDLE

PLYWOOD BOTTOM

Organizing Wine Storage

1 Installing the diagonal divider. Cut five 12-inch-wide pieces of ¾-inch exterior-grade plywood for each wine-storage unit. Make the top and bottom pieces the planned overall size of the square, the two sidepieces 1½ inches shorter. To determine the length of the divider, assemble one corner of the square by gluing and nailing the bottom to one side. Then mark a line ¾ inch in from the free end of the bottom, and measure the diagonal distance from this line to the inside edge of the free end of the side. Mark off this distance on the plywood for the divider, and cut a 45° inward bevel at each mark to trim the divider to size. Use fourpenny galvanized finishing nails to fasten the divider in place, putting one end flush with the line drawn across the bottom, the other end flush with the top of the side.

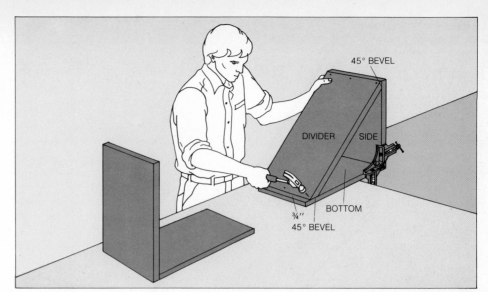

2 Finishing the square. To complete the wine-storage unit, glue and nail one end of the remaining sidepiece into the ¾-inch space between the divider and the bottom. Then glue and butt-nail the top onto the two sidepieces. Countersink the nailheads, fill the holes with wood putty, and sand the surfaces smooth. Because humidity in the storeroom will be quite high, you should finish the storage unit with either marine paint or polyurethane varnish.

3 Bracing stacked units. To join wine-storage units into stacks or rows, align them at floor level so that the divider boards form a V, and clamp the adjoining sides together. Drill a pilot hole through the clamped sides, as close to their centers as the divider boards allow, and drive in a 1¼-inch flat-head screw. Remove the clamps, and turn the joined units over to repeat the procedure from the other side. Join adjacent horizontal and vertical units in the same way, positioning them so that the dividers form a pattern of interior squares (*inset*). To keep stacked units from tipping away from the wall, secure them to the studs with corner braces.

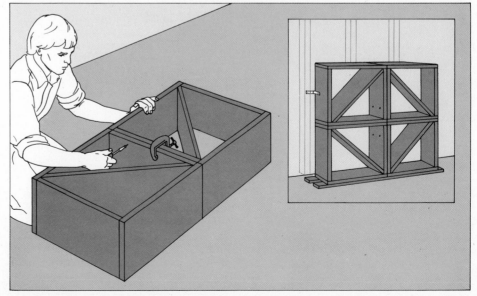

Aids to Make Life Easier for the Disabled

One of every 10 Americans suffers from some form of physical disability. For many of them, houses and public buildings present a maze of barriers to mobility and independence—a threshold that must be crossed, a light switch out of reach from a wheelchair, a faucet too difficult for an arthritic hand to turn.

Just as these annoyances are being removed in many public buildings, they can also be eliminated at home: You can modify a room to serve the needs of someone with physical limitations. Be-

cause of special strength or design requirements, it often is best to use commercially made equipment in these adaptations. But you can also construct many useful aids and make slight alterations in, say, the height and depth of storage shelves—without great expense and without introducing an institutional atmosphere to your home.

Often only simple changes in the furniture are needed. Moving your chairs and tables so that you open a 5-foot circle in the center of a room offers the turning

area needed for a wheelchair. A non-wheelchair user with limited mobility might find a typical office chair on casters a boon, and the installation of electric control devices at a bedside table *(page 30)* allows a bed-ridden person to turn off lights or control other devices without summoning help.

Other changes require more effort, but still are easily managed. By substituting single-motion lever-type doorknobs and faucet handles for the kind that must be grasped and turned, you will help an ar-

Two Rooms with Comfort Added

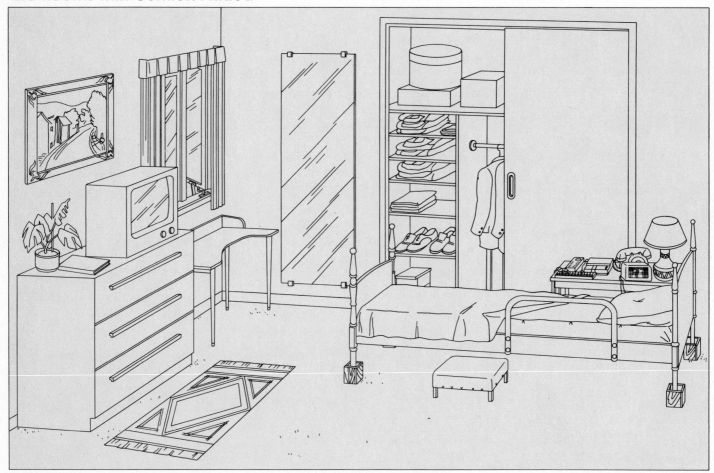

A bedroom for the disabled. Small adaptations and additions such as those shown in this bedroom can greatly ease the life of an invalid. The bed, for example, is made more accessible to a wheelchair user—or the person attending a bed-ridden patient—by being raised on wooden blocks so that the mattress height is 20 inches or more. On a bedside table are an intercom and

an array of electronic and electric controls that regulate such devices as lights and a television.

The closet pole is lowered to 42 inches—within reach from a wheelchair—and enough shelves are set between 15 and 54 inches above the floor to keep essential clothing accessible. A sliding door is the easiest kind to use from a wheelchair.

A specially constructed worktable, whose 30-inch height and contoured front are designed for the comfort of wheelchair users, stands underneath a window that can easily be opened by means of a crank. A bureau no higher than 36 inches, a mirror for dressing and a footstool to make it easier for the invalid to get dressed while seated complete the room.

thritic or anyone with limited strength in the hands. Replacing high thresholds with ones that are gently beveled and are no thicker than ½ inch helps persons who use walkers as well as those who move in wheelchairs. Floors can be covered with cork tiles, vinyl asbestos or any nonskid material, or with securely anchored low-pile carpeting.

A doorway must have a clear opening of 30 inches to permit passage of the smallest wheelchair. If the doorway itself is wide enough but the edge of the open door interferes, you can remove the door altogether or rehang it on swing-clear hinges *(page 33)*, which allow the entire

door to pivot out of the way. When the arc of an opening door is awkward for someone in a wheelchair or a walker to manage, replace the door with a folding or sliding type.

Always consider the specific needs and preferences of the disabled individual before buying, building or installing helpful equipment. Check, for example, the preferred height of a grab bar in the bathroom or the most useful length and height for rails above a bed, to see if they differ from the standard dimensions given on page 32. If you build a lightweight worktable for a person in a wheelchair, check the person's reach and the height

of the wheelchair arms—you may want to alter the standard dimensions of the one shown on page 31.

Physical and occupational therapists can offer guidance on adaptations, as can organizations devoted to the interests of the disabled. Among the nationally known are the National Easter Seal Society and the Office for Handicapped Individuals of the U.S. Department of Health and Human Services. In addition, there are hospital-supply stores and mail-order catalogues of self-help aids, both of which offer an array of equipment designed for virtually every need of invalids and the disabled.

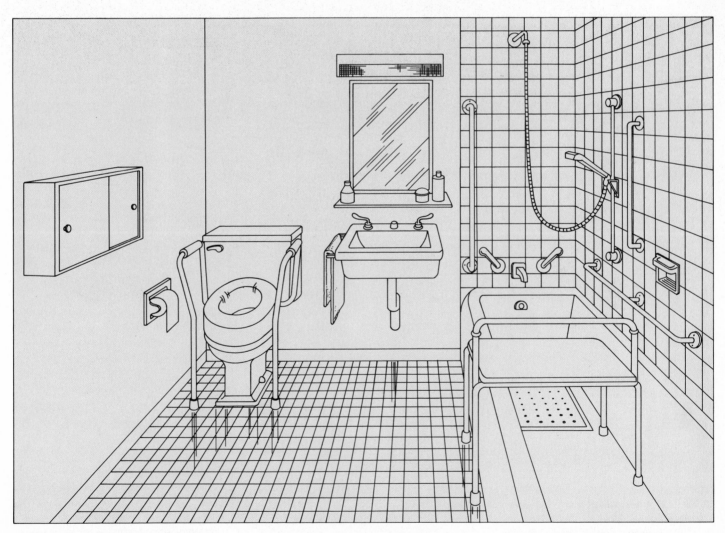

A bathroom for the disabled. A bathtub seat with nonskid rubber feet straddles the bathtub edge and facilitates tub access for someone with limited use of the legs. Above the seat, a shower head on a flexible hose slides along a vertical bar to bring the hose within reach. A non-slip mat clings to the tub floor. Rails set 33 to 36 inches above the bathroom floor provide grips over the bathtub and beside the toilet, which also has an elevated plastic seat. Lever-type faucet handles, which require only light pressure to operate, are installed at tub and sink. A mirror with shelf and a storage cabinet are mounted with their lower edges 30 to 40 inches above the floor, within reach of a wheelchair user.

Homemade and Commercial Helpers

A handy control center. Numerous controls for electrical devices, located on a bedside table, offer a measure of independence to a bedridden person. Available from several manufacturers in various models, the controls perform useful tasks. A multiple-outlet strip equipped with switches for each receptable turns lamps and other appliances, such as radios, on or off. A wireless remote-control unit operates a television set. A telephone amplifier allows the user to answer the phone or make a call without lifting the receiver. And an intercom facilitates communication with family members in other rooms.

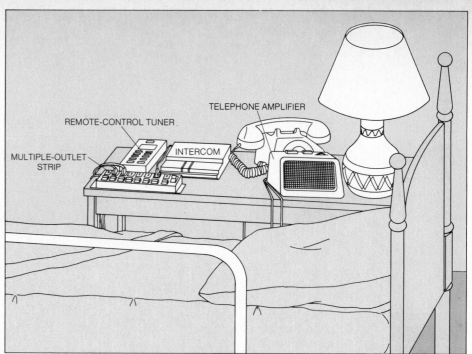

REMOTE-CONTROL TUNER.

TELEPHONE AMPLIFIER

MULTIPLE-OUTLET STRIP

INTERCOM

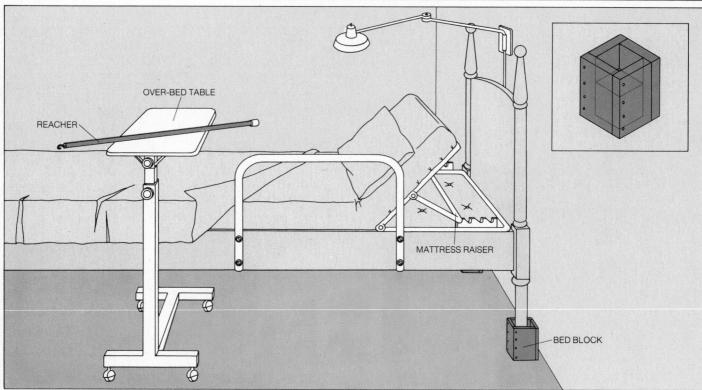

OVER-BED TABLE

REACHER

MATTRESS RAISER

BED BLOCK

Accessories for invalids. A folding metal mattress brace and a hospital-style over-bed table, both available from hospital-supply stores, are for people confined to bed for long periods. The brace locks at various angles under the mattress, to hold a reclining person in a comfortable position; the table rolls into place on casters and adjusts to an appropriate height. The bed is raised on 4-by-4 blocks, fenced in by ¾-inch plywood walls that rise 4 inches above the blocks (*inset*). A useful homemade reacher is fashioned from a length of ½-inch dowel, with a metal hook screwed into one end and a rubber walking-cane tip slipped over the other. The hook helps in retrieving three-dimensional objects; the rubber tip allows a wheelchair-bound person to pick up a piece of paper by pinning it against the floor, wall or table and pulling it within reach.

Making a
Wheelchair Worktable

1 Attaching the legs and cleats. With a saber saw, cut a rounded opening 24 inches long and 9 inches deep in the middle of one side of a 24-by-36-inch piece of ¾-inch plywood. On the underside, screw on metal base plates for 30-inch legs, then screw 1-by-2 cleats between the plates along the sides and back, placing the cleats flush with the edges of the table. Finally, screw the legs into the base plates *(inset)*.

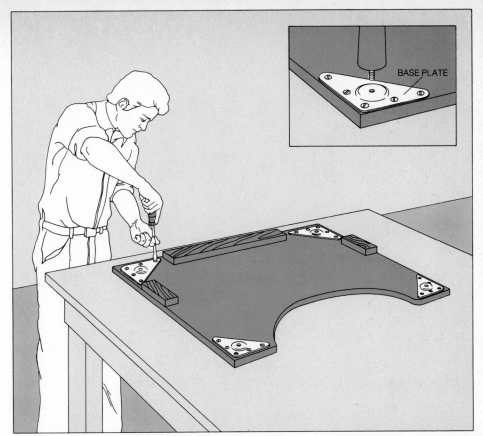

BASE PLATE

2 Adding a backboard and sideboards. Cut a 3-foot-long backboard and two 1-foot-long sideboards from 1-by-6 lumber, and round the top front corners of the sideboards with a saber saw. Have a helper hold the backboard against the table, its lower edge flush with the bottom of the 1-by-2 cleat, and drill pilot holes for 1-inch No. 8 screws through the backboard into the cleat. Glue and screw the backboard into place. Attach the sideboards to the side cleats and the edge of the backboard in the same way. Sand and finish the table as desired *(inset)*.

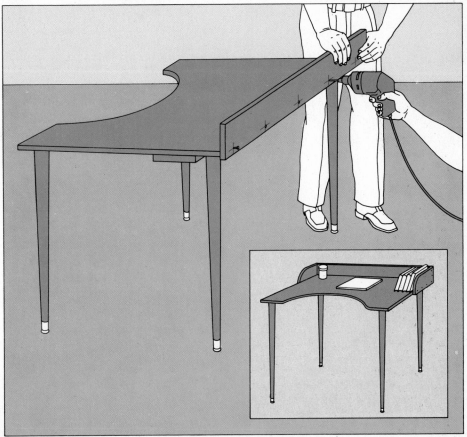

Fabricating a Tubular Bedrail

1 **Bending conduit.** Slide a conduit bender, available from an electrical-supply company or a tool-rental agency, over a length of ¾-inch thin-wall electrical conduit cut to fit the dimensions of the bed. For each rail, measure from the bottom of the bedframe to a point 6 inches above the mattress, and mark the conduit at that point. Then measure 30 inches and make a second mark. Finally, measure and mark the second leg of the rail, equal to the first, and cut off the excess conduit with a hacksaw.

Line up the arrow on the conduit bender with the first mark, place one foot on the rocker tread and pull the handle of the bender until the spirit level on the bender indicates you have made a 90-degree bend. Slide the bender onto the other end of the conduit, and line up the arrow with the second mark. Have a helper hold the first leg of the bedrail perpendicular to the floor while you make the second bend.

Cut two ½-inch dowels, one to fit inside each leg of the rail, and slide them into place. With a helper holding the rail against the bedframe, drill two holes through each leg and the frame.

2 **Mounting the bedrail.** With a helper holding the bedrail in place, pass a 2-inch-long stove bolt through the holes in the rail and frame, and secure it with a lock washer and a nut. Repeat for each mounting hole (*inset*).

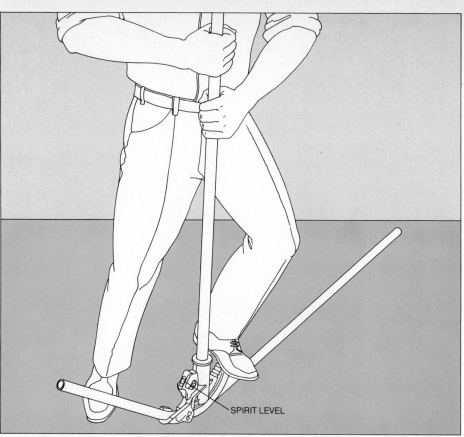

SPIRIT LEVEL

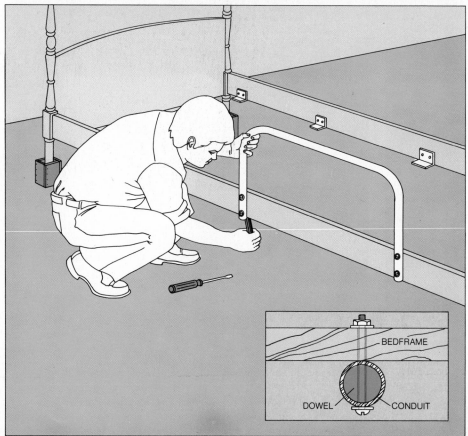

BEDFRAME

DOWEL — CONDUIT

Installing Special Hardware

Anchoring a grab bar to tile. Hold the grab bar against the wall at the desired height, preferably so that the ends align with the centers of two tiles, and mark the hole locations. Tap the tile with a center punch at each mark. Drill through the tile at each mark, using a masonry bit and a variable-speed drill set at a low speed. Use a masonry bit slightly larger than the diameter of the screws, and then a smaller wood bit when you hit a stud. Attach the grab bar to the wall.

When possible, position grab bars so that they can be screwed into studs, located as shown on page 112. If you cannot screw into studs, use toggle bolts in a plaster wall, Molly bolts in a wallboard wall, in each case drilling holes through the tile and wall to the diameter that is specified by the bolt manufacturer.

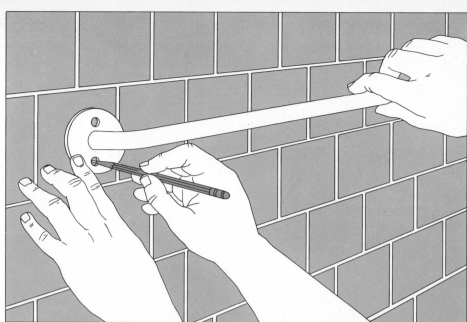

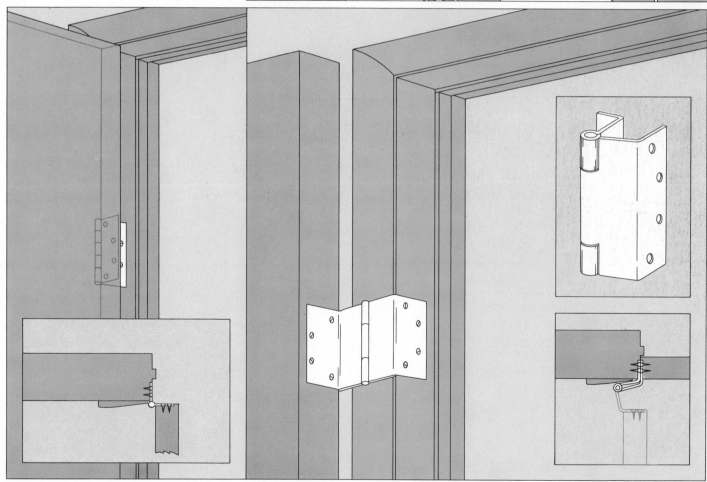

Installing a swing-clear hinge. When the edge of a door is an impediment to wheelchair access through the doorway *(left)*, the standard hinge can be replaced with one of the swing-clear type *(right)*. First remove the hinge leaves from both the door and the jamb. Check the leaves of the swing-clear hinge against the mortise for size. You probably will not have to remortise, but you may have to change the size or the position of the holes. To do so, cut lengths of dowel to fit into the existing holes, coat the dowel pieces with glue and then hammer them gently into the holes. Allow the glue to dry overnight, then drill pilot holes for attaching the new hinges and rehang the door.

A Showcase for Your Books: The Home Library

Books have a way of accumulating. Whether you are buying paperbacks or first editions, the acquisitive instinct never seems to wane; soon you have run out of storage space. Floor-to-ceiling bookshelves covering an entire wall—perhaps even more than one wall—may supply the answer. Treated architecturally and provided with such amenities as a built-in ladder and a lighted reading ledge, the wall of books becomes a library—a gracious addition to any home.

Although a bookcase that covers an entire wall may look imposing, it is relatively simple to construct. Rather than building one monolithic cabinet, you can assemble the book wall in modules—small, sturdy, self-contained units that are screwed to the wall studs and to each other and rest on a common base.

Modular construction offers some distinct advantages. Since each unit is relatively light, it is easy to move. Thus you have the option of doing most of the work in your shop and assembling the finished unit on site. Perhaps more important, the short shelves of a modular unit, with their built-in vertical supports, are less apt to sag than a bookcase with a continuous span of longer shelves. Paper, remember, is heavy: The kind used in most books weighs about 58 pounds per cubic foot, and a typical 3-foot shelf fully loaded with hard-cover books is supporting more than 100 pounds.

This book weight is an important factor in your decision on where to place a library wall. A fully loaded, 3-foot-wide floor-to-ceiling module in an 8-foot-high room may weigh over 700 pounds, and a row of such modules adds up to considerable weight on the floor. On floors above ground level, an outside or load-bearing wall is the most desirable place for the library, and ideally the shelves should sit on floor joists that run perpendicular to the wall. In most houses the joists run across the shorter dimensions of the house, but if your house is constructed differently and you suspect you may run into structural problems, you should check out your library design with a structural engineer.

The most efficient wall in terms of book storage space obviously is one without doors or windows. But the modules can be adapted to surround a window or to pass over a door—although this is likely to place the top shelf so high that you will need to plan for access to it. The floor-to-ceiling bookshelves shown here, for instance, are designed with a top shelf 12 inches below the ceiling in an 8-foot-high room. This puts the top shelf within arm's reach of the average person. If you are taller or shorter, you may want to change the height of the top shelf. Or you can install a ladder, which puts even high shelves within easy reach.

To design a library wall that is balanced and pleasingly proportioned, plan it on paper first. Start by making a scale drawing of the area the bookcases will cover, indicating the position of any architectural features or electric outlets. Divide this scale drawing into equal-sized sections no more than 38 inches wide, the optimum span for a bookshelf. If you are planning to cover one wall only, calculate the divisions corner to corner, allowing at least 1 inch of clearance for installation. At each of these divisions, mark off the width of the modules' vertical supports.

If you are covering two adjacent walls with shelves, lay out and build the longer wall first, the shorter wall second. Subtract from both walls the depth of the completed bookcase (the total width of the standards, the back and the face frame). Add 1 inch to the length of the longer bookcase or the one that is built first. This provides a surface for joining the two bookcases, leaving an inaccessible dead space in the corner.

At this stage in your planning decide what else, in addition to standard-sized books, you may want the library wall to hold. If you have oversized art books, you will probably need extra-deep shelves. You may want slanted display shelves for magazines, a well-lighted reading ledge for reference books, or cabinets for stereo components. Finally, to complete your scale drawing, calculate in linear feet the amount of shelving you will need for your books, and decide how many shelves you can fit in each module. In general, shelves are spaced 10 to 12 inches apart for hard-cover books, 8 to 10 inches apart for paperbacks; an average of seven books will fit into a running foot of space. But these figures can vary widely, and the spacing of your present shelves may be the most accurate guide.

Once you have found a design that suits your needs and looks attractive, preview it in full scale by sketching it lightly on the wall. Since the bookcase modules have backs, the marks will later be concealed. Then, in preparation for building the modules, measure the distance from ceiling to floor at several points along the wall. The vertical standards for the modules will be cut to a length equal to the height of the lowest point on the ceiling line minus the height of the common base and less an additional inch for clearance during installation. If there are any irregularities in the ceiling line, they will be concealed by moldings attached to the finished units. In addition, during installation you will use shims to compensate for any irregularity in the back wall (Step 1, page 38).

A library built in modules. The unbroken expanse of bookshelves in this library is actually composed of a series of relatively narrow floor-to-ceiling modules resting on a common base that matches the height of the existing baseboard. The modules are attached side to side with wood screws and are screwed to the wall studs through a horizontal hanging bar inside the back of each unit. Each module has two vertical standards cut from ¾-inch plywood or, where ceilings are more than 8 feet high, from solid lumber. The inner face of each standard is rabbeted top and bottom to take the top and bottom of the module, and dadoed slightly below its mid-point to accept a stationary center shelf. A ¼-inch plywood back reinforces these connections. In a typical module the shelves are 10 inches deep and, except for the stationary center shelf, rest on adjustable shelf pins. The same basic module can be modified to incorporate slanted display shelves and cabinet doors. Similarly, a reading ledge can be fitted into dadoes in the sides of one module, replacing three shelves. The shelf unit that spans the top of the door is simply a box, attached to the flanking modules with screws. A movable ladder (*page 40*) hooks over the stationary shelf to provide access to the upper books.

A face frame of solid lumber hides the module joints and conceals the rough plywood edges. A fascia board spans the tops of the modules and supports a cornice molding; it and the floor-line shoe molding serve to conceal any floor or ceiling irregularities and make the library wall look as if it is permanently built in.

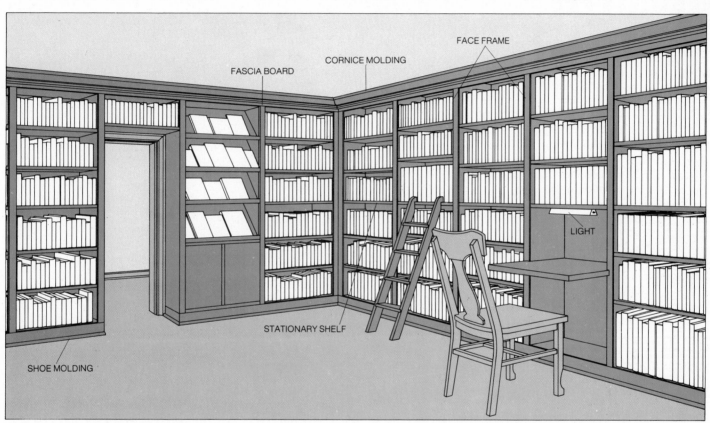

FASCIA BOARD • CORNICE MOLDING • FACE FRAME • LIGHT • STATIONARY SHELF • SHOE MOLDING

Building a Bookshelf Module

1 Cutting the plywood components. Cut standards to the desired width from large sheets of ¾-inch plywood; crosscut each standard to the desired length. Cut a top, bottom and stationary shelf for each module, making these pieces the same depth as the standards and as long as the planned inside width of the modules plus ¾ inch. Cut adjustable shelves ⅛ inch shallower than the standards and less the thickness of the shelf edging you plan to use. Shelves are ¼ inch shorter than the inside width of the modules, to accommodate shelf pins. Cut a 4-inch-wide hanging bar for each cabinet, the inside width of the modules. Cut back panels from ¼-inch plywood or hardboard, the full outside dimensions of the modules.

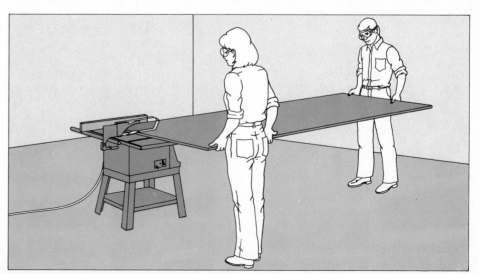

2 **Positioning the shelves.** With a pencil and a combination square, mark a line for a ¾-inch-wide rabbet at each end of all standards, and a ¾-inch-wide dado for the center shelf, positioning the dado at the midpoint of the standard minus the height of the base (*Step 2, page 38*). Measuring carefully, mark the positions of holes for the shelf pins 1 inch from the front and back edges of each standard. Space these marks 2 inches apart, beginning 1 foot in from the ends of the standards and stopping 1 foot short of the marks for the dadoes.

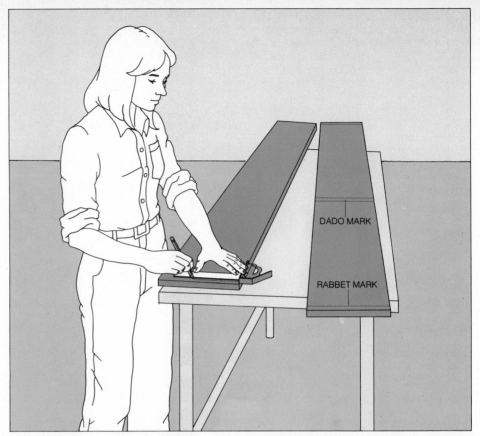

DADO MARK

RABBET MARK

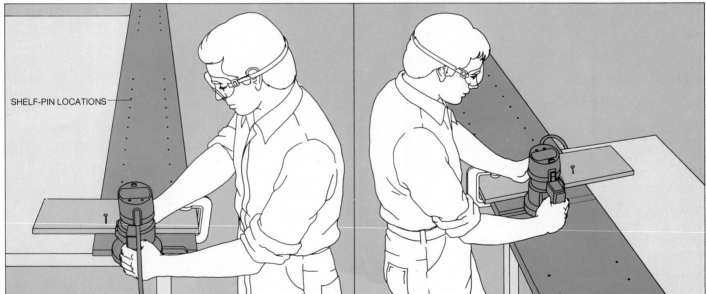

SHELF-PIN LOCATIONS

3 **Cutting the shelf supports.** Clamp a length of straight-edged scrap wood to one end of a standard, as a guide for the router base, and cut the first rabbet ⅜ inch deep and ¾ inch wide. In order not to splinter the corner of the plywood, begin the rabbet 2 or 3 inches in from one edge. Guide the router to complete the forward cut first, then bring the router back to complete the rabbet. Reposition the guide, and cut an identical rabbet at the opposite end of the standard.

The top and bottom of the module will fit into the rabbeted ends of the standards.

Use the same length of scrap wood to guide the router between the dado lines marked for the stationary shelf, making this cut, too, ⅜ inch deep. Finally, use an awl to make a slight depression at every shelf-pin mark, and drill a ¼-inch hole ½ inch deep, taping the bit ½ inch from its tip to keep from drilling too deep.

4 **Assembling the frame.** Working with a helper, test-fit the joints between the standards and the top, bottom and stationary shelf of each module. If necessary, use a hammer and a block of wood to seat the center shelf snugly. If the fit is not perfect or the modules do not line up precisely, adjust the depth of the rabbets and dadoes until they do. Then assemble the pieces with glue and sixpenny finishing nails. Spread glue on the ends of the horizontal pieces as well as inside the rabbets and dadoes. Drive the nails partway into the center line of the rabbets and dadoes, spacing the nails 4 inches apart and at least 1 inch from the edge of the standard.

5 **Squaring the frame.** To make sure the frame is squared, measure diagonally between opposite corners while the glue is still moist. If the measurements are not exactly equal, push the corners with the longer measurement toward each other, then measure again. Repeat until the measurements are identical, then set all of the nails. Apply glue to the ends and top edge of the hanging bar. Slide it into the top back of the module. Secure the bar with sixpenny nails, putting two through each standard; nail every 6 inches through the top.

Glue and nail the ¼-inch-thick back panel into place. Drive ¾-inch box nails through the panel into the edge of the frame at 3-inch intervals. Drive two rows of nails at 3-inch intervals through the back panel into the hanging bar. Paint or finish the completed module as desired.

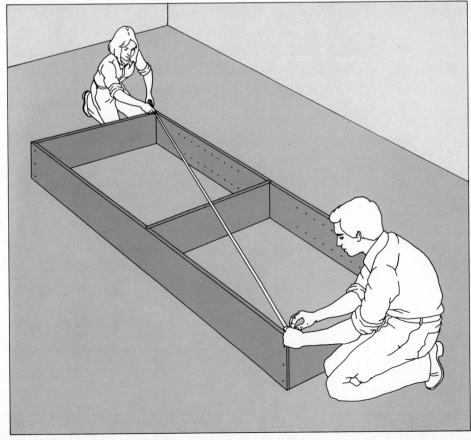

Installing the Modules

1 Preparing the wall. Remove the shoe molding and baseboard along the planned location for the bookcases; sweep the edge of a straight 6-foot board across the wall and mark any pronounced bumps in the surface. Determine the height of these bumps by holding a carpenter's level against the board, to make sure it is perfectly vertical, and measuring the depth of the gaps between the edge of the board and the low points on the wall. Note your findings on your scale drawing (*page 34*) or on the wall. In installation, the base of the unit and the hanging bar in each module must be shimmed until they are flush with the highest point in the wall.

Mark the location of every wall stud at the top and bottom of the wall. Extend the top marks out onto the ceiling, far enough to clear the front edge of the modules when they are set in place.

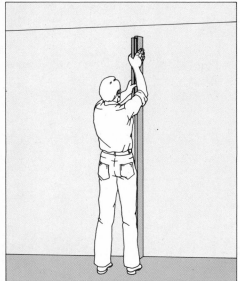

3 Installing the modules. With a helper, place the first module at the end of the base. Use the carpenter's level to check vertical alignment and, if necessary, have your helper slide a horizontal shim behind the hanging bar to plumb the module before you screw it in place. Drill two pilot holes through the hanging bar and shim into each stud, one above the other and 2 inches apart, using the stud marks on the ceiling as a guide. Secure with 3-inch flat-head screws.

Butt the second module against the first. Align their front edges, then clamp them together with C clamps, using scraps of wood under the clamp jaws. If necessary, shim the second module before you screw it to the studs. Drill pilot holes for two 1¼-inch wood screws 1 inch in from the edge at the top and bottom of the adjoining standards and below the stationary shelf, and screw the modules together.

2 Making the common base. Using a continuous strip of plywood or lumber, cut to the height of the room's baseboards, assemble a common base that will support all the modules. Cut the front and back rails to the planned total length of the bookcase less 1 inch; cut the end-pieces and the interior braces—known as spreaders—to the width of the standards minus the combined thickness of the front and the back rails. Set the four framing pieces on edge, forming a rectangle, and butt-join each corner with three sixpenny finishing nails driven through the rails. Nail the spreaders inside the frame, at intervals of 2 feet.

Move the base into position and, if necessary, shim it out from the wall at the studs to the distance that you determined in Step 1. Level the base by tapping shims under its corners as necessary, as well as into any gaps beneath the spreaders. Then fasten the base to the wall by driving two eightpenny nails into each stud in the wall behind, through the back rail and the shims. Use sixpenny finishing nails to toenail through the spreaders and the shims into the floor. If the ends of any shims protrude beyond the base, use a chisel to notch them; then break them off flush with the bookcase by pulling up firmly on the protruding ends.

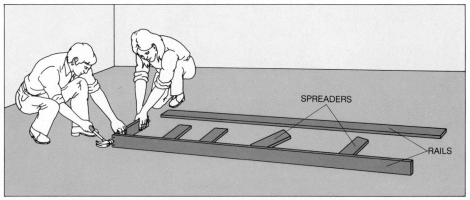

4 **Attaching the facings.** Using solid lumber, cut a fascia board to span the top of all the modules, a rail to span the bottom, and vertical stiles—as wide as the combined thickness of two adjoining standards—to cover up the front edges. The bottom rail can be one long board or several boards butted together. First install the fascia board, aligning its top edge with the top edges of the modules. Secure it with sixpenny finishing nails every 10 inches, setting the nails.

Next attach vertical stiles, cut to fit between the bottom edge of the fascia board and the top edge of the module bottoms. At the two ends of the wall, align the outside edges of the stiles with the outside edges of the standards, allowing the inside edges to lap over the shelves. Cut horizontal facings to fit between the vertical stiles at each stationary shelf, and nail these facings to the front edge of each shelf. Finally nail on a bottom rail, flush with the bottoms of the stiles.

Cover the nailheads with wood putty, and paint or stain the facings to match the modules. To cover any gaps between the ceiling and the fascia board, install a cornice molding, mitering joints if the bookcase covers more than one wall. Nail shoe molding at the base of the bottom rail. If one end of the library wall will be exposed, conceal the back edge of the end module with a length of quarter-round molding.

FASCIA BOARD

STILES

5 **Trimming the shelf edges.** Conceal the front edges of plywood shelves either with ¼-by-¾-inch pine edging strips *(above, left)* or with veneer tape *(above, right)*. To attach the edging strips, clamp the shelf in a woodworking vise and cut a section of edging to match. Spread yellow glue on the shelf edge and on one face of the strip. Press the surfaces together and secure them at 8-inch intervals with 1½-inch finishing nails, set-

ting the nails. Cover the nailheads with wood putty, and finish to match the shelf.

To use veneer tape, cut a strip of tape 1 inch longer than the shelf. Spread contact cement on the shelf edge and allow it to soak in. Add a second coat and at the same time spread cement on the back of the tape. Place three or four small wooden dowels on the shelf edge—to keep

the glued sides from sticking—then carefully line up the tape with the shelf edge. Working from the center outward, press the tape onto the edge, removing dowels as you go. Roll the tape smooth with a larger dowel, then rub the dowel over the corners of the shelf to crease the excess tape, and cut off the excess with a razor blade. Sand the tape edges with 120-grit sandpaper, blending them into the edges of the shelf.

Amenities That Enhance a Library's Appeal

Like libraries of grander scale, a home library benefits from such accessories as a ladder for reaching high shelves; slanted shelves for displaying magazines or, if rare books are your passion, prized editions; and the convenience of a reading ledge perched amidst the books.

Traditional library ladders are elegant oak assemblies that roll on wheels and hang from tracks. Such ladders are still available from manufacturers and, if your floor is relatively flat, can be installed in your home library. Look for the names of producers under listings for rolling ladders in the Thomas Register, a reference work found in most public libraries.

A more modest but equally useful ladder can be built from 1-by-4 hardwood stock or 2-by-4 softwood. The four-tread ladder (right) is sturdy but lightweight and easily moved. The notches in its rails are cut at a height to hold the ladder at a comfortable angle when it rests on the stationary center shelf of a bookcase module. If the stationary shelves in your modules are more than 48 inches from the floor, you will have to add extra treads to the ladder—one tread for every 12 vertical inches.

Support for display shelves or a reading ledge can be dadoed into the standards along with the dadoes for the stationary shelves, without major changes in construction procedures (Steps 1-3, pages 35-36). A display shelf requires a lip at its front edge to keep its contents from sliding off; the lip can be cut from the same wood as the cabinet facings. The reading ledge should be fashioned from 1½-inch or 2-inch stock—a slab of butcher block is one possibility—and should not extend more than 12 inches beyond the front of the standards without additional bracing. Lighting for the ledge can be fastened to the bottom of the shelf above or provided by a small desk lamp. Plan ahead, however, so that wiring can be connected to a nearby outlet.

A Library Ladder to Build

1 **Making ladder rails.** Prop a 1-by-4 or 2-by-4 board on edge against the stationary shelf so that one corner rests 27 inches out from the base of the bookshelf, and at least 4 inches extends above the stationary shelf. With a straight scrap of wood, mark a horizontal line for the bottom of the rail; cut there. Mark a horizontal line where the rail meets the top of the stationary shelf. From the inside, cut along this line 1½ inches, then cut at a right angle to make a notch that will fit over the shelf (inset). Leave at least 3½ inches between the notch and the top, and round the top with a saber saw. Use this rail as a pattern for the second one.

With a T bevel locked at the bottom angle, mark four dado lines on the inside of each rail, making them equidistant but not more than 10 to 12 inches apart. Cut the dadoes ⅜ inch deep on 1-inch stock, ½ inch deep on 2-inch stock.

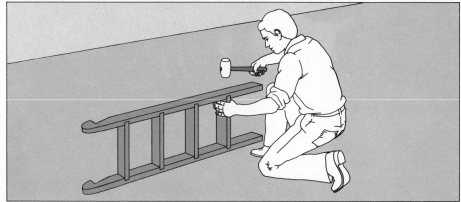

2 **Installing the treads.** Cut treads from the same stock used for the rails; make them 12 to 14 inches long and bevel their front edges to match the angle of the rail edges. Test-fit the ladder. If the fit is precise, drill pilot holes for two flat-head screws at each end of every tread. Use 2-inch screws on 1-by-4 stock, 3-inch screws on 2-by-4s. Disassemble the pieces, counterboring the holes to sink screwheads. Apply glue to the dadoes and treads; reassemble the ladder, immediately setting the screws. Conceal the screwheads with wooden plugs or wood putty. Paint or stain the wood as desired. Glue rubber strips to the underside of the top notch and the bottom of the ladder, to prevent slippage and surface marring.

A Roll-around Ladder
to Assemble from a Kit

Anatomy of a rolling ladder. This factory-built
rolling ladder runs along a slotted metal track that
is fastened with brackets to the edges of the
bookshelf standards. Such ladders are built to order and are sold complete with all their hardware. Here the track is bent to curve around a
corner; other designs permit the ladder to be
lifted from its track and shifted to another track in
a separate part of the library. The slide fixtures
at the top of the ladder permit the ladder bottom
to swing inward, flush with the face of the
bookshelf, when the ladder is not in use. Wheels
with rubber tires roll quietly across the floor.

Wide Shelves That Slant,
A Desk Shelf for Reading

Shelves for display and reading. The slanted
shelves join dadoes cut to the same depth as
those for the stationary shelves (*page 36*). The
dadoes are angled 20° to 30° from the horizontal,
depending on the size of the items to be displayed—the larger the item, the greater the angle
needed. Dado angles are marked on the standards with a protractor and a T bevel. The front
and back edges of the shelves are cut to fit
flush with the front and back edges of the standards. Edgings on the front are cut wide enough
to provide a lip ½ inch above the shelves.

Set into dadoes in the standards, a 1½-inch- to 2-
inch-thick ledge projects 10 to 12 inches beyond the front of the module to provide space below for the knees. The dadoes, positioned to
hold the working surface of the ledge 30 inches
above the floor, are cut with several passes of
a router. The ledge is fastened with glue and 2-
inch wood screws, driven through the sides
of the standards. Facings on the standards are
notched to fit around the ends of the ledge.

The shelf just over the ledge should be at least 18
inches above it. If you mount a light fixture on
the bottom of this shelf, dado the shelf into place.
Before the book wall is assembled, cut a hole
to expose the electric outlet.

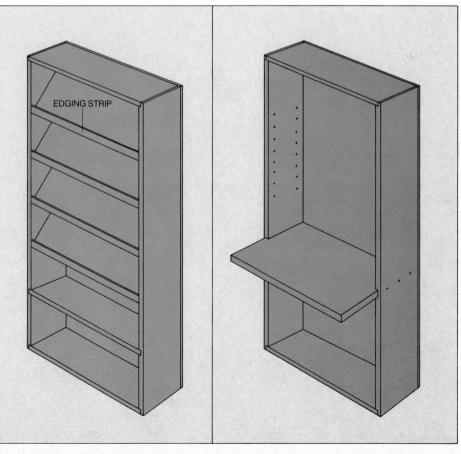

EDGING STRIP

In Pursuit of Serious Avocations

Ingredients of high-fidelity sound. A system of speakers, such as the one shown at left with its grille removed to expose the low- and the high-frequency speaker cones, is a key element of a stereo listening room. Surprisingly, the 2-by-4s next to the speakers are key elements as well. Nailed together, they frame a sound baffle; when strategically placed, baffles help the speakers and the room to work together to ensure that sounds of varying frequencies are all heard with equal volume and clarity.

A hobby is by definition a random activity worked into the overall fabric of our lives. But in recent years, as shorter working hours have produced an increase in leisure time, many a part-time pursuit has developed into a space-consuming passion. An indoor garden that started as a single shelf of plants can rapidly blossom into a room-sized showcase for a particularly prized species. A Sunday painter can develop into a serious artist needing a permanent place for supplies and work in progress.

When a hobby expands in seriousness and begins to overrun the house, the ideal solution is to find or make a space that can be permanently devoted to the hobby. Choosing and planning the appropriate area depends on the nature of the hobby and its particular requirements. A few hobbies, such as woodworking and metalworking, can be more noisy than is comfortable for other members of the household; they are best relegated to a far corner or to the basement. Some, such as sculpting and pottery making, tend to be messy and need easy access to washing-up areas so that budding artists need not walk through the living room with dripping hands. Other hobbies, such as spinning and weaving, are relatively sedate but need plenty of space to spread out and can easily end up taking over an entire room.

A prime consideration for housing a hobby is its special requirement for storage: A good rule of thumb is to plan for twice as much storage as you think you will need. Storage areas do not have to be built in; movable, modular units that can be expanded or rearranged to suit your needs are the most useful. Where closet space is available, adjustable shelves are ideal for storing extra supplies that are not needed within arm's reach.

Even when space has been found that is perfect in size and location, adaptations in lighting and plumbing may be necessary. Walls and floors may need protective finishes or coverings. The changes can be minimal or radical, depending on the extent to which you are willing to make the room cater to your needs.

But even when a particular pursuit requires a very special environment, you do not have to relinquish an entire room. An aquarium or aviary built into a wall will allow you to raise tropical fish or breed exotic birds without changing the function of the room at all, and the components for listening to high-fidelity music can be so carefully incorporated into the décor and structure of a room that while the use of the room changes, its appearance remains the same. Indeed, both the hobby and the room's primary use can benefit from such a doubling up of form and function, with one purpose enhancing the other.

For the Artist, a Quiet, Well-lighted Studio

Whether you are a full-time or a part-time artist, having a room of your own in which to paint or take pictures or work with clay makes the occupation much more enjoyable. The ideal is a well-lit, private space with abundant storage, but when such a place is not available, you can convert part of a family room, spare bedroom or basement into a compact studio for your work.

There are several things to consider in selecting an area for a studio. Depending on your particular pursuit, you may, for example, need special utilities. If you plan to put in more lights or install heavy-duty electrical equipment such as a potter's kiln, you may have to upgrade the area's electrical capacity. Or you may want water; if this is the case, you should check for a wall where there are existing plumbing lines to be tapped.

Crafts involving the use of dyes, toxic chemicals, or intense heat require an area with excellent ventilation from an exhaust fan or windows. Also consider accessibility for bringing in supplies—locating a pottery studio in a second-story bedroom, for instance, will mean carrying 50-pound bags of clay upstairs.

Another consideration is the light. For painting and sculpture, abundant natural light is desirable—ideally from a northern exposure because such light is diffuse and relatively consistent—in which case you may decide to add window area (pages 118-123). Where this is impractical, or if you will be painting at night, you can simulate natural light with special color-rendering fluorescent tubes. The light qualities of such tubes are expressed in units called Kelvins. Closest to a natural north light are 7,000 K fluorescent tubes, but many artists who want their work to look good in incandescent light (about 3,200 K) compromise by working in the range of 4,200 K to 5,000 K.

An art studio should accommodate the potential side effects of a pursuit. If noise accompanies the craft, the studio may need to be soundproofed. If mess and clutter are inevitable, an easy-to-clean floor is essential and adequate storage space for supplies simplifies tidying up.

If a studio must double as a guest or family room, as much equipment as possible should be stowed out of sight when not in use. A caster-mounted taboret that rolls into a closet and a worktable that can be disassembled speed the conversion of a studio to other uses.

Places to Suit Painters or Potters

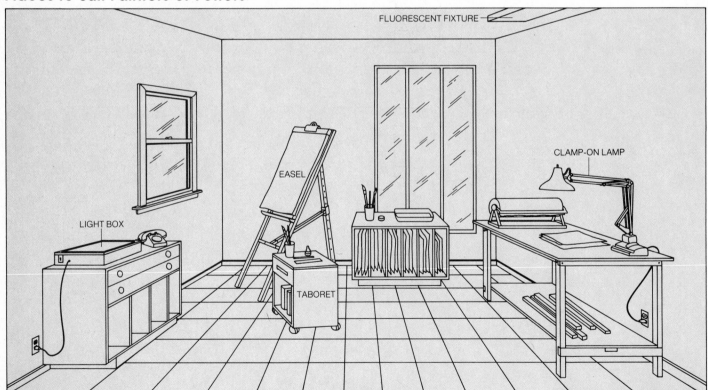

Features of a painter's studio. Because natural light is the most important aspect of a painter's studio, in this one an existing window has been lengthened and a trio of long stationary windows have been added between studs. Above the worktable at right, used for planning and framing, a fluorescent fixture with tubes that do not distort colors provides a diffuse light; a clamp-on incandescent lamp aids close work. The table provides protective storage below for stretchers and canvas. Stretched canvases and finished work stand in a unit with vertical partitions. A second storage unit, at left, holds a homemade light box and contains shallow drawers for large sheets of watercolor paper and posterboard. A special cabinet called a taboret is available at art-supply stores; it rolls to the easel with paints and brushes, and some models have a top of clear plastic that can double as a palette. The vinyl-tile floor makes cleanup easy, but a drop cloth could be spread under messy projects.

Layout of a potter's studio. In a potter's studio, safety and logical traffic flow are the main concerns. The electric kiln must be 8 to 10 inches off the floor on a metal stand, and 2 feet away from any wall. If the floor beneath the kiln is wood or tile, it should be protected with a layer of fire brick. An exhaust fan near the kiln pulls heat out of the room during firing; the fan can be installed through the wall or in a window.

Equipment is arranged to save steps. A wedging table for kneading raw clay is near the wheel where the clay is shaped. Glazing chemicals are stored in pails beneath the worktable and on shelves above (*page 15*), close to the banding wheel where the glazes are applied. A water pail on a dolly is used for rinsing hands, thus keeping corrosive clay out of the plumbing system. Although most of the clay will collect as sediment in the bottom of the pail, the utility sink (*page 8*) has a plaster trap for extra protection.

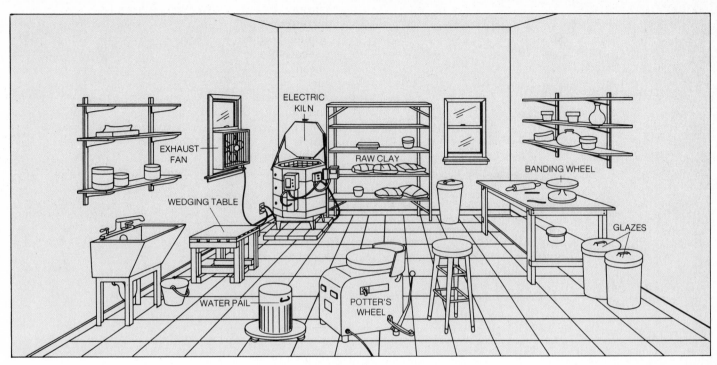

A Multipurpose Worktable

1 Notching the legs. Cut four 2-by-4 legs, ¾ inches shorter than the table height desired; then notch each leg at two points along one edge. Cut one notch at the top of the leg, a second 6 inches from the bottom, making each notch 1½ inches deep and 3½ inches long. Use two saw cuts to make the top notch. To remove the waste wood from the lower notch, make parallel saw cuts, or kerfs, into the notch and use a mallet and chisel to cut out the wood, holding the chisel so that the bevel faces the kerfs. When all the legs are notched, drill two ⅜-inch boltholes through the top of each leg, alongside the notch and near the midpoint of the remaining wood (*inset*).

Cut four 2-by-4 end rails to the planned width of the leg assembly. In two of the rails, cut a 1½-by-3½-inch center notch in one edge; fit these rails, notched edge up, into the notches at the bottom of the legs and secure them with 2½-inch screws. Fit the two remaining end rails into the notches at the top of the legs and secure them, taking care to place the screws where they will not penetrate the boltholes.

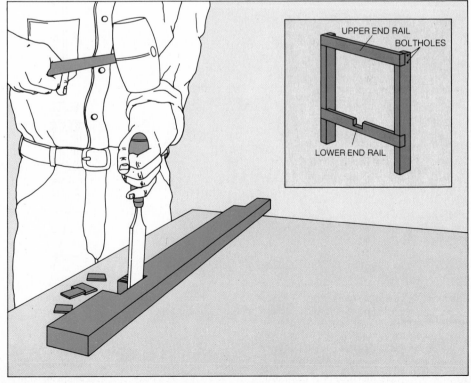

2 **Bolting the frame pieces.** Cut 2-by-4 front and back rails, 3 inches shorter than the planned length of the table frame, and clamp them edge up between the two leg assemblies. Position them inside and flush with the tops of the legs. Use a pencil to mark through the boltholes at the top of each leg, to match their locations on the rails. Unclamp the rails, and drill ⅜-inch holes at the marks. Then reposition the rails, and bolt them to the legs with 3½-inch-long ⅜-inch carriage bolts, using nuts and washers to tighten them against the back of the rails.

Cut a 2-by-4 center support the full length of the frame, fit it into the notches on the lower end rails, and secure it with 2½-inch screws.

3 **Attaching the top.** Place a top of ¾-inch plywood face down on the floor, and position the frame upside down over it, adjusting it for the desired overhang (usually about 4 inches all around). Attach the top to the frame with metal angle braces outside the front and back rails. Position one brace 2 inches from each leg, and put additional braces at about 2-foot intervals.

Turn the table right side up; nail or screw a ½-inch plywood shelf atop the lower end rails.

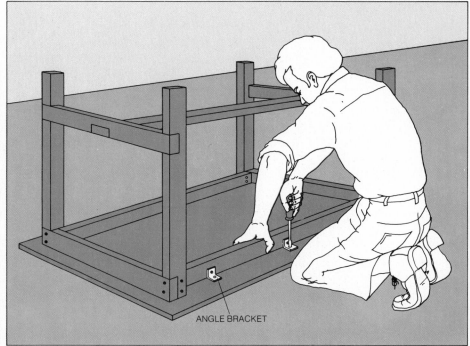

ANGLE BRACKET

An Adjustable Drafting Top

1 **Adapting the basic table design.** Construct the same worktable frame, but cut the front rail 3 inches longer and bolt it to the front of the legs instead of behind them. Position the frame upside down on the underside of the tabletop, 4 inches in from the front edge. Place three butt hinges along the outside of the front rail, one near each leg and one in the middle. Use an awl to punch starting holes for screws; attach one leaf of each hinge to the underside of the top, the other leaf to the outside of the front rail.

For the drafting top (inset), cut two 18-inch arms of 2-by-2; drill ⅜-inch holes through them, 1 inch apart, starting 3 inches from one end. Use a T hinge to attach the undrilled end under the tabletop—just outside an end rail, 4 inches from the back rail; keep the drilled holes perpendicular to the end rail. Screw the strap leaf of the hinge to the arm's front face, the square leaf to the underside of the top.

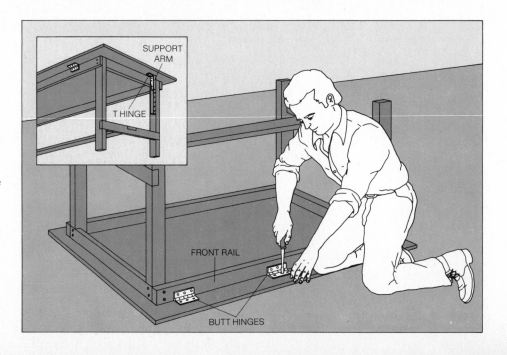

SUPPORT ARM

T HINGE

FRONT RAIL

BUTT HINGES

2 **Marking hole locations on the end rails.** With a helper, turn the table right side up and lift the back of the top to a preferred drafting angle. Position each support arm vertically, with one hole near the back of each end rail. Mark and drill a ⅜-inch hole through each end rail at that location. Align corresponding holes in the support arms with the holes in the two end rails, and slip 3½-inch long ⅜-inch bolts through the arms and rails to support the tabletop at the desired angle. If you want, glue and nail 1¼-inch molding to the front edge of the top, creating a pencil lip.

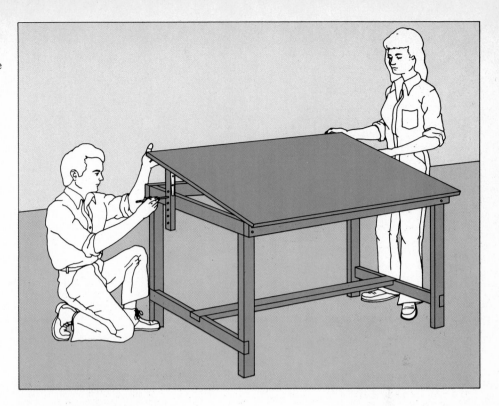

Specialized Equipment for a Diversity of Hobbies

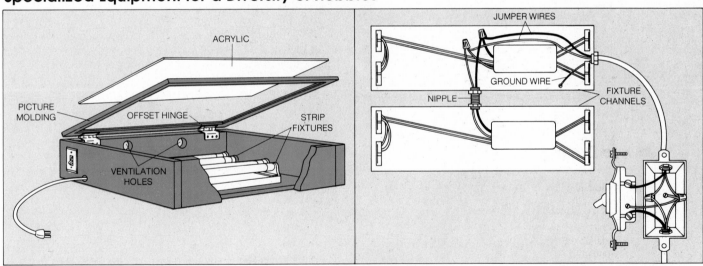

A homemade light box. A light box for viewing transparencies or making tracings should not be less than 14 inches long inside, to allow for the shortest fluorescent-strip fixtures available. The frame is made of ½-inch plywood, glued and nailed together with butt joints. The sides are 6 inches high, allowing clearance above two 20-watt, two-tube fixtures mounted on the bottom. A square hole in one side accepts the light switch, and the power cord exits through a hole below the switch. Several ½-inch holes along the back of the box provide ventilation; a high-gloss white paint covers the box's interior, to maximize the reflection of light.

The lid is a ¼-inch sheet of translucent white acrylic in a picture-molding frame, attached to the box with two offset hinges. The frame is the same size as the box, the plastic sheet ½ inch smaller. Glazier's points pressed into the lip of the picture molding hold the plastic in place.

In the wiring that connects the fixtures to the switch (*above, right*), wires run from one fixture into the other through a metal nipple, passing through knockout holes in the sides of the channels. Wire caps connect the fixture wires to each other—black to black and white to white—and to jumper wires. The jumper wires, along

with a ground wire that is screwed to the channel, are then fed through a thin-wall conduit into the switch box. There the black jumper wire is connected to one of the switch terminals, and the white jumper wire is connected to the white wire of a three-conductor No. 14 cord that runs from the switch box to a nearby outlet. The ground wires from the fluorescent lights and from the power cord, the jumper wire from the grounding screw on the switch, and a jumper from the ground screw on the switch box are all joined together with a wire cap. The black wire of the power cord is then connected to the remaining free terminal on the switch.

A light table. You can convert one end of a worktable into a light table by cutting an opening in the tabletop to receive the light box shown on page 47. The box is attached to the underside of the tabletop with two 2-inch angle brackets on each side. For convenience, the light switch is mounted in a hole in the top of the table instead of on the side of the box. The plastic surface can be made flush with the tabletop if you cut the opening to match the outside dimensions of the box and attach the angle brackets ½ inch below the top edge of the box, leaving a ¼-inch ledge for the plastic. When it is set flush, the plastic is left unframed and is cut to exactly the same size as the opening.

Alternatively, the box can be attached flush with the underside of the table, and picture molding can be nailed—notched side up—around the opening, with the plastic set in the notch. If you choose, you can splice a line switch into the supply cord, to eliminate the need for a switch on the light box or light table.

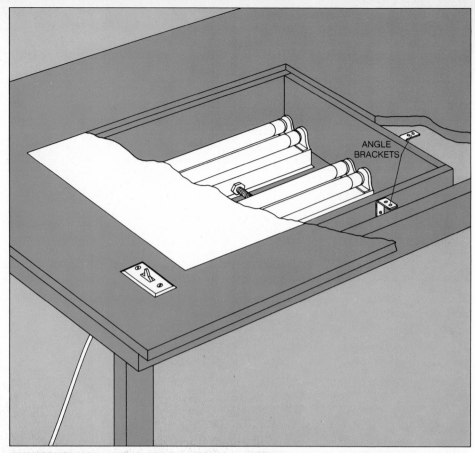

ANGLE BRACKETS

Supports for paper backdrops. Two vertical stands, almost ceiling high, support several rolls of colored, seamless background paper for photography. The I-shaped base of each stand consists of two 18-inch-long 2-by-6s, set on edge and nailed to a pair of 1-foot-long 1-by-6 crosspieces, also on edge. The crosspieces are spaced 1½ inches apart so that the stand's 2-by-2 vertical pole can be sandwiched between them. Two 3½-inch-long ¾-inch bolts secure each pole between its crosspieces. Adjustable furniture glides are screwed into the bottom of the base at each corner to level it.

Metal hooks, such as those sold for supporting hanging plants, are screwed into one face of each pole at several levels to hold the ends of the paper roll. Each stand can also be used individually to support clip-on studio lights or, with white posterboard tacked on, to serve as a reflector.

A sturdy wedging table. This 30-inch-high canvas-covered table, built of 2-by-4 lumber, provides potters with a strong, solid surface on which to work clay before it is shaped on the wheel. As the clay is kneaded, the canvas soaks up excess moisture. Doubled 2-by-4 legs and 2-by-4 rails are attached with tenpenny common nails. The front and back upper rails are fastened to the outside of the legs, to allow for maximum work surface; all the side rails are fastened to the inside of the legs, to brace the frame. The front and back lower rails rest on the lower side rails, to provide toe space.

Lengths of 2-by-4, spaced evenly and face up, are nailed across the frame top to support the ½-inch plywood top, cut to the same size as the base. Canvas is stretched over it and stapled underneath; the top is then nailed at the corners.

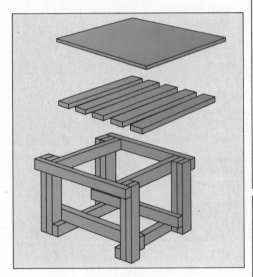

Drawers and bins for art supplies. Flat storage for large sheets of paper and posterboard and upright storage for finished work are both accommodated in this art-supplies unit, adapted from the yarn-storage unit shown above, right. The shell can be filled entirely with drawers, with vertical partitions or, as shown, with a combination of the two. Wide, shallow drawers (*inset*) consist of ½-inch plywood sides dadoed ¼ inch deep ¾ inch from the lower edge, to take a ½-inch plywood bottom. A 1-by-2 center support, glued and nailed under the drawer bottom, provides strength. The drawers are fitted with drawer glides attached as in Step 3, page 13, and each drawer has a false front, 1 inch wider than the actual drawer front, attached with screws from behind, to hide this hardware. Drawer pulls are attached through both fronts.

Below the drawers, a center shelf is dadoed into the sides, and vertical partitions of ½-inch hardboard are held between strips of 1-by-1 glued and nailed to the bottom of the cabinet and the underside of the center shelf.

A catacomb for yarn. Cubicles 24 inches deep and 8 inches square, each one sized to hold eight hanks of yarn, keep various textures and colors separated. The ¾-inch plywood sides are dadoed ¼ inch deep to receive two ¾-inch plywood shelves. The shelves and the top and bottom, also made of ¾-inch plywood, have dadoes ¼ inch wide and ¼ inch deep to hold the vertical dividers of ¼-inch hardboard. The shell has butt joints, glued and nailed, with nails countersunk and filled with wood putty. A ⅛-inch hardboard back is tacked on for rigidity, and the unit sits on a 2-by-4 frame that is 3 inches smaller than the unit on each side, to allow toe space. On the end, hooks and dowels in a pre-drilled board hold tools and loose yarn.

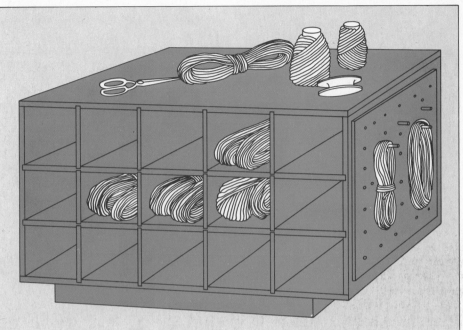

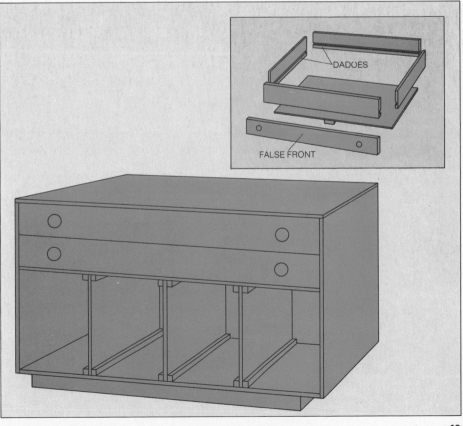

DADOES

FALSE FRONT

Three Approaches to a Photography Darkroom

Whether shoehorned into a closet or occupying spacious quarters of its own, a photographic darkroom needs to be designed for the careful, efficient work that printmaking demands. Most obviously, the room must be totally dark at times, so that you can avoid fogging undeveloped film or paper. It must also have two separate areas—a wet side and a dry side—to let you avoid contaminating negatives and photographic papers with chemicals and wash water; ideally these areas should be across an aisle from each other, but if space is limited, a splashboard separating the enlarger from the processing trays will do. Finally, in a room full of chemicals, good ventilation is crucial.

To make a darkroom permanently dark, you can paint the windows black or cover them with black adhesive paper. But temporary darkening is often more practical, especially if the room is also used for other purposes. Windows can be temporarily sealed with sheets of photographic cloth, cut to size and fastened to the window frames with the hook-and-loop tape sold under the trade name Velcro. Panels of thin plywood, cut to fit snugly, are equally effective. These too can be secured with Velcro tape or held in place with screws.

To be sure a room is lightproof, stand in it with the lights out for at least five minutes. When your eyes have adjusted, hold a sheet of white paper at arm's length in front of you. If you can see the paper, check the room further for leaks. Small light leaks around the windows can be caulked or sealed with black tape, and doors can be lightproofed with weather stripping.

To provide ventilation in a room with sealed doors and windows, you will probably need to purchase a special baffled, lightproof vent and exhaust fan, available at photographic-supply stores. The fans are rated according to the cubic feet of air they move in a minute (CFM). An adequate darkroom ventilation system changes the air every six to eight minutes. To keep moist fumes from spreading through the room, the system should be installed so that fresh air will enter on the dry side of the darkroom and exit over the wet side.

Two other darkroom necessities, electricity and water, may already be present in the room in some form. Ideally, electrical outlets are located just above worktable height—convenient to safelights, enlarger and timer. You can install new outlets if you need them (page 130); a satisfactory shortcut is to attach multiple-outlet strips just above the worktables and plug them into existing outlets.

For water, you can rely on the nearest sink. Running water, though convenient, is not crucial within the darkroom. Once prints are fixed, they can accumulate in a large tray of water and be carried out of the room to be washed. In the long run, however, you will save time and effort by modifying your plumbing (pages 124, 128) so that you can supply running water inside the darkroom and install a special darkroom sink.

Although there are stainless-steel and plastic sinks that are made for darkroom use, the custom-made fiberglass-lined wooden sink has become almost a symbol of the craft of photography. The one depicted on pages 52 and 53 is 6 feet long by 2 feet wide—large enough that it can accommodate three 11-by-14-inch trays and a print washer.

You can, of course, tailor your own sink to suit the size of your darkroom and your processing needs. But construct the sink so that its sloping ½-inch plywood bottom is about hip height, and cut its front and sides from 2-by-10 boards, wide enough that the sink will be comfortable to lean on. The ½-inch plywood back should extend 8 inches above the sink rim to protect the wall from splashes.

Wooden darkroom sinks are customarily waterproofed with a combination of fiberglass cloth, to seal the joints, and several coats of polyester resin. This material gives off extremely noxious fumes, so apply it outdoors if possible. If you must apply polyester resin indoors, take care to ventilate the area and to close off the area from the rest of the house. Wear a respirator with an activated-charcoal filter. Both the fiberglass cloth and the polyester resin are generally available at marine-supply stores.

In a Closet, a Bathroom or Luxurious Space

A closet darkroom. Tucked into a space as small as 3 by 4 feet, this darkroom contains everything needed for printing photographs. The ¾-inch plywood shelves—one of them a work surface—rest on 1-by-2 cleats nailed to studs in the walls. A splashboard, installed with screws and angle irons, divides the work surface into wet and dry sides. Center dividers, dadoed in place, compartmentalize the lower shelves and keep the shelves from sagging in the middle.

The dry side accommodates the enlarger and a multiple-outlet strip that plugs into a receptacle outside the closet. The wet side houses a stepped, three-tier tray rack that organizes the printing chemicals vertically. On the shelf below the tray rack, a larger tray filled with water holds the fixed prints until they can be washed elsewhere. The safelight is clipped onto an overhead shelf; a smaller shelf at eye level keeps the timer and small utensils handy.

In such a confined space, adequate ventilation is especially important. Install an exhaust fan through the ceiling or wall. The door is a convenient place for an intake vent.

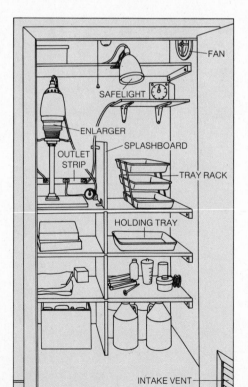

FAN
SAFELIGHT
ENLARGER
SPLASHBOARD
OUTLET STRIP
TRAY RACK
HOLDING TRAY
INTAKE VENT

A full-scale darkroom. This well-equipped darkroom occupies a 6½-by-8-foot space. Its wet and dry areas are separated by a 30-inch-wide aisle. The wet side features a fiberglass-and-resin-sealed wooden sink (*page 52*) with a high back to protect the wall from splashes. The sink base (*page 54*) has built-in tray-storage racks and supports for print-drying screens. The two mixing faucets have short hose attachments to direct wa-

ter flow; one faucet is fitted with a thermometer for precise temperature adjustment. The shelf over the sink holds a timer and small utensils. Negatives can be clipped to dry on the clothesline overhead. A wall-mounted exhaust fan removes moist fumes. On the dry side, a counter stretching the length of the room provides space for an enlarger, a print-viewing light, a light box for negative viewing (*page 47*) and a

paper cutter. Underneath, cabinets and shelves provide storage space. Safelights and other electrical fixtures plug into outlets at worktable height. A dowel board near the sink holds graduates and funnels, a pegboard next to the enlarger organizes negative carriers, and processing notes are displayed on a cork bulletin board. The stool and the resilient floor mat help ease tired feet during long hours of printing.

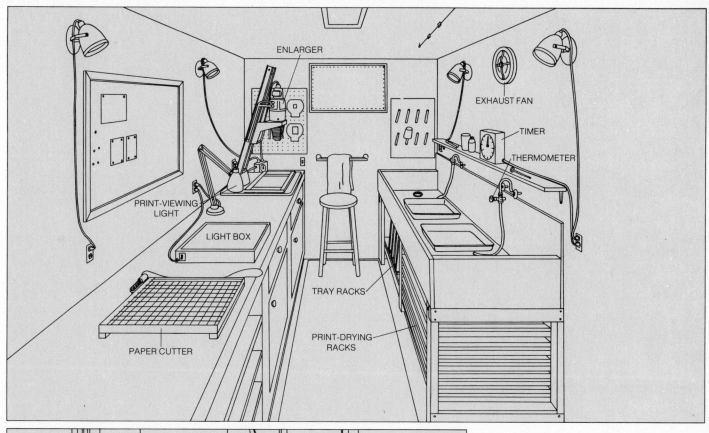

ENLARGER

EXHAUST FAN

TIMER

THERMOMETER

PRINT-VIEWING LIGHT

LIGHT BOX

TRAY RACKS

PRINT-DRYING RACKS

PAPER CUTTER

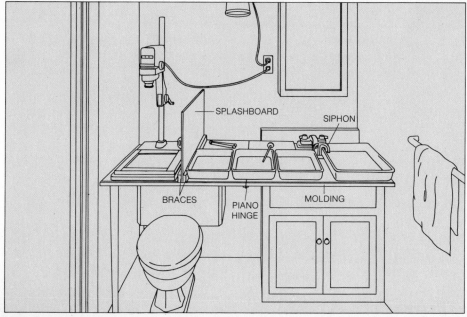

SPLASHBOARD

SIPHON

BRACES

PIANO HINGE

MOLDING

A foldaway darkroom. This portable 58-by-24-inch work surface is tailored to the dimensions of a 5-by-7-foot bathroom and will accommodate a small enlarger, three 8-by-10-inch processing trays, and an 11-by-14-inch wash tray. Made of ¾-inch plywood and designed for easy storage, the work surface is joined at the middle with a piano hinge and has removable, screw-on legs at one end to bring that end to the height of the lavatory. The front edge of the work surface is finished with a molding, and a cutout in the back edge makes room for a siphon running between the faucet and a wash tray. Adhesive pads underneath the work surface keep it from sliding off the lavatory counter.

A removable ¼-inch hardboard splashboard separates the work surface into a wet and a dry area; it slides into place between 1-by-2 braces that are glued, edge up, on the work surface. The enlarger and the safelight plug into an existing electrical outlet.

A Commodious Wooden Sink

1 Installing the bottom cleats. Cut a 2-by-10 front piece the full length of the sink, and mark its bottom edge 2½ inches in from the end where the drain will be located. Then cut a 1-by-2 cleat 5 inches shorter than the sink front; align one end of the cleat with the bottom edge of the sink front at the mark, and tack it loosely in place with a fourpenny nail. Swing the opposite end of the cleat so that its bottom edge is ½ inch above the bottom edge of the sink front; then nail both ends of the cleat firmly in place. At the center of the cleat, measure the distance between its bottom edge and the bottom edge of the sink front; the distance should be ¼ inch. If necessary, force the cleat up or down into line, and nail its center in place. Then drive nails through the cleat every 8 inches, staggering the nail positions to avoid splitting the cleat.

Repeat this procedure to attach a cleat to the bottom of the 18-inch-wide plywood back of the sink, but this time use threepenny nails. Cut two 2-by-10 sidepieces and two 1-by-2 cleats to the inside width of the sink. On the sidepiece for the drain end, nail a cleat flush with the bottom edge; on the other piece, nail the cleat ½ inch above the bottom edge.

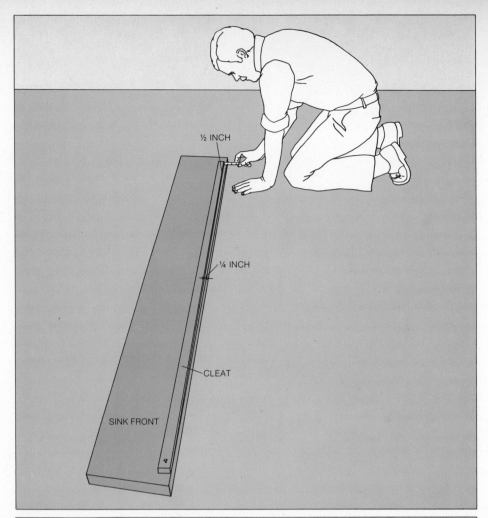

½ INCH

¼ INCH

CLEAT

SINK FRONT

2 Assembling the sink. Attach the sink front to the sides by drilling pilot holes for four 2½-inch wood screws at each end; screw the front in place. Then attach the sink back to the sides with four 1¼-inch wood screws at each end. Align the pieces so that the cleats form a continuous rim around the inside bottom of the sink.

Measure the inside length and width of the sink just above the cleats. Cut a piece of ½-inch plywood to these dimensions for the sink bottom.

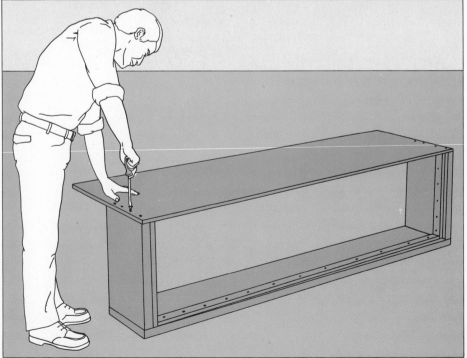

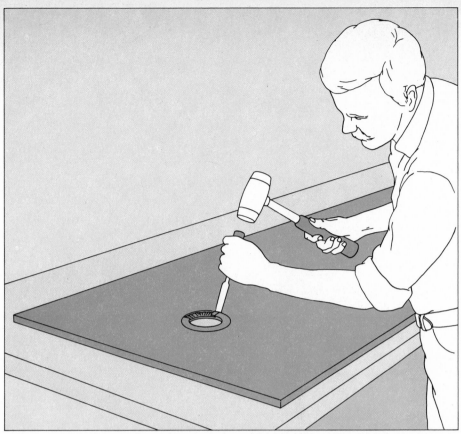

3 **Adding a drain.** With a hole saw or a saber saw, cut a hole 4 inches from the drain end of the plywood bottom and chisel a rim around the hole to match the flange of the drain. Cut the hole to the size specified by the drain manufacturer; then insert the drain fitting, trace around its flange and firmly score the marked line with a utility knife. With a ½-inch chisel blade held bevel side down, chip out the top layer of plywood between the drain hole and the scored outline. Test-fit the drain; for the sink to drain properly, the flange must be flush with the surface of the sink bottom. When you have the flange snug and level in its bed, line the plywood recess with silicone caulk, and press the drain fitting permanently in place.

Push the plywood bottom down into the sink until it rests on the cleats, with the drain at the lower end. The bottom should fit very snugly; use a mallet if necessary to seat it on the cleats. Carry the sink outdoors and, in a clean coffee can, mix a half pint of polyester laminating resin according to the manufacturer's instructions.

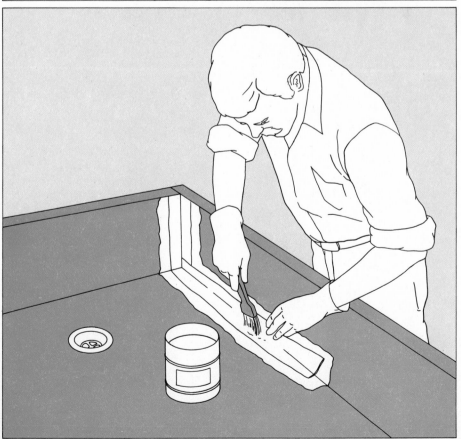

4 **Making the sink watertight.** Wearing rubber gloves and using a 2½-inch paintbrush, spread the resin generously along the interior joints, working it well into any cracks. Press 4-inch-wide strips of 2½-ounce fiberglass cloth into the resin along the joints, using the brush to force the cloth into the corners and to smooth out bubbles and wrinkles. When you join strip ends, overlap the cloth ½ inch.

When all the joints are sealed with cloth, mix more resin as needed and coat the entire sink interior, spreading the mixture generously over the fiberglass strips and the interior wood surfaces, including the top edges. Apply two additional coats of resin as soon as the previous coats are no longer tacky. Finally, paint the exterior of the sink, using either moisture-resistant enamel or polyurethane varnish.

A Sink Base with Space to Dry Prints, Store Trays

1 Building the base. Assemble a base as on pages 45-46, proportioning the rail lengths so that the outermost corners of the base fit flush beneath the corners of the sink. But instead of a single center brace at the bottom, install rails across both the front and the back at the same height as the lower rails on the sides. Bolt these rails in place through predrilled holes, attaching them to the inner surfaces of the legs.

Drive 2½-inch wood screws through predrilled holes to attach 2-by-2-inch vertical cleats spanning the centers of the front and back rails (*inset*). Cut a ¾-inch plywood shelf to fit over the lower rails, inside the legs. Tilt the shelf so that you will be able to slide it through the legs at one end of the base and into position.

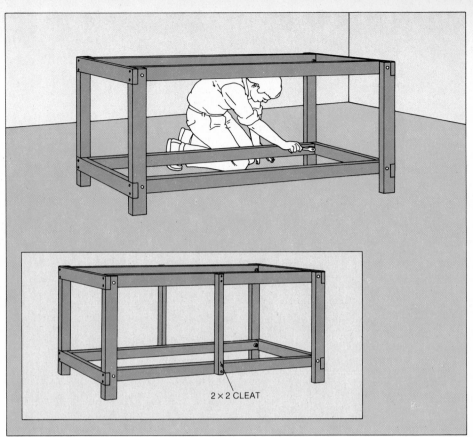

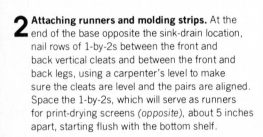

2 × 2 CLEAT

2 Attaching runners and molding strips. At the end of the base opposite the sink-drain location, nail rows of 1-by-2s between the front and back vertical cleats and between the front and back legs, using a carpenter's level to make sure the cleats are level and the pairs are aligned. Space the 1-by-2s, which will serve as runners for print-drying screens (*opposite*), about 5 inches apart, starting flush with the bottom shelf.

At the opposite end of the base, nail ¾-by-¾-inch molding strips every 6 inches along the bottom shelf. Position the first strip 6 inches from the vertical cleats and the last strip at least 6 inches from the legs. Nail a matching set of molding strips to the underside of the top rails but, to leave space for the sink drain, omit the strip closest to the legs, and instead attach a last strip flush with the edges of the vertical cleats. Insert ¼-inch plywood panels at a slant between these molding strips (*inset*), to make compartments for storing and drying trays.

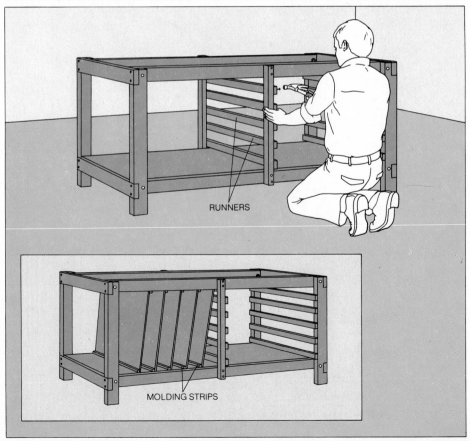

RUNNERS

MOLDING STRIPS

Making Print-drying Screens

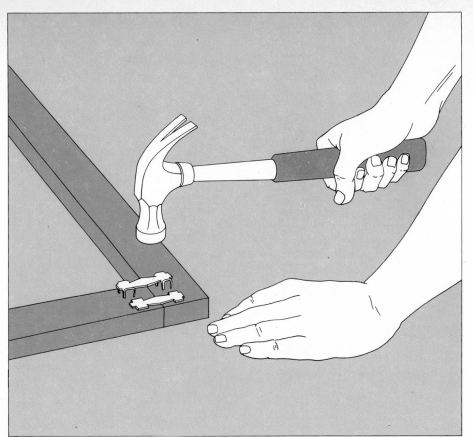

1 **Making a frame.** Build a lightweight frame by assembling four 1-by-2s with butt joints, securing the joints with toothed fasteners. To determine the dimensions of the frame, measure the length of the runners in the sink base, and cut side-pieces 3 inches shorter than this length. Then measure the distance between the outside edges of opposite runners, and cut front and back pieces for the frame ¼ inch shorter than this distance. Check all the cut ends with a combination square to be sure they are perfectly square.

Butt the ends of the sidepieces against the edges of the front and back, and drive two toothed fasteners spanning the joint. Turn the frame over, and drive a third fastener in each corner, midway between the other two.

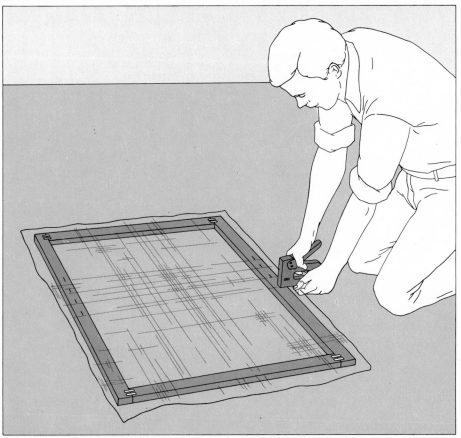

2 **Stretching the screen.** Cut a piece of fiberglass window screening slightly larger than the outside dimensions of the frame and staple it at the center of each side. Stretch the screening just enough to make it taut, keeping the mesh square with the sides of the frame. Add a staple on each side of the existing staples, ½ inch away, continuing in this sequence until you reach the corners of the frame. Then trim the edges of the screen ½ inch outside the staples. Dab varnish over the staples and toothed fasteners to prevent them from rusting.

Room for Appreciating Music–or Recording It

The exhilarating experience of listening to music in a good concert hall can be duplicated in a music room at home if you apply the principles of acoustics that were used to tune the hall. Or you can use these principles to fine-tune a home studio for recording high-fidelity sound.

In both a listening room and a recording studio, the goal is to create an even level of sound intensity at all frequencies throughout the room. Most rooms produce uneven sound patterns, reinforcing some frequencies and muffling others as sound waves interact with structural materials and furnishings in dissimilar ways.

For a recording studio, you may even need to provide sound absorbers to shield performers from each other so that the sounds of their individual instruments do not mix too much, resulting in a distorted recording. And you may need to surround the room with acoustic insulation to prevent sound from entering or leaving the studio.

Audible sound, the common denominator of these two projects, consists of waves of air pressure striking the listener's eardrums. One of the standard characteristics of sound is the frequency of these waves—the number of wave cycles per second—measured in Hertz (Hz). The range of human hearing extends from the very low tones of 20 Hz, with waves longer than 50 feet, to the high-pitched tones of 20,000 Hz, with waves about ½ inch long. The long waves of low-frequency sounds tend to flow around objects and make the surfaces of a room's long, hollow walls, floor and ceiling vibrate. The short waves of high-frequency sounds travel by more direct routes and have a tendency to be absorbed by porous and irregular surfaces.

The acoustic properties of a room—the ways in which it reponds to these waves—are determined partly by its size and shape. You can calculate a room's lowest audible frequency by dividing the speed of sound, 1,130 feet per second, by two times the room's longest dimension: In a room 20 feet long, for example, you can hear tones as low as 28½ Hz.

Similarly, the room's shape may distort sound waves of certain frequencies by causing so-called standing waves, accumulations of reflected sound waves that build up like waves of water sloshing against the sides of a bathtub. Low-frequency standing waves sound unnaturally loud in some parts of a room and soft in others. High-frequency standing waves produce a ringing sound (flutter echo), most noticeable in empty rooms.

The materials that make up the room's structure and furnishings also affect its acoustic properties. Dense materials such as glass, painted brick and troweled cement reflect the most sound waves. Carpets and heavy curtains absorb the short waves of high-frequency sound, which dissipate their energy among the fibers, but allow most of the medium and long waves of lower-frequency sound to pass through. The floor beneath a carpet or windows behind curtains will, however, trap medium- and low-frequency sounds, causing the longer waves to bounce back and forth inside the air space until their energy is dissipated.

Some structural features of a room improve its acoustics. Irregular shapes or openings, such as bay windows, nonparallel walls or open archways, diminish the standing-wave effect by dispersing the sound. Carpets and curtains can be used to reduce reflected sound by absorbing some frequencies, although you may need to make special baffles to trap certain frequencies.

These baffles and other sound-shaping accessories are especially important in a sound-recording studio, where small areas must be partitioned from each other to prevent too much mixing and consequent blurring of sound. Movable baffles called gobos, hinged to the wall or mounted on casters, are good for shielding performers from each other. To disperse sounds most evenly, you can build a hollow, semicylindrical absorber called a poly. An angled wall in a studio also helps disperse sound and break up standing waves, and a control-room wall like the one shown here provides soundproof separation between the studio players and the person doing the recording.

To find the acoustic properties of a room and tune them for best effect, you will need to be able to measure the sound intensity (expressed in decibels, or db) of various frequencies at several places in the room. A good way to make these measurements is with a sound-level meter, which can be rented from a recording-equipment supplier or purchased at some audio shops. To generate the test sound, you can use several musical instruments with different ranges (see chart, page 58) or a special test record that produces either pure tones or so-called pink noise.

Once you have a profile of the room's acoustics, you can modify the room with furnishings and special accessories to suit your needs. Materials for the accessories are available at building-supply stores. For acoustic sealant, commonly used in controlling sound, buy any caulking compound that remains resilient.

Means of Manipulating Stereophonic Sound

A listening room. This living room has been transformed into a room for listening to recorded stereophonic sound by a blending of good acoustics with the usual amenities. The two speakers are placed in opposite corners of a short wall, facing the long axis of the room. This position accentuates the sound of low frequencies; draperies over the glass wall and a large painting on canvas trap and muffle these low tones. But the curtains and the painting also prevent the formation of so-called standing waves, which would upset acoustic balance.

The chairs are positioned for optimum listening, at a distance from the speakers where direct and reflected sound blend. To further improve the room for high and mid-range frequencies—and to compensate for the sound-absorbing qualities of upholstered furniture—the wood floor is covered only by an area rug, leaving some of its sound-reflective surface exposed. Small rugs laid under the speakers prevent the passage of structure-borne sound to other rooms. Various irregular surfaces—a bay window, a large leafy plant, and the bulky furniture itself—help prevent the formation of standing waves to which this nearly square room would otherwise be prone.

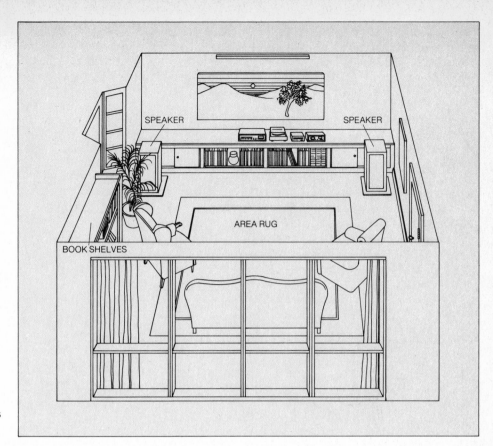

A Studio for Taping Music

A home recording studio. This basement room has been converted into a recording studio by the construction of a soundproof diagonal wall to isolate a corner control booth and the addition of accessories to insulate, disperse or absorb conflicting sounds of various instruments. Carpet on the cinder-block walls and concrete floor reduces standing waves, which distort sound. The 2-by-4 studs in the partition are staggered; none contact both sides of the wall. The wall is filled with fiberglass insulation, covered with a double layer of wallboard on each side and caulked with acoustic sealant. A special double-paned window allows soundproof viewing, and two weatherstripped solid-core doors provide insulation against sound. Magnetized latches prevent the sound leaks caused by the holes cut for standard door latches. The studio consists of a drum booth with thick rugs on the floor and a low-frequency absorber hanging from the ceiling to deaden the drum sound. Movable gobos, or sound baffles, shield performers from each other. Acoustic polys—semicylindrical sound absorbers—help disperse sound. In the booth, speakers for monitoring the performance hang on the wall above the recording console, to avoid emphasizing low-frequency sound.

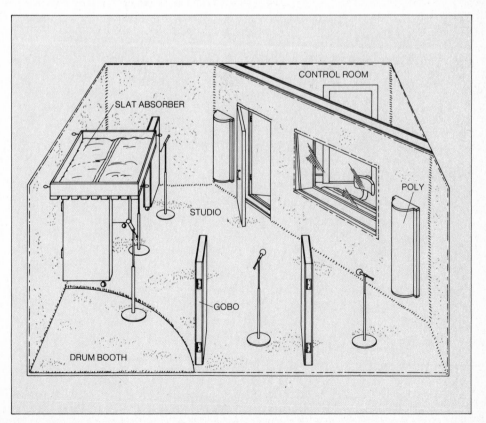

The Wide Spectrum of Audible Sound

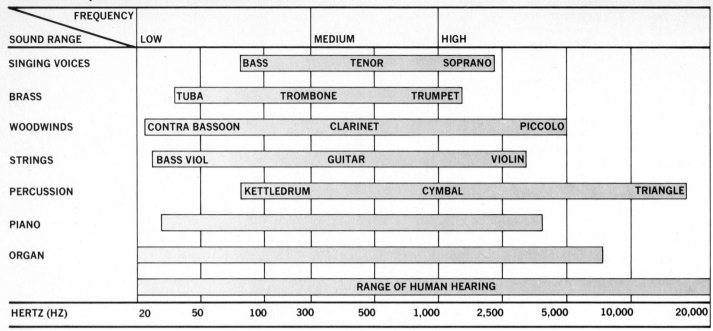

FREQUENCY SOUND RANGE	LOW		MEDIUM		HIGH				
SINGING VOICES		BASS	TENOR		SOPRANO				
BRASS	TUBA		TROMBONE		TRUMPET				
WOODWINDS	CONTRA BASSOON		CLARINET			PICCOLO			
STRINGS	BASS VIOL		GUITAR		VIOLIN				
PERCUSSION		KETTLEDRUM		CYMBAL				TRIANGLE	
PIANO									
ORGAN									
			RANGE OF HUMAN HEARING						
HERTZ (HZ)	20 50	100 300	500	1,000	2,500	5,000	10,000	20,000	

A palette of sounds. As this chart shows, most musical instruments, including the human voice, produce sound waves in a range of frequencies—expressed in Hertz (Hz)—that fall within the limits of human hearing. But whether you actually hear those sounds depends on the acoustics of your listening room or sound stu-dio and on the fidelity of your sound system. The best systems reproduce sounds from 20 to 20,000 Hz, the limits of human hearing. But the shape of the room can boost certain frequencies, especially low frequencies, and give an un-natural quality to the kettledrum, contra bassoon, tuba and bass viol. And hollow objects in the room can attenuate, or muffle, the same in-struments; soft or porous objects can render the high-frequency ping of a triangle almost inau-dible. For playing and listening to a particular in-strument, tune the room to produce a flat (even) response to sounds in the instrument's range, by adding or removing sound-absorbing elements.

Building Simple Baffles for Shaping Sound

1 Assembling the frame. Construct a four-sided frame, open front and back, for a baffle. First cut the top, bottom and sides, then drive sixpenny box nails through the sides and into the ends of the top and bottom. Cut the frame pieces from 1-by-2s for absorbing high-frequency sound, or from 1-by-4s or 1-by-6s for mid-range and low-frequency absorption. The frame should be about 2 feet wide by 3 feet high.

Cut four triangular corner brackets from ⅛-inch plywood or hardboard, with the right-angle sides about 4 inches long. Nail one bracket over each corner on the back of the frame. Using a utility knife, cut fiberglass insulation for a snug fit in the frame, and set it into the frame from the front. For high- and mid-frequency baffles, use insulation as thick as the frame; for a low-frequency baffle, use insulation that is half the thickness of the frame.

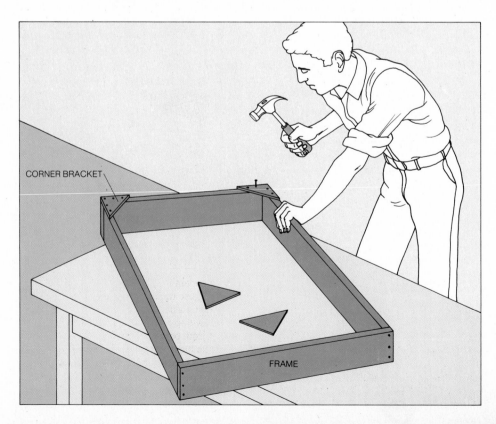

CORNER BRACKET

FRAME

2 **Adding cloth facing.** Lay the insulated frame face down on a piece of cotton, burlap or perforated vinyl fabric large enough to stretch over the front and sides of the frame, with a 1-inch overlap on the back. Staple the fabric to the back edge of the frame, folding in the V-shaped excess fabric at each corner. If you are making a low-frequency baffle, push the insulation gently against the cloth facing.

Turn ½-inch eye screws into the back edge of the frame, 7 to 10 inches down from the top; stretch picture wire between the two eyes, for hanging the baffle on the wall.

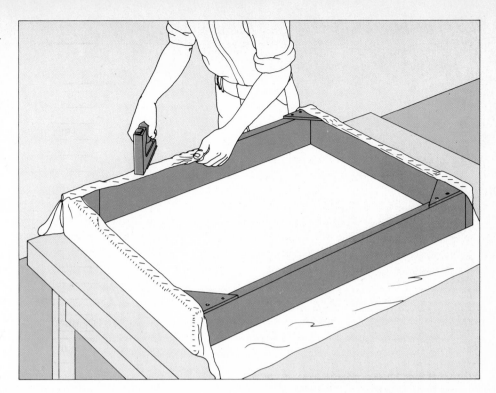

Varying Baffles for Highs and Lows

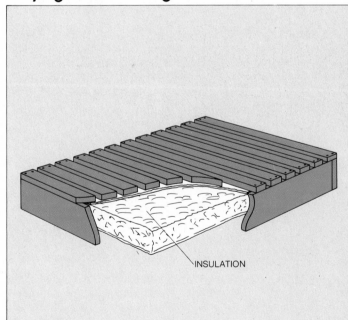

INSULATION

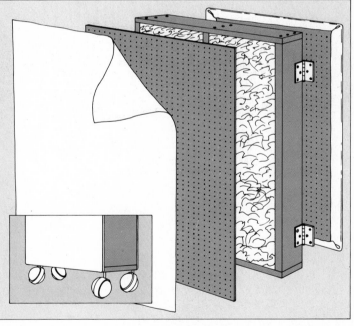

A slat absorber. To make an absorber for low frequencies, construct a frame 8 inches deep and cover the front with slats rather than cloth (*left*). For the frame, use 1-by-8s or 8-inch-wide strips of ¾-inch plywood, cut to produce a frame 48 inches square. Add corner brackets on the back as in Step 1, opposite; then nail 1-by-3 slats across the front of the frame, spaced ³/₁₆ inch apart. Fill the frame with one layer of 4-inch fiberglass insulation, pressed against the slats. To adapt the slat absorber for mid-range frequencies, use two layers of 4-inch insulation. For hanging a baffle from the ceiling as a low-frequency trap over a drum booth, as on page 57, put cloth between the slats and the insulation, to contain the glass fibers. Drive four ¾-inch eye screws into the sides of the frame, one near each corner, and suspend the baffle flush with the ceiling, using picture wire and four 3-inch eye screws driven into ceiling joists.

A gobo (*right*), used as a shield to reflect and absorb sound, has a frame of 2-by-4s, a front and back of ⅛-inch pegboard, and a core of 4-inch fiberglass insulation. The pegboard is covered with cloth, folded and glued to the edge of the underside before the pegboard is screwed to the frame. The gobo can swing from the wall like a door, on 3-inch butt hinges; or you can make it to roll on the floor, by attaching small ball-type metal casters at each corner of the base (*inset*).

A Poly to Disperse Sounds

1 Assembling the frame. Build a frame for the poly by screwing two long bevel-edged braces to the sides of a backing board of ½-inch plywood. Cut the backing board at least 14 inches wide and 36 inches long; then cut two 1-by-2 braces the same length. With a table saw or a jack plane, bevel one edge of each brace at an angle of 65° (inset). Apply a thin coat of yellow carpenter's glue to the narrow face of one brace, and use C clamps to secure it along one edge of the backing board, bevel facing in. Drill pilot holes at 6-inch intervals through the backing board into the brace, and secure the brace with 1-inch screws. Attach the second brace to the other edge of the backing board.

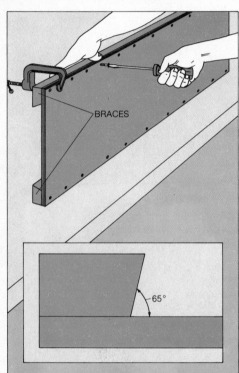

2 Stretching the skin. Cut a skin for the poly from three-ply ⅛-inch plywood, and bend it into a curve between the two beveled braces. The skin should be as long as the backing board and about half again as wide, with the surface grain of the plywood running parallel to the long edges. Butt one long edge firmly against the brace at one side of the back, and gently bend the skin so that the other edge fits inside the opposite brace. If the plywood resists and begins to crack, reduce the curvature by trimming ½ inch from one long edge. Repeat the bending process, trimming until the skin fits easily but snugly between the two braces.

Remove the skin and apply acoustic sealant along the inside edge of each brace. Replace the skin, bedding it firmly into the sealant.

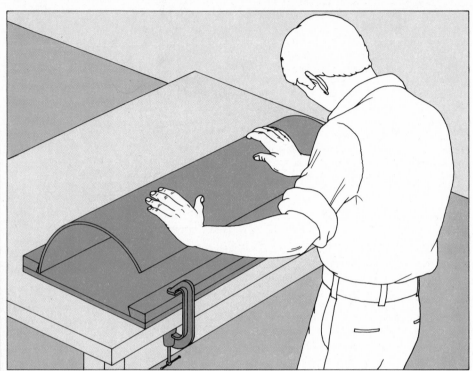

3 Cutting the endpieces. Trace two semicircular outlines of the poly's end onto a sheet of ½-inch plywood, and use a saber saw to cut along the lines, making two endpieces. Apply a bead of acoustic sealant to the edges of the backing board and the curved skin; then press one endpiece into position on top of the sealant, and drive 1¼-inch brads through the endpiece into the edge of the backing board and the ends of the braces. Wipe away excess sealant.

Stuff the poly with fiberglass insulation, if desired (page 59), to increase the poly's absorption of mid-range sound. Seal and close the open end with the second endpiece.

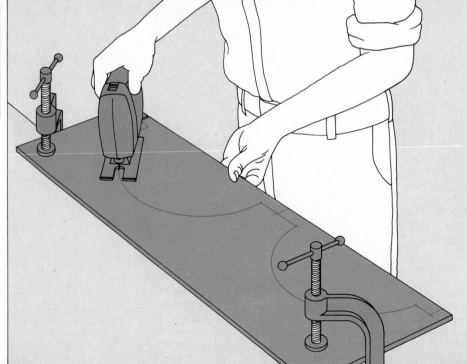

A Soundproof Wall Designed for a Recording Studio

Anatomy of a staggered-stud wall. This soundproof wall, here enclosing a corner of a basement, is built so that only a few framing members extend all the way through, reducing structure-borne sound transmission. Fiberglass insulation inside the wall, a double layer of wallboard on each side, windowpanes set at an angle, and acoustic sealant in all seams help muffle airborne sound. The wall is framed with 2-by-6 top and sole plates, and the 2-by-4 studs are staggered so that they are flush with alternate sides of the plates. Jambs for the double doors and the window are made of 1-by-8s, nailed to pairs of 2-by-4 studs set with their wide faces parallel to the wall. The 3-by-4-foot window has double glass panes about 4 inches apart. The 30-inch-wide solid-core doors have magnetic catches and are acoustically sealed with weather stripping around the opening.

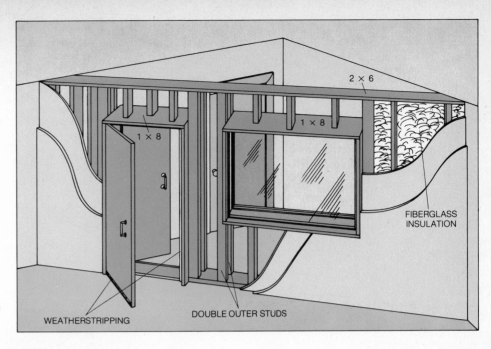

2 × 6

1 × 8

1 × 8

FIBERGLASS INSULATION

WEATHERSTRIPPING

DOUBLE OUTER STUDS

Building a Barricade to Block Sound

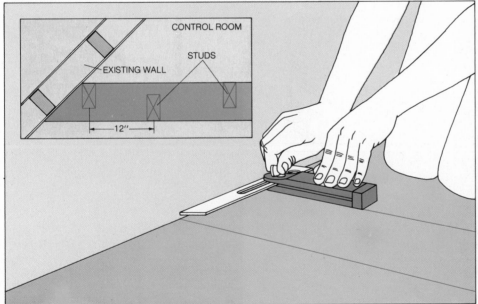

CONTROL ROOM

STUDS

EXISTING WALL

12"

BEVELED END STUD

1 Setting in the wall. Mark the position for a 2-by-6 sole plate on the floor, then use a T bevel to measure the angles where it will meet the existing walls. Transfer these angles to the ends of two 2-by-6s, and cut a sole plate and a top plate for the new wall. If there are studs in the existing walls, lay out the new wall with each end intersecting the adjacent wall at a stud, to provide backing for the new wall's corner studs (*Step 2*). Mark the top and sole plates for staggered 2-by-4 studs. Position the first stud flush with, and at the end of, the control-room side of the wall. Following the method shown on page 112, Step 1, set the studs on alternate sides of the plates, spaced 12 inches center to center

(*inset*). At the door and window locations, mark positions for one pair of studs to frame each side of each opening. Make the openings 2 inches wider than the planned width of the finished door and window, and set the framing studs with their wide faces parallel to, and flush with, the edges of the plates. With all of the stud positions marked, nail studs to the top plate, then erect the wall as shown on page 114, cutting out the sole plate between the studs framing the door. Toenail a header between these framing studs, 6 feet 9½ inches above floor level. Add cripple studs between the header and the top plate, following the same staggered pattern that was used for the full-length studs.

2 Adding the beveled end studs. With a table saw or a jack plane, bevel the end studs on the studio side of the new wall so that they will fit flush with the existing wall, cutting the bevel at the same angle as the end of the sole plate. Then nail the studs to the existing wall.

3 **Making the window frame.** Cut two 1-by-8 side jambs for the window, the same length as the planned height of the window. Nail them to the framing studs of the window opening at the desired height above the floor. Center each jamb so that it overlaps the framing stud on each side of the wall by 1 inch.

Cut a head jamb and a sill from a 1-by-8, making them long enough to fit the width of the rough opening. Nail them in place at the top and bottom of the window opening, as you would a door header (*Step 2, page 115*). Then cut and nail cripple studs to fit between the sill and the sole plate and between the head jamb and the top plate, following the same staggered pattern used for the regular studs (*inset*).

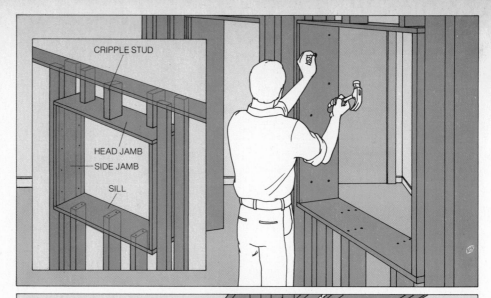

CRIPPLE STUD

HEAD JAMB

SIDE JAMB

SILL

4 **Making channels for the windowpanes.** On the studio side of the wall, nail lengths of ¾-by-¾-inch molding down the inside of the side jambs and across the head jamb and sill, creating a continuous channel for one pane of glass. Position the top molding 1¾ inches from the edge of the head jamb, and the bottom molding 2¾ inches from the edge of the sill; angle the side moldings to fit snugly between them, beveling their ends accordingly.

On the control-room side of the wall, construct a similar channel for the second pane of glass, but position both the top and the bottom moldings 1¾ inches from the edge of the sill and jamb. Lay a thick bead of acoustic sealant against the outside edge of each channel.

STUDIO SIDE

ANGLED SIDE MOLDING

ACOUSTICAL SEALANT

5 **Setting the glass.** Have a helper lift one windowpane into the frame, seating the bottom edge against the bottom molding. Then push the top edge firmly against the top molding. Lay a thick bead of acoustic sealant around all four edges of the pane, and secure it with an outer channel of ¾-by-¾-inch molding. Push the molding firmly against the glass, and nail it to the window frame. Install the second windowpane in the same manner. Caution: Handle the glass with work gloves, and nail the molding carefully to avoid shattering the pane.

Installing Soundproof Doors

1 Assembling the doorframe. Make a finished frame for the door opening by cutting two 1-by-8 side jambs, 2½ inches longer than the doors, and a 1-by-8 head jamb, ¾ inch wider than the doors. Using a router, cut a ¾-inch-wide, ⅜-inch-deep dado into each side jamb; the distance from the bottom edge of the dado should be 1 inch greater than the height of the door. Assemble the jambs on the floor, securing the joints with glue and 1½-inch screws, countersunk and driven through the side jambs. Square the corners of the jamb assembly, then nail two temporary 1-by-2 spreaders across the side jambs *(inset)*. Install the jamb assembly, centering it in the rough door opening. Shim and nail the assembly as shown on page 117, Step 1.

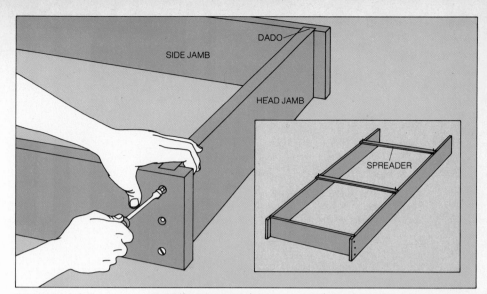

2 Hanging the doors. While a helper holds one door flush with the edge of the frame, use shims to wedge the door against two fourpenny nails used as spacers between the top of the door and the head jamb. Mark the position of a 3½-inch butt hinge on one edge of the door and the adjacent jamb, 7 inches below the top of the door. Mark for the lower hinge, 11 inches above the bottom. Remove the door, and with a chisel and mallet cut two hinge mortises on the jamb and the door edge, the same depth as one hinge leaf, with the hinge pin extending ¾ inch from the edge *(inset)*. Remove the hinge pin, screw one leaf to the door and the other to the jamb, then reposition the door and replace the pin. Hang the second door on the other side of the opening, with its hinges along the same jamb. Cut a 1-by-10 threshold to fit snugly between the side jambs, bevel the top edges, and nail it to the floor, centered in the opening.

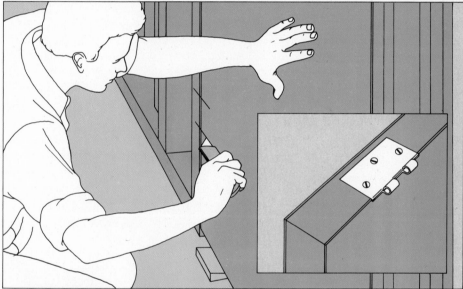

3 Finishing the doors. Cut a piece of doorstop molding the same height as the doors, and nail the stop to one side jamb, with its edge barely touching the back of the closed door. Nail similar stops to the opposite side jamb and to the head jamb. Install a magnetic cabinet latch at a height of 36 inches, attaching the magnet to the doorstop and the strike plate to the door. Screw a door pull to the outside of the door at the level of the catch. Install a doorstop, latch and pull for the other door in the same way. Screw sweep weather stripping to the bottom of each door *(inset, top)*, and attach neoprene-gasket weather stripping to the doorstop, positioned so that the gasket compresses slightly when the door is closed. Staple 3-inch-thick, 24-inch-wide fiberglass insulation to alternating studs. Encase the wall with two layers of ½-inch wallboard *(page 116)*, staggering it so that the seams of the first layer are covered by the second layer. Caulk gaps with acoustic sealant.

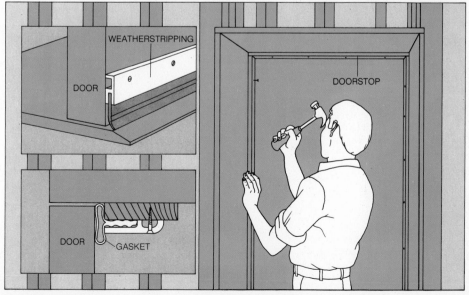

Creating a Home within Your Home for Plants

For people who like plants, a gardening room is both a place to work and a showcase for the results of their labors. It should be equipped with attractive display units, but it should also contain such workaday elements as a potting bench and a nursery unit for starting new plants or caring for ailing ones. Also desirable is storage space for such gardening essentials as soil, fertilizers, chemicals for pest control, tools, pots, stakes and string, and a watering can.

Among possible locations for an indoor garden are a heated garage, an enclosed porch or a basement—areas where the existing flooring is more or less impervious to water damage. Ideally, the site should admit some natural light, preferably from south-facing windows. If natural light is limited, you can increase it by lengthening existing windows or setting glass panels into spaces between studs (page 118). Or you can substitute fluorescent lights.

Although there are full-spectrum fluorescent tubes made especially for indoor gardening, good results can be ob-tained with a fluorescent fixture that combines two 40-watt tubes—one cool white, the other warm white—mounted in a reflector. The most common tubes are 48 inches long, but tubes ranging from 18 inches to 8 feet are available; for high-intensity light, they can be mounted in banks of multiple-tube fixtures.

For many situations you will want fluorescent fixtures that hang from chains, so that their height can be changed. This arrangement allows you to raise the fixture as plants grow and also to alter the light levels to suit the needs of different plants. In adjusting light levels, remember that fluorescent tubes are brighter at the ends than in the middle and that they will lose strength in time. They should be changed after about 9,000 hours of use—about two years, allowing 12 hours of operation a day. Mark the date of installation on the tubes with a grease pencil, to keep track of their age. Also dust the tubes regularly, as well as the plant leaves, since dust sharply cuts the intensity of the lights.

Because plants have varying needs for darkness, you will probably want to plug your lights into timer switches. To handle the lighting needs of plants, plus in some cases supplemental electric heaters for warmth, you may want to install a new electric circuit for the room (page 130). Be sure all fixtures, switches and receptacles are grounded, since a gardening room inevitably involves using water.

Water, in fact, is the other necessity for an indoor garden, essential for watering plants and for scrubbing pots. Ideal for these purposes is a utility tub (page 9) that taps into existing supply and drain lines (pages 124, 128). The tub should be fitted with a mixing faucet, so that water temperatures can be adjusted to suit the requirements of various plants.

For durability, structures in the gardening room should be made of redwood, cedar or a wood that has been pressure-treated with a wood preservative, and should be put together with galvanized or aluminum nails. And, for convenient watering, none of the planting units should be deeper than arm's length—usually about 24 inches.

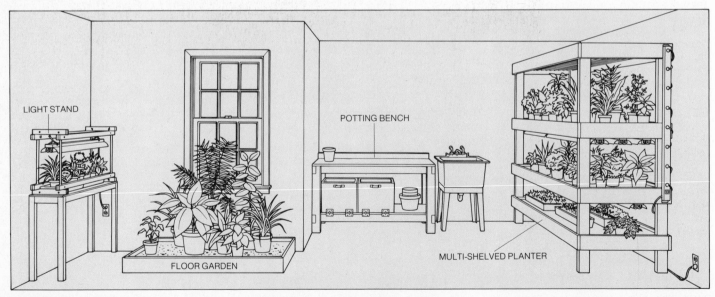

Furnishings for an indoor garden. In this room for nurturing and displaying plants, the working units consist of a sturdy potting bench with storage space for soil, sand, vermiculite and the like, and a multishelved fluorescent-lit planter fitted with slats for holding plastic or aluminum trays. The potting bench is a simple table made from 2-by-4s, covered with a ¾-inch plywood top and fitted with plywood bins hinged to a bottom shelf. The tiered planter is built in sections from two ladder-like endpieces joined by front and back rails whose inside ledges support the slats. It is lighted by either fixed or movable fluorescent fixtures, as many as six tubes per shelf, that plug into a multioutlet unit mounted vertically on the back of the unit.

The two display units featured in this room are a floor-level garden and a table-height plant stand that has its own built-in lighting. The floor garden has a traylike aluminum bottom that rests on slats inside a shallow wooden frame. The light stand's demountable parts consist of a conduit tubing that has been fitted and clamped into holes drilled in paired wooden frames.

A Potting Bench with Bins

1 Building the bench. Build the basic bench frame as shown on pages 45 and 54, but omit 2-by-2 uprights at the center front and back unless you want to provide shelves alongside the bin. Add a 1-by-8 backboard to the design, drilling boltholes in the backboard so that the same bolts that hold the back rail to the legs will also engage the backboard. Make a ¾-inch plywood bench top to fit flush with the outer faces of the side rails and the front legs. Install a lower shelf as shown on page 46. If you are adding shelves alongside the bin, construct runners for them as shown on page 54.

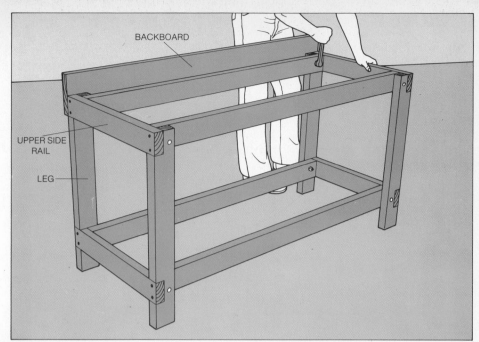

2 Building bins for potting soil. Cut pieces for the front, back, sides and bottom of a trough-shaped bin from ¾-inch plywood, following the exploded drawing above. Make the top of each endpiece 3 inches wider than the bottom, but be sure the diagonal measure of the end-pieces is less than the distance from the upper front rail to the lower shelf so that when tipped, the bin clears the upper rail. Bevel the front and back edges of the bottom to fit the front and back pieces. Drill several ¼-inch holes in the bottom for ventilation, and staple metal screening over them. Screw handles to the front pieces. Finally, assemble the bins with waterproof glue and angle brackets, attaching an endpiece to the bottom, then lapping the back over it and attaching the second endpiece and finally the front.

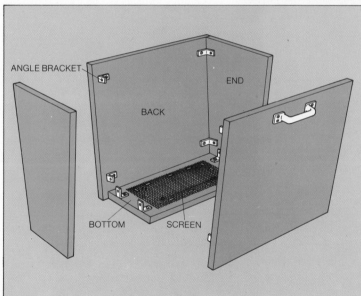

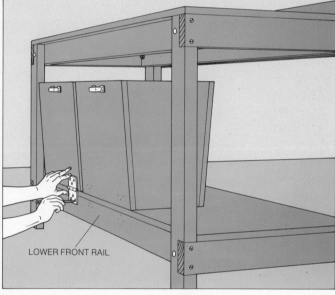

3 Hinging the bins to the bench. Place the bins on the lower shelf of the bench, making the front edge of each bin flush with the front edge of the shelf. Mark the screw holes for two loose-pin hinges on each bin and the lower front rail. Drill pilot holes for the hinge screws, and attach the hinges. Attach a screw hook to the back of each bin, another to the back rail of the bench. Run chain between the hooks, selecting a link size strong enough to hold the loaded bin in the tilted position. To free the bins for cleaning, unhook each chain and pull out the hinge pins.

Boxing In a Floor Garden

1 **Attaching supports for slats.** Measure and cut four pieces of 1-by-6 lumber for the box sides, mitering their ends at a 45° angle; plan the inside dimensions of the box to enclose the aluminum liner. Nail two supporting ledges of 1-by-2 lumber to the inside face of two parallel sides of the box, positioning each ledge ½ inch above the lower edge of the box and flush with the ends of the side. Use threepenny nails, spaced 6 inches apart, to secure the ledges.

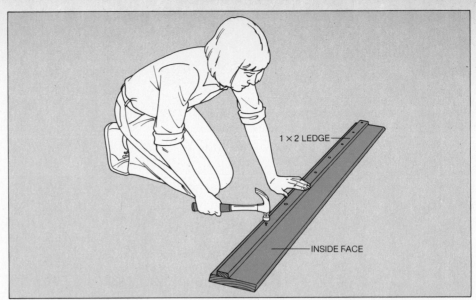

1 × 2 LEDGE

INSIDE FACE

2 **Assembling the box.** Place two adjoining sides in a corner clamp, and check the joint for fit. If the mitered ends do not fit snugly, remove the sides from the clamp and lightly sand the high spots. Repeat the clamping and sanding procedure until the two ends fit exactly. Apply a waterproof glue to both surfaces of the joint, and clamp until dry. Before removing the clamp, drive two finishing nails into the joint from each side; set them with a nail set. Repeat for the remaining joints. Fill the holes with wood putty.

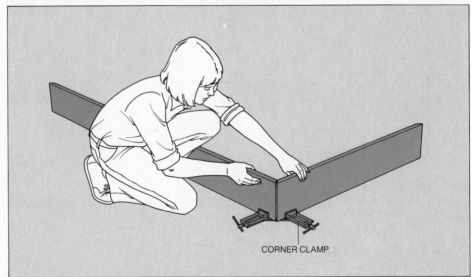

CORNER CLAMP

3 **Finishing the bottom.** Cut 1-by-2 slats to fit on edge between the ledges; space the slats about 8 inches apart. Nail a slat across the two ledges at each end of the box, using eight-penny nails and butting each end slat against the short sides of the box. Add remaining slats.

4 Making an aluminum liner. From a roofer or sheet-metal supplier, obtain a sheet of .025-inch aluminum 4 inches wider and longer than the inside of the box. Place the sheet on a work surface at least 4 inches shorter and narrower than the sheet, and allow one edge of the sheet to overhang 2 inches. Put a weight on the sheet and then, wearing work gloves, bend down the overhanging edge, pounding the crease smooth with a rubber mallet. Slide the sheet until a second, adjoining edge overhangs the work surface by 2 inches and, with tin snips, cut along the crease for 2 inches, forming a 2-inch-square tab. Snip about an inch off the end, and taper the two vertical edges of the tab; then bend and smooth the second edge of the sheet, and tuck the tab under the first edge. Crease the sheet, cutting and forming tabs to shape the edges. Caulk the tabs with silicone sealant (*inset*). Set the liner in the box. Place potted plants in the liner, over a layer of pebbles or marble chips.

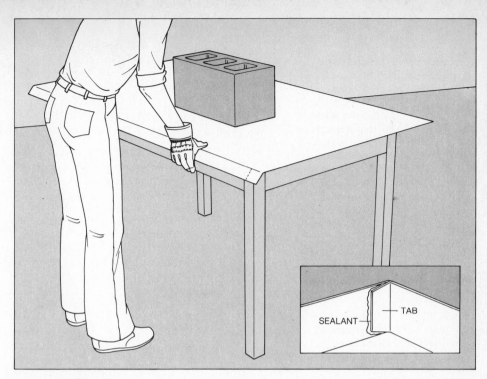

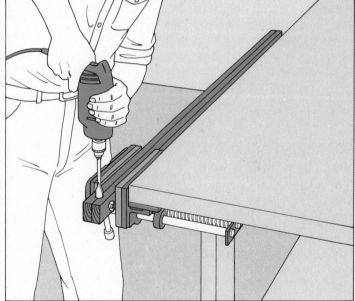

An Adjustable, Demountable Light Garden

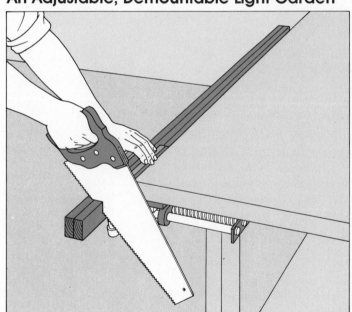

1 Making the framing sections. To construct a stand that will hold a 48-inch fluorescent fixture, measure, cut and drill four pairs of 1-by-2s, each 53 inches long, and four pairs 12 inches long. To simplify cutting and drilling, clamp paired 1-by-2s in a vise and cut them to the required length. At one end of each clamped pair drill a ¼-inch hole, positioning the hole 2½ inches from the cut end and at the midpoint of the lumber's 2-inch face. Slip a 2-inch-long ¼-inch stove bolt with a washer into this hole, and fasten it with another washer and a wing nut.

2 Drilling holes for conduit pipe. Keeping the paired 1-by-2s clamped in the vise, drill a hole for the conduit pipe down through their adjoining edges, using a ¾-inch spade bit and positioning the hole 1 inch in from the cut end of the lumber. Then reverse the paired 1-by-2s in the vise, and drill a hole for a stove bolt and a conduit hole at the opposite end. Repeat both of these drilling operations at the ends of all the other paired 1-by-2s. Finally, cut four pieces of ½-inch heavy-wall metal electrical conduit; these will serve as the uprights of the unit.

3 **Assembling the stand.** Place two paired 53-inch sections across two paired 12-inch sections, aligning the holes for conduit pipe. Loosen the wing nuts, insert the pipe and tighten the nuts. Loosen the nuts on the four remaining paired sections, and slide one 53-inch section down over two conduit-pipe uprights, until the top edge of the section is 1½ inches below the top of the pipes. Tighten the wing nuts at each end. Similarly position the other 53-inch section, and fasten it onto the other two pipes. Then slip the remaining 12-inch sections over the pipes, resting them on the 53-inch sections, and tighten the wing nuts on the short sections.

4 **Hanging the light fixture.** At the midpoint of the two top 12-inch sections, install a screw eye into the bottom edge of the inner board. Loop a length of chain (usually provided by the manufacturer) under the metal hanger at one end of a 48-inch, two-tube fluorescent fixture, and slip the two ends of the chain onto an S hook. Hook the top of the S into the screw eye. Repeat at the opposite end. To change the height of the fixture, adjust the chain links on the upper S hooks. Place two 2-foot-square plastic trays in the bottom frame, and lay a piece of egg-crate diffuser grid, 23 inches square, over each. Set potted plants on top of the grid.

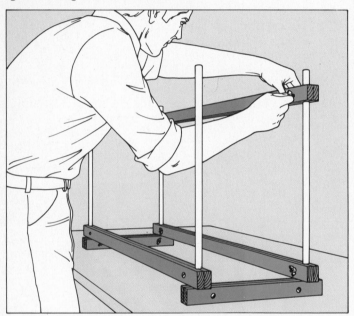

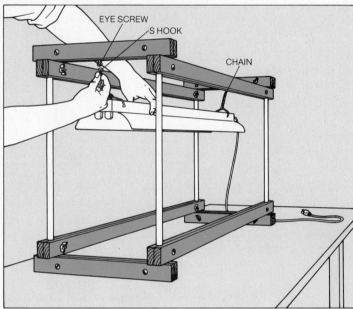

EYE SCREW

S HOOK

CHAIN

A Many-Splendored, Multishelved Planter

1 **Building the end ladders.** Cut four 2-by-4 uprights to the desired height of the unit, and at least eight 1-by-6 crosspieces—four for each set of uprights—allowing for a minimum distance of 16 inches between shelves and for a space of at least 4 inches between the bottom shelf and the floor. Make each crosspiece 1½ inches shorter than the planned depth of the unit. Lay two uprights flat, and join them at one end with a crosspiece, setting the top edge of the crosspiece ¾ inch from the ends of the uprights; secure each side with three eightpenny nails. Position a second crosspiece so that its top edge is at least 16 inches below the top edge of the first crosspiece, and nail it in place. Attach other crosspieces in the same way. Then assemble an identical ladder for the other end.

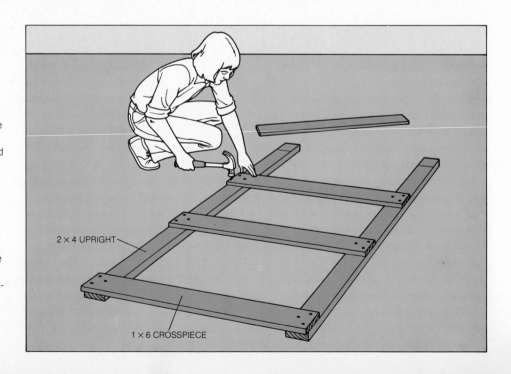

2 × 4 UPRIGHT

1 × 6 CROSSPIECE

2 **Attaching the rails.** Cut 1-by-6 front and back rails for each shelf, making them the planned length of the unit. Nail a 1-by-2 ledge to the inside face of each rail, making the ledges 3 inches shorter than the rails. Set each ledge 1½ inches in from the two ends of the rail and ½ inch in from one long edge. Set one ladder on end and rest a 1-by-6 rail against its top crosspiece, positioning the rail so that its ledge lies at the top of the unit. Align the edges of the rail and crosspiece, and make sure the rail is at right angles to the upright; then drive three eightpenny nails through the rail into the upright. Similarly join the other end of the rail to the other ladder.

Nail remaining rails to one side of the unit, positioning their ledges toward the bottom. Then turn the unit over and attach rails to the other side in the same way. Cover the top of the unit with ½-inch plywood or particle board cut to fit the unit's inside dimensions. Rest the top against the recessed ledges along the top rail, and nail it to the recessed ends of the ladders.

Cut 1-by-2 slats to fit between the ledges on the front and back rails. Set them on edge against the ledges, spacing them not more than 15 inches apart, always butting one slat against the uprights at each end of the shelf. Fasten the slats to the ledges with sixpenny nails.

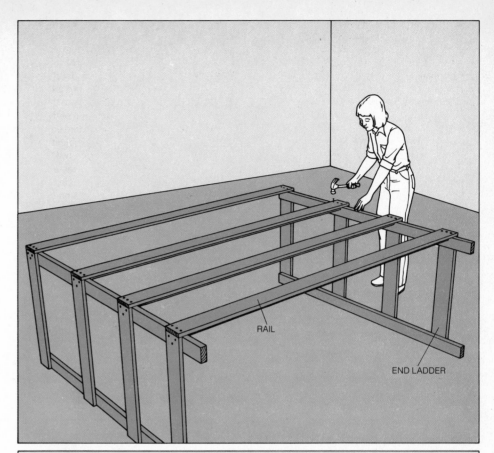

RAIL

END LADDER

3 **Adding the lights.** Attach a multiple-outlet strip to the back edge of one or both ladders, depending on the number of fluorescent fixtures you plan to install. Fasten the strip to the ladder, following the manufacturer's instructions. Attach as many as three rows of fixtures under a shelf 24 inches deep, depending on the light requirements of the plants. Fasten the lights to the underside of the slats—or to the underside of the top shelf—with screw eyes, chains and S hooks as in Step 4, opposite. Alternatively, use fixtures that can be screwed directly to these supports. Plug the lights into the outlet strips, and plug the strips into timers. Then connect the timers to a grounded receptacle.

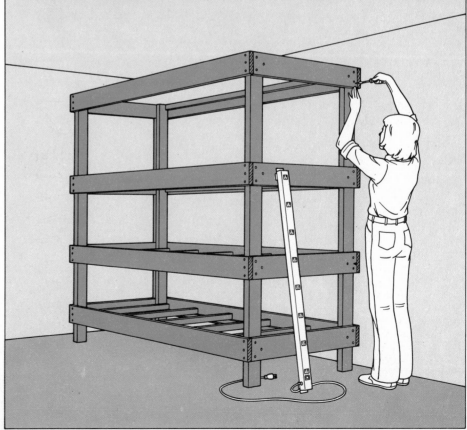

Hydroponics: Soilless Gardens

For a gardener who wants to grow more plants in less space and spend less time taking care of them, a hydroponic unit is ideal. Hydroponics—a technique for raising plants without soil—carries nutrients to the roots by putting mineral salts into the water. Systems range from a single pot in a water-filled container with a window of clear plastic to show the nutrient level, to more elaborate pump-operated units like the one shown here.

This unit includes the three basic elements required for hydroponic gardening: a container for the plants, a medium to support the roots—in this case, sphagnum moss—and a reservoir for the nutrient solution. It also has a circulation system that maintains a constant flow of nutrients through the unit.

The plastic pots, sphagnum moss and fiberglass window boxes used for the plant box and reservoir are available at garden-supply centers. The plastic tubing, siphon, pump and aerator connector for the circulation system can be obtained at aquarium-supply stores. Standard tubing with a ½-inch outside diameter is used here; if you use another size, check for a tight fit with the other accessories, and in drilling outlet and drainage holes use a drill bit of the same size.

To garden successfully with a hydroponic unit, you will have to pay attention to the level and content of the nutrient solution. In the system shown here, the solution flows at a rate of about a quart every four minutes; that should keep the growing medium as damp as a wrung-out sponge—a good index of proper flow. If you plan to build a larger unit, be sure the circulation system is adequate; you may have to install a larger pump.

Nutrient mixes for hydroponics are available at garden-supply centers or from special hydroponic-gardening suppliers, which advertise in garden magazines. The mixes vary depending on the specific plants and on whether you are using natural or artificial light. If you plan to mix the nutrients with ordinary tap water, you will also need a kit to check the water for its pH level: Excess acidity or alkalinity can harm plants. When your unit is in use, it should be topped off with fresh solution about once a week to maintain the original volume, and the solution should be drained and replaced once a month. When you change the solution, flush the pots with tap water to rid them of excess mineral salts.

Anatomy of a hydroponic unit. In this pump-operated hydroponic unit, two 6-inch-deep fiberglass window boxes are placed on shelves 9 inches apart. The plant box on the upper shelf is 36 inches long, the reservoir box on the lower shelf 24 inches long. The nutrient solution flows through plastic tubing from an outlet hole in the reservoir box to an aerator connector—a bubbler—which is connected with narrow air-line tubing to an aquarium air pump. Bubbles generated by the pump draw the solution up through a 10-inch length of tubing and a curved siphon tube hooked over one end of the plant box.

In the plant box, the solution soaks through sphagnum moss in plastic pots perforated with two bands of holes, one band about halfway up the side of the pot, the other around the bottom. The solution drains through a hole at the other end of the box, positioned at the same level as the top band of holes in the pots. Plastic tubing carries the solution back to the reservoir box. A backup drain with identical tubing is placed slightly higher than the first and prevents overflow if the lower drain should clog. The tubing is fastened in place with silicone sealant.

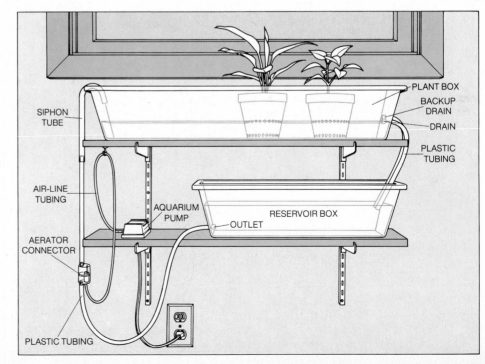

SIPHON TUBE

AIR-LINE TUBING

AERATOR CONNECTOR

PLASTIC TUBING

AQUARIUM PUMP

OUTLET

RESERVOIR BOX

PLANT BOX

BACKUP DRAIN

DRAIN

PLASTIC TUBING

An Experiment to Try

1 Drilling outlet and drain holes. Drill two ½-inch holes at one end of the 36-inch plant box. Position one hole at the height selected for the top row of holes on the pots, and center it between the two corners of the box. Position a second hole 1 inch above the first, and slightly offset from it. Then drill a ½-inch hole in one end of the 24-inch reservoir box, 1 inch above the bottom and centered between the corners.

Scribe a line around the pots at the height selected for the upper row of holes. Measure and scribe a second line around the bottom of the pot. Drill ¼-inch holes around the pots at regular intervals, ¼ to ⅜ inch apart.

2 Attaching plastic tubing. Insert a 13-inch length of plastic tubing into the lower drain hole of the plant box, allowing ½ inch of the tubing to protrude inside the box. Set the box and tubing on a level surface and run a thin bead of silicone sealant around the tubing, first on the inside of the box, then on the outside, making sure the seam between the tubing and the box is completely filled. Spread the sealant with a wet stick or wet knife blade; allow the sealant to set, without moving the tubing, for 20 to 30 minutes. Connect a 14-inch length of tubing to the other drain hole and a 20-inch length of tubing to the outlet hole in the reservoir box. Let the sealant cure for 24 hours.

3 Setting up the unit. Place the plant box on the top shelf and the reservoir box on the bottom, positioning them with their outlet and drain holes at opposite ends. Cut 10 inches of plastic tubing, slip it inside a rigid aquarium-siphon tube, and hook the siphon over the end of the plant box. Attach the other end of the tubing to the stem at the top of the aerator connector. Connect the outlet tubing from the other box to the large stem at the base of the aerator connector, which should now hang below the lower shelf.

Place an aquarium pump on the lower shelf and attach one end of a 27-inch length of air-line tubing to the stem on the pump. Attach a cup hook to the bottom of the top shelf, loop the free end of the air-line tubing through the hook, and slip it over the small stem at the base of the aerator connector. Loop the drain tubes from the plant box into the reservoir box; shorten them to end slightly below the water level.

Fill both boxes with water and let stand for 24 hours, to check for leaks. Apply more silicone sealant if necessary. Then run the pump for 24 hours, again checking for leaks and resealing if necessary. Add nutrients, and place sphagnum moss and plants in the perforated pots.

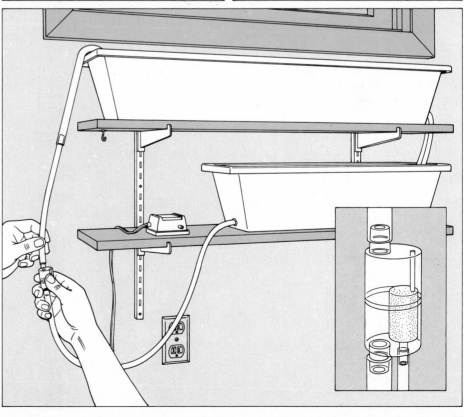

Built-in Aquariums for a Spectacular Wall

A frieze of built-in aquariums can turn a blank wall into a showcase or divide a large room with a wall of live entertainment visible from both sides. Whether your built-in holds a single aquarium tank or a series of them, the project requires consideration for both your fish and your house. The tremendous weight of water in a tank necessitates strong support, and the filtration system must be unobtrusive but easily accessible.

In setting up a large aquarium, location is important. You must place the tank or tanks well away from sunlit or drafty windows, since most kinds of fish cannot endure rapid changes of temperature. Space, however, is usually not a problem, because even the largest aquarium tanks are compact. A typical 50-gallon tank is 36 inches long, 18 inches wide and 18 inches high, and a 100-gallon tank is the same width and height but twice as long. If you have room for a sizable aquarium, using several small tanks instead of one large one has several advantages. It prevents the spread of disease and enables you to separate incompatible species of fish. With smaller tanks it is possible, for example, to regulate the environment of each species individually and keep both salt-water and fresh-water fish.

In a room with limited floor space and a closet wall you may be able to build the aquarium into the closet by cutting a tank-sized opening in the wall and constructing a platform inside the closet to hold the tank. This arrangement allows you to service the tank from inside the closet, but it does involve some structural changes. In cutting into the wall (page 77), you will remove sections of studs, leaving an opening that must be framed.

To support the weight of hundreds of pounds of water—100 U.S. gallons weighs 833 pounds—an aquarium cabinet like the one shown below must be much stronger than an ordinary built-in, and the floor beneath the cabinet must be strong enough to bear this weight. Structural engineers advise that no more than 50 gallons of water can safely be placed at the center (the weakest point) of a wood-framed floor. Greater amounts must be placed against a bearing wall or on a floor surface over a concrete slab.

Although technically it is feasible to build your own tanks, manufactured tanks are much less prone to leaks or ruptures—and the damage that even a small leak can do to floors, ceilings and fish can be catastrophic. The tanks are available at pet shops, in sizes up to 150 gallons and in a rectangular shape that allows the necessary oxygen exchange at the top of the tank and an adequate swimming area for the fish. For best visibility, select a tank glued along the corners with transparent silicone rubber and framed with angle irons along the top and bottom edges only.

Design the upper and lower cabinet sections so that the tank appears to float between them, at eye level, forming one continuous unit. To achieve this effect, suspend the upper cabinet (of exterior-grade plywood) from the ceiling and build both cabinets almost flush with the sides of the tank, allowing them to overlap the tank slightly. Choose an inconspicuous filter system consisting of a pump hidden in the upper cabinet and a plastic tray placed on the bottom of the tank and covered with gravel.

For lighting, you can install inexpensive fluorescent aquarium fixtures in the bottomless upper cabinet. Electricity for the lights and filtration equipment can be brought into the upper cabinet from the ceiling or floor (page 130) or, if it is against a wall, from the wall behind.

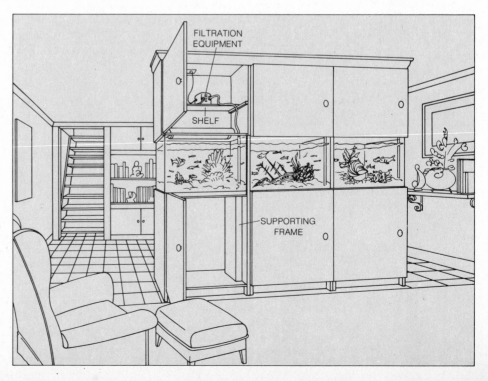

An aquarium room. This trio of floor-to-ceiling cabinets intersected by a row of glass tanks actually functions as a single unit, turning one end of a basement family room into an aquarium. The lower section of each cabinet houses a supporting frame for the tank's great weight: a wall-like internal structure of 2-by-12s and plywood, which may be fitted with shelves for storing nets, thermometers and other aquarium accessories. The frame is sheathed with a back, sides and a door of ¾-inch plywood. The upper section of the cabinet, which is attached to the ceiling joists, is designed to allow easy access to the top of the tank for cleaning, and to provide a shelf for the filtration apparatus.

Constructing a Sturdy Aquarium Base

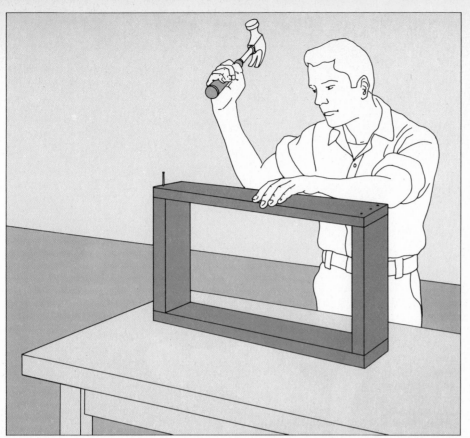

1 **Building the cabinet base.** Cut front, back and sides for the cabinet base from 2-by-4 lumber, and assemble the base by nailing the front and back pieces to the ends of the side-pieces. Make the front and back pieces ½ inch longer than the bottom of the aquarium tank; the sidepieces should be 5½ inches shorter than the overall width of the tank.

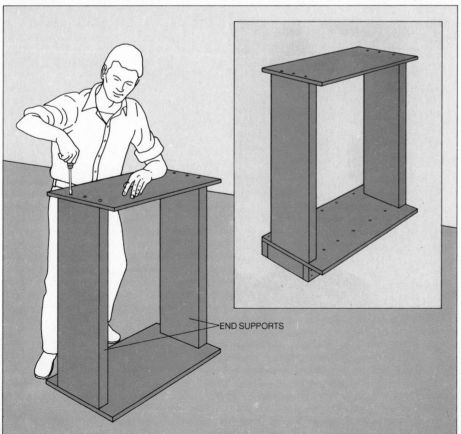

END SUPPORTS

2 **Building the supporting frame.** Assemble a frame by screwing top and bottom pieces of ¾-inch plywood to 2-by-12 vertical supports. Cut the top and bottom pieces ½ inch wider and longer than the tank bottom, and the vertical supports 5 inches shorter than the planned height of the bottom of the tank. Make enough vertical supports to provide one at each end of the frame plus additional supports at intervals no greater than 34 inches. Center the plywood pieces on the end supports, aligning the ends of the plywood with the outer face of the supports, and secure them with 3-inch flat-head wood screws. Fasten the other supports at regular intervals between the two ends.

Set the bottom of the supporting frame on the cabinet base, aligning the rear edges of the frame and base (*inset*). The front frame edge should overhang the front of the base by about 3 inches. Drive eightpenny common nails through the frame bottom into the front and back edges of the base at approximately 6-inch intervals.

3 **Assembling the cabinet walls.** Make a back and sides for the supporting frame from ¾-inch plywood, cutting these pieces 1½ inches longer than the height of the base-and-frame assembly to provide a lip around the bottom of the tank. Cut the back ¾ inch wider than the back edge of the supporting frame. Cut each sidepiece 1½ inches wider than the end of the supporting frame, then use a router and guide board to cut a dado down the length of each sidepiece. Make the dado ¾ inch wide and ⅜ inch deep, and position it ¾ inch in from the back edge.

Position the back against the back of the frame so that it overlaps ⅜ inch at each side; nail it to the back edge of the plywood top and bottom of the frame with finishing nails. Spread yellow carpenter's glue in the dadoes of the sidepieces, tap them into place over the projecting edges of the back piece, and use finishing nails to secure them to the frame and back (inset).

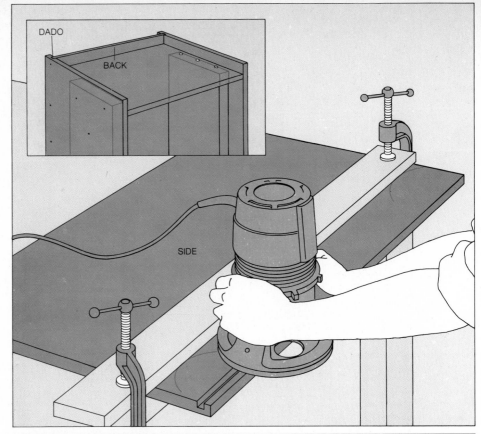

4 **Attaching the door.** Make a door of ¾-inch plywood to cover the front of the cabinet. The door should be as wide as the cabinet and high enough to reach from the bottom edge of the supporting frame to the top edge of the sides, including the top lip. The hinges should be positioned 5 inches from the top and bottom. If you are building a group of adjacent cabinets with flush doors that must open alongside each other, use special concealed spring hinges that require no clearance or catch, available at cabinet-supply stores. To attach a spring hinge, outline the circular end of the hinge on the inside of the door, drill out the circle to a depth of ½ inch and screw the hinge to the door and side of the cabinet. Attach a door pull.

If your cabinets will not be adjacent, use standard offset hinges (inset). Place the flat leaves of the hinges against the inside of the door, mark their outlines with a pencil, and cut mortises as deep as the thickness of the hinge leaves, using a chisel and mallet. Screw the hinges into the mortises, hold the door against the cabinet, and outline the offset hinge leaves on the front edge and inside face of the side of the cabinet. Cut these mortises and fasten the offset leaves. Install a magnetic catch and a door pull.

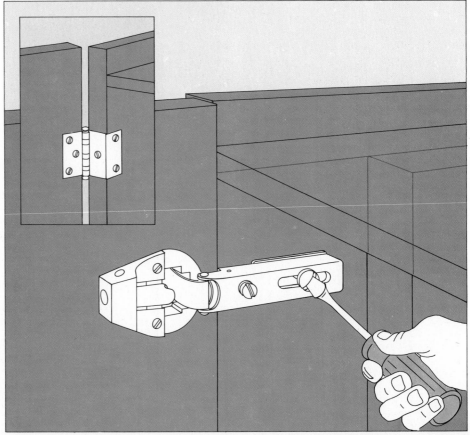

Above-the-Tank Cabinet

1 **Assembling the cabinet.** Make the sides and back for the upper cabinet the same width as those of the lower cabinet, and long enough to reach from the ceiling to a point 1½ inches below the top of the tank. Dado the sides and attach them to the back as in Step 3, opposite.

Cut a cabinet top to fit snugly between the sides and back, apply glue to its side and back edges; attach it with screws through the sides and back. Nail a 1-by-4 board across the top of the cabinet front, providing a nailing surface for crown molding. Cut a door and mount it (*Step 4, opposite*). Install cleats for a shelf about 12 inches above the open bottom of the cabinet (*page 18*), and cut a shelf to attach to the cleats after the cabinet is mounted. To protect the upper cabinet from water vapor, use exterior-grade plywood and finish all inside surfaces with spar varnish or polyurethane exterior varnish.

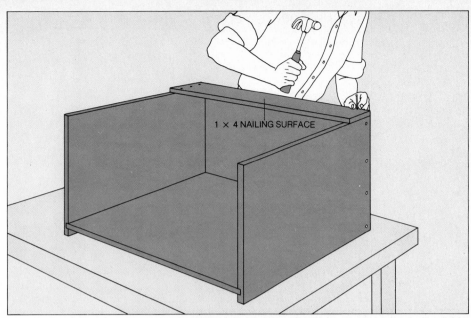

2 **Mounting the upper cabinet.** Find the positions of the ceiling joists (*page 112*), and mark guidelines for the upper cabinet. Then have a helper hold the upper cabinet against the ceiling while you drill pilot holes through the plywood top and into the joists. Secure the cabinet with 3-inch screws at 12-inch intervals along each joist.

3 **Attaching crown molding.** After all the upper cabinets are in place, measure the length and width of the entire unit, and cut crown molding to fit, mitering the corners. Use fourpenny finishing nails to fasten the molding to the back, side and front nailing surfaces of the cabinets at about 12-inch intervals.

Using a plumb line, position the lower cabinets directly beneath the upper cabinets. Then open the doors and slide in the tanks.

A Through-the-Wall Aviary to Display Birds

Pets often absorb large blocks of their owners' time—but not necessarily their living spaces. An exception is this aviary, which links two rooms and, for a bird lover, probably monopolizes both. The aviary is built into the wall and on one side extends into the room the depth of the base cabinet. On the other side it is flush with the wall. In the dimensions given, the aviary is large enough for a number of small birds that in general require about 1 cubic foot each.

You can put such an aviary anywhere in the house, with two limitations. Place it where stray feathers and occasional spilled bird seed will not cause difficult cleanup problems. And put it in a nonbearing wall, since you may want to re-move studs to widen the cage. Look at the rafters in the attic or the joists in the basement: A nonbearing wall is one that runs parallel to them.

The height and width of the aviary can vary, but it should not be less than 3 or 4 feet tall, since birds need a chance to fly upward. Plan the opening in the wall so that when you remove studs, the aviary will fit exactly between the two outer studs remaining. These studs will form the sides of the frame that supports the aviary. The depth of the cage should be at least 18 inches, again for the comfort of the birds. In the aviary pictured below, the height of the cage bottom is dictated by the height of a purchased cabinet incorporated in the design.

Assembling building materials for the aviary is a simple matter; all of them are standard items. The top and bottom of the cage are made of ¾-inch plywood, the sliding tray on the cage bottom of ½-inch plywood. For a wall of average thickness (less than 5 inches) the cage's vertical and horizontal framework is made of 1-by-2 and 1-by-6 lumber. The pieces are held together with glue and screws or with T plates; the latter are good for hard-to-reach joints that are subject to little or no stress. The frame is enclosed with ¼-inch woven-wire mesh. Finish the raw edges of the constructions with quarter-round molding and 2-inch picture molding; if you paint the aviary, use lead-free, nontoxic enamel.

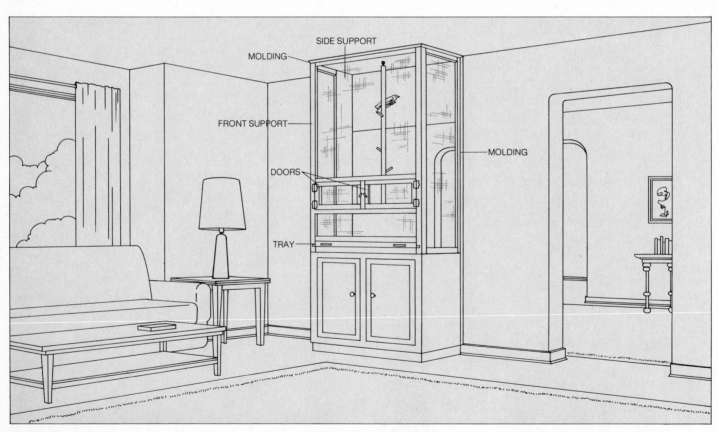

An aviary set in a wall. The aviary above is 3 feet 10½ inches wide, the distance between studs after two studs have been removed, and 5 feet tall, the distance between the top of a purchased cabinet and the ceiling. This makes the cage large enough to house comfortably 10 to 20 small birds, such as parakeets, or a half dozen larg-er birds, such as parrots. The cage extends about 14 inches into one room but is flush with the wall in the adjacent room. The cage bottom is cantilevered from a rough sill 3 feet off the floor and rests on the cabinet, which is both a structural support and a storage space for bird food and accessories. The cage ceiling is nailed against the wall's top plate; the 1-by-6 supports at the rear of the cage are nailed to the adja-cent studs. The doors open for removing or adding birds, and a sliding tray at the cage bottom simplifies cleaning. Cut edges of the surrounding wallboard are hidden by quarter-round mold-ing on the protruding side of the cage, picture molding on the flush side. The perch, hung from the ceiling, can be a length of closet pole or 2-by-2, studded with ⅜- to ⅝-inch dowels.

Building the Birdcage

1 **Cutting an opening in the wall.** Cut away both wallboard surfaces, using the technique shown on page 10; on the vertical cuts, you can saw through both surfaces at once if you use a keyhole saw. On the horizontal cuts, remove the sections of wallboard separately. Then remove intervening studs by cutting them flush with the bottom of the opening and pulling them loose from the nails that hold them to the header at the top. Cut a 2-by-4 sill to fit the width of the opening. Toenail the sill into the studs framing the side of the opening, and butt-nail through the sill into the ends of the intervening studs.

2 **Assembling the cage floor and ceiling.** Cut a ¾-inch plywood ceiling and floor, the planned depth of the cage and the width of the opening less a 1½-inch allowance for the thickness of two sidepieces. Then cut the two 1-by-6 side supports, making them the same length as the height of the opening. Glue and screw the supports into the cage floor, with the back edges flush and the floor ¾ inch in from the ends of the supports. Fasten the cage ceiling to the top ends of the supports in the same way, but make the ceiling top flush with the supports.

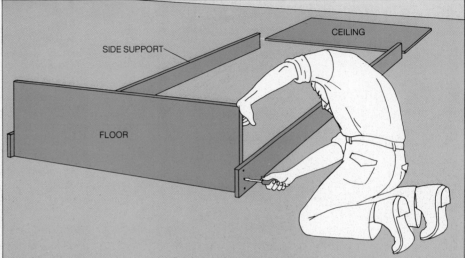

3 **Making the front supports.** Cut two pairs of 1-by-2 strips to match the height of the opening, and glue each pair together at right angles to form the front corners of the cage. Then drive 1½-inch wood screws at 8-inch intervals through the face of one strip into the edge of the other, countersinking the screws and concealing the heads with wood putty (*center right*). Glue the front supports onto the corners of the plywood ceiling and floor, placing the corners flush with the top of the ceiling but recessing the floor ¾ inch, as in Step 2. Drive screws through both faces of the corner supports into the plywood edges (*bottom right*). Cut a notch for a sliding tray in the front edge of each of the corner supports. Position the notches directly above the floor of the cage, making each one ½ inch wide and ¾ inch deep (*inset*).

4 **Adding the crosspieces.** Cut five 1-by-2 crosspieces to fit between the front corners of the cage, and secure them inside the cage with glue and T plates. Use two crosspieces to frame the tray opening, two to frame the door and one to brace the top. Place the first crosspiece flush with the cage bottom, the second one 2 inches above the first, the third 24 inches above the cage floor, the fourth 10 inches above the third. Put the last one flush with the cage ceiling. Divide the door opening in half with a 10-inch vertical support cut from 1-by-2 lumber. Then brace the sides at the top and the bottom with two 1-by-2 crosspieces, fitted between the front and rear supports for the cage.

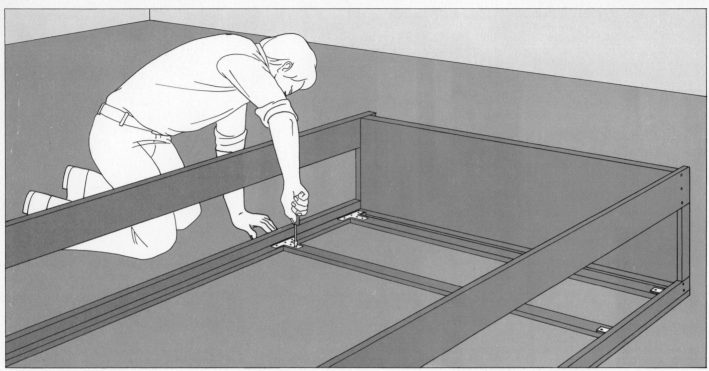

5 **Making the doors and tray.** For each hinged door, cut four 1-by-2s to fit the opening, allowing ⅛ inch of clearance horizontally and vertically for door movement. Glue and screw the pieces together to form a rectangular frame, and cut a ¼-inch wire-mesh rectangle for each frame, allowing for ¼ inch of overlap on all four sides. Staple the mesh to the inside of each frame; finish the cut edges of the mesh with ¾-inch quarter-round molding. Then fasten each door to a front corner support, using two ornamental hinges, and add swivel catches at the vertical center support.

Cut a tray from ½-inch plywood, making it ¾ inch narrower than the width of the cage floor and ¾ inch deeper than the depth of the floor. Glue a strip of quarter-round molding to the back of a lip made from 1¾-inch lattice; glue and screw the lip to the front of the tray, and attach a brass pull to each side of the lip (*inset*).

If you are painting the aviary, paint the doorframes before you attach the wire mesh, and the tray lip before you attach the pulls. Paint the bare frame of the aviary at the same time.

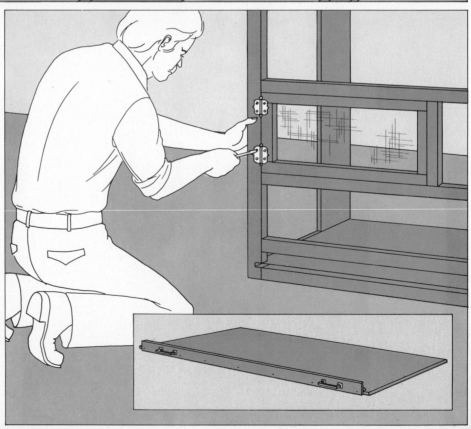

6 **Stapling on the wire mesh.** Cut ¼-inch wire mesh to fit the openings in the front and sides of the cage, allowing for ¼-inch overlap on all four edges of each piece. Set the cage upright, and, working from the inside, staple the wire mesh first to the center points of each opening; then work out to the corners, pulling the mesh taut as you go and placing staples at 2-inch intervals. Cover the cut edge of mesh with quarter-round molding, and paint it to match the aviary.

Make a 3-foot-long perch-support from a closet pole or 2-by-2 lumber, and drill holes along its length for ⅜-inch to ⅝-inch dowels, to serve as perches. Cut the dowels 6½ inches long, and glue them into the holes. Screw an eye hook into the cage ceiling and another hook into the top end of the perch support.

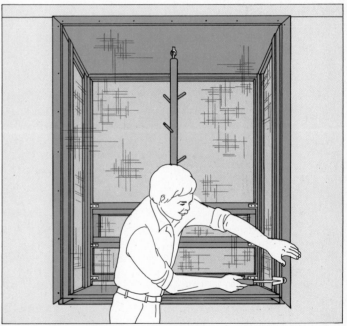

7 **Installing the aviary in the wall.** With a helper, lift the cage into the wall opening by resting the bottom edges of the rear supports against the sill and tilting the cage upright, lining up the back of the cage with the wall surface. Drive sixpenny nails through the rear supports, into the studs that frame the opening, placing the nails at 8-inch intervals. Then nail through the ceiling of the cage, into the top plate. Hang the perch, and then cut ¼-inch wire mesh to fit the back opening, allowing ¼ inch of overlap on all edges. Staple the mesh to the edges of the ceiling, the floor and the rear supports as in Step 6, above.

8 **Adding the trim.** Nail a 1-inch wood strip, cut to the thickness of the wallboard, to the rough sill on each side of the wall, bringing the sill out flush with the surrounding wallboard. Then cut and miter the corners on four strips of 2-inch picture molding, to frame the back of the cage. Glue and nail one lengthwise strip in place, flush with the edge of the opening; then add the remaining strips consecutively. On the other side of the wall, glue and nail strips of ¾-inch quarter-round molding, to frame the projecting top part of the cage and also the entire wall on each side of the opening.

Rooms with Split Personalities

Using a room for more than one purpose is not a new idea: It undoubtedly was the first domestic arrangement. Families gathered around the fire to socialize and withdrew from the fire to sleep, both activities sharing the same room. The doubling up then was a practical measure: It promoted the most efficient use of heat. In a modern house, rooms are made to double their function for other reasons. Space usually is at a premium and families have a diversity of interests. Individual passions for photography, exercise, gardening, weaving and even swimming put strains on all but the biggest houses, and only an arrangement of shared space can possibly contain them.

When a room must serve two functions, careful planning is essential for the merger to succeed. Sometimes the two uses can exist simultaneously in time and in space, like the wine cellar-office on page 83, which belongs to a wine critic.

In some dual-purpose rooms, the room itself changes, like a chameleon. With the flick of a light switch and the removal of a few chairs, the quiet dining area on page 85 becomes a razzle-dazzle disco dance floor. In other cases, two purposes are served by dividing a room into two smaller spaces, by such visual definitions as the combination of conventional and stadium seating that demarcates the living room-screening room on page 84.

The secret of success in subdividing space for several functions is to end with the same sense of spaciousness you had at the beginning. Otherwise, the room will look cramped. Designers often achieve a sense of spaciousness by using purely visual devices, such as different wall or floor coverings that separate one part of a room from another: They combine bare floors with wall-to-wall carpeting, wood floors with tile, wallpaper with painted or paneled walls.

You can also divide space with such unobtrusive physical barriers as a change in floor level or the addition of a low screen—a row of freestanding bookcases, for example, or a row of plants. Even furniture itself, like Thomas Jefferson's alcove bed shown opposite, can demarcate a change of function within a room.

With imagination and a determination not to be ruled by the conventional uses of living, dining, cooking and sleeping rooms, you can house special activities in any room. If you like, you can have a swimming pool in your kitchen or a garage in your living room. Unlikely, you may say; but for proof that pools can coexist with kitchens, and cars with Oriental rugs, turn to pages 86 and 87.

Dual-duty bedroom. Thomas Jefferson's elegant combination of bedroom and study was his own design. The alcove bed, common in drafty 18th Century houses, was moved away from the wall and used as a room divider. The study, in the foreground, was furnished with a chaise-longue arrangement consisting of a padded bench and a swivel chair in which Jefferson could sit half-recumbent, a position that favored his rheumatic back. The bureau table, visible in the bedroom beyond the bed, held grooming articles and, on top, Jefferson's medicine chest.

Rooms with a Work Complex

In pursuit of a profession or of a serious avocation, more and more people are creating work spaces in their homes. This approach not only saves the cost of office or studio space; it provides a convenient and comfortable work environment for people who must juggle professions or hobbies with domestic responsibilities.

In homes with limited space, a work area can coexist with a leisure area without being a visual blight, if there is a well-planned storage system for work materials. Often these materials are shut away, but they can enhance a room's beauty. A writer's books, a weaver's spools of yarn or a composer's elaborate audio equipment can add warmth and visual excitement to a room's decor.

Sociable studio. Lined with sound-enhancing wall paneling and gauze-covered paper, this music room, with its piano and projection equipment, was designed for Oscar-winning composer Marvin Hamlisch as a place to work and entertain. A control unit in the coffee table in front of the sofa projects film onto a large mechanized screen that drops down over a window; the television projector hangs from the ceiling on a metal frame. In daytime the screen is raised to admit sunlight and a view of New York's Park Avenue.

Three-dimensional tapestry. A 16-harness loom and a wall of brightly colored wool yarns are displayed in this weaving studio that doubles as a living room. A low wall divides, but does not hide, the two areas from each other, giving the artist an opportunity to expand his working space. Usually an upright frame loom is positioned against the brick wall in the living area and is used to create large works, such as the two panels shown, which are part of a triptych inspired by the work of the French artist Sonia Delaunay.

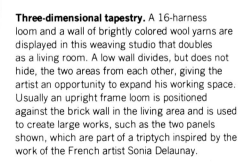

Live-in cave. Wine critic and writer Charles Turgeon converted a 10-by-14-foot corner of his basement into a wine cellar and office. Up to 1,000 bottles can be stored on the plywood shelves, which Turgeon designed and built. The bottles are separated from one another by heavy wire that has been strung through holes drilled in the shelves, a partitioning device that saves space as well as money.

Rooms That Entertain Fantasies

Sometimes it is easier, less expensive, and more fun to exercise and entertain at home than to go out to the discotheque, the health club or the movies. Such pursuits can often share a room originally intended for more traditional activities, and the recreation half can even set the dominant decorative theme. For example, in an area that doubles as a bedroom and exercise room *(below)*, a king-size bed takes its cue from the rinks and ballet bars in the background and masquerades as a gym mat.

But sometimes the secondary use of a room is more effective when it can come as a surprise. With the flip of a few hidden switches, a seemingly ordinary living room *(right)* is transformed into a discotheque that pulsates with colored lights and sound.

Miniature theater. Stadium-like seating and a huge screen in the living room of a Washington, D.C., film executive turn one end of the room into a television screening room. Matching fabric on the stadium cushions and the swiveling armchairs integrates the room's two functions, and what appears to be a coffee table in front of the special seating is the control panel for projecting images on the screen.

Designer gym. A New York fashion designer for whom exercise is a daily rite had this gymnasium built into the sleeping area of her loft home. Flying rings and ballet bars are reflected in the mirrored panels, blending their utilitarian forms into the loft's simple lines. The bed is on a carpeted platform, backed by movable clothing cabinets facing each other across a corridor.

Deceptive disco. At night a startling change comes over the quiet beige, plum and gray furnishings in the living-dining area of this home belonging to a professional magician. A mirrored ball is lowered from the ceiling, the dining area is cleared for dancing, neon lights glow in pink, lavender and blue, and colored spotlights pulsate, synchronized with the room's music system.

Rooms with an Outdoor Look

With daring and a great deal of imagination, the unlikeliest combinations of room usage can be made to work. You can have a garden path that meanders through one end of your living room, a swimming pool in the kitchen. Or you can garage a suitably decorative car in the room where you entertain.

When you bring such outdoor elements indoors, common sense dictates that you put them in a logical place. A garden needs sunlight, a pool good plumbing, a car access to the street. You must also make some concessions to the comfort and health of the human beings who will be sharing the space. The plants that grow in the indoor garden, right, are species whose temperature and humidity requirements are similar to those of people. The fumes briefly given off by the car in the garage-living room below rise through the lofty space overhead and exit through slotted windows with sliding panes in the roof.

Quick dips. In this Texas kitchen, the outdoors is brought indoors with a 12-by-15-foot swimming pool. Waterproof decking normally associated with outdoor installations surrounds the pool and runs diagonally up the kitchen wall. The roof is pierced by a number of long, narrow skylights; the columns and beams are reminiscent of the airy structure of an arbor.

A tree in the house. A two-story slanting wall of insulating glass creates a sunlit setting for a landscaped indoor garden that includes, in the foreground, a weeping fig tree and a lemon bush. The garden can be enjoyed from a living room below or a sitting area above. Special equipment controls humidity and temperature, and a screen rolls down to provide shade when needed.

Overtime parking. A party-loving Brazilian architect incorporated his garage into his living room to gain more space for entertaining. In doing so he got two bonuses: overflow seating and automatic car care—the maid who cleans the house also dusts and polishes the Porsche. Car and couches are separated by an enormous cement-slab coffee table sheathed in aluminum.

3 Fun and Fitness in Family Rooms

A swing for the playroom. Though usually suspended from a tree, a swing can also hang from a ceiling joist and be an indoor delight. Metal eye screws anchored in the joists provide solid support; nylon ropes threaded through these eye screws are locked in place with steel clips. The rounded contours of a rubber seat fit many anatomies and make the swing less hazardous in the limited space of a playroom.

Conventional wisdom dictates that the harder one works, the more one needs to play. For that reason, active recreation in leisure time becomes a significant need amid the work tensions and everyday pressure of modern life. A room in the house dedicated to giving body, mind or spirit a chance to recoup is a room put to good use.

But recreation can encompass a wide range of activities—and may require various types of facilities—depending on personal life style. To a sedentary office worker, strenuous exercise may be the ideal tonic, and a room equipped for weight lifting or dance exercises could be the perfect retreat. To a person whose work is physical, the opposite may be true: A recreation room may mean a special place to watch television or a room set up for playing board games with the children. To a parent who spends long hours with children, the perfect recreation room may be simply a place that keeps tricycles out of the living room and isolates noisy play.

The age span of children is a major factor in planning a recreation room. School-age children need a place to burn off excess energy. But to a smaller child, play is not a relief but the main business of living. For toddlers, therefore, a playroom should be a source of stimulation—but also a place where they can play in safety.

Planning a single room to satisfy the recreational needs of the entire family can be complicated, but a few basic guidelines are helpful. First of all, the design and construction of the room should anticipate change. As children grow, interests wax and wane, and the family's life style evolves, the room will probably have to be adapted to new purposes. Consequently, major installations such as a wet bar should never be positioned where they will prevent later changes in the room. Equally important is the division of floor space and the arrangement of lighting so that one person's activity does not conflict with other activities going on in the room. A light over a pool table, for instance, should not be placed where it interferes with the projection of a big-screen television; and the table itself must have adequate clearance for players wielding cues 5 feet long.

Planning should also take creature comfort into account. Given its usual location—somewhere on the periphery of the main living areas—a recreation room may need the extra warmth of a space heater or perhaps a dehumidifier to dry out the air. Entertaining may put a strain on the room's natural air circulation, suggesting the installation of an exhaust fan to carry off stale air. Finally, the room should be as carefree as possible. Spilled drinks, dropped ashes, stray apple cores and sandwich crumbs should fall on surfaces and materials that naturally resist abuse—or have been coated with abuse-resisting finishes. When the party is over, the cleanup should be easy.

Equipping a Place to Help You Keep in Shape

Healthful regular exercise is indisputably good for you, but it can also be an inconvenience. If you exercise outdoors, you are at the mercy of the weather, and using a gym or a health club usually involves travel time. By outfitting a room in your home with exercise equipment, you can bypass both problems and save money too—setting up an exercise room generally costs less than the yearly membership in many health clubs and will serve your family for years to come.

The equipment you choose for a home exercise center and the way you arrange it will naturally reflect your own interests and needs. Some items may have to be purchased, such as an exercise bicycle or weight-lifting pulleys. But you can build certain standard pieces of equipment yourself. Two of the most versatile are a padded press bench for working with weights and a ladder-like set of stall bars for chinning and limbering exercises. The press bench doubles as a storage box for weights and other equipment. The stall bars double as support for a padded slant board, used in toning stomach muscles.

Given sufficient space, the exercise room could also contain a mirror and a dancer's handrail, instructions for which appear on pages 20 and 33 respectively. And for most exercise programs you are likely to need mats to cushion your body from the floor or wall. Available in various sizes through stores that sell sporting goods or gym supplies, these mats are often fastened to the wall, either for use or for storage, with a nylon hook-and-loop tape called Velcro, which separates with a quick tug. The hook section of this tape is easily mounted on the wall in two parallel strips that match the loop section on the edges of the mats, which often is factory-installed and, if not, can be installed at home.

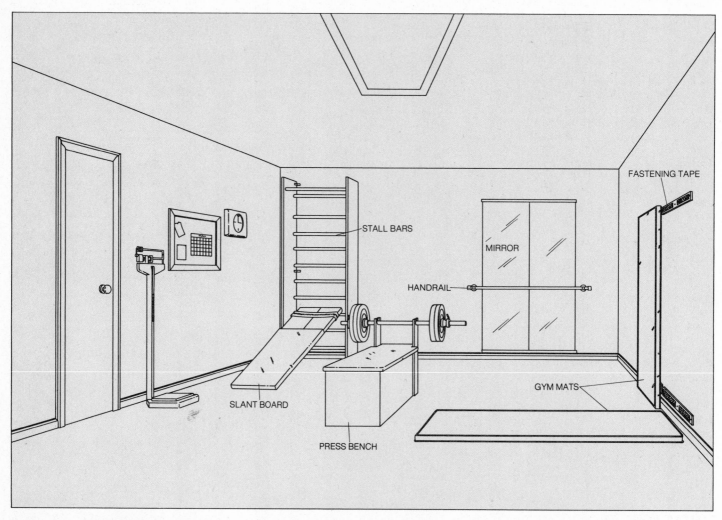

STALL BARS

FASTENING TAPE

MIRROR

HANDRAIL

SLANT BOARD

GYM MATS

PRESS BENCH

Layout of an exercise room. The room shown here is equipped for various physical-fitness activities. Mats pull down from the wall to create an area for gymnastics, martial arts and floor exercises; each mat is mounted to the wall by special hook-and-loop fastening tape, one section of which is attached to plywood strips that are screwed to the wall. A press bench at center has the requisite weight rests and a removable padded top so that the base can be used for storage. Stall bars, anchored to wall studs, support a slant board, used for sit-ups; a mirror and handrail are bordered by enough open space for dance practice. A wall clock, bulletin board and weight scale complete the equipment.

Tumbling Mats to Pad the Wall or Floor

Securing the tapes. Cut two 4-inch-wide strips of ½-inch plywood to match the length of the mat, then attach 1¾-inch hook-and-loop tape to both strips. If the mat is factory-equipped with the looped half of the tape, cut matching sections of the hooked half, and position them on the strips so that they line up with the tape on the mat. If the mat is without tape, cut 12-inch sections of complete tape assembly, both hook and loop halves, one section for each 3 feet of mat length; but make sure there will be a section of tape at each end of the mat.

Glue the hooked tapes to the plywood strips with the adhesive recommended by the tape manufacturer, or use an adhesive with a methyl-ethyl-ketone base. Then staple the hooked tapes to the plywood at 3-inch intervals, placing the staples along the edge of the tape. Mark the position on the wall for the plywood strips, using the size of the mat as a guide. Screw the strips to the wall, using one screw at every stud and driving the screws at least 1 inch into the studs.

If necessary, attach looped tapes to the top and bottom edges of the mat, aligning the tapes with those mounted on the wall (*inset*). Glue the tapes to the mat with glue recommended by the tape manufacturer. Then reinforce the tapes by stitching all along the border of each section of tape with an upholstery needle and heavy-duty nylon thread.

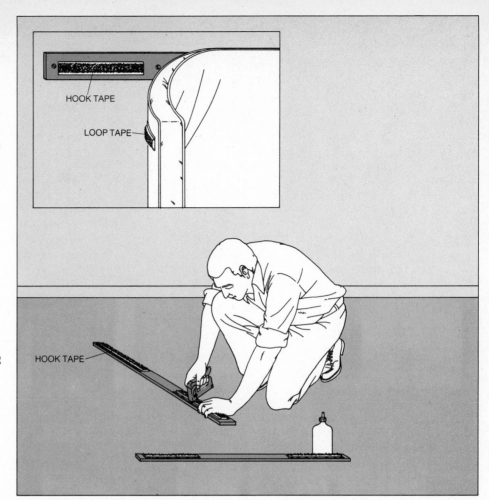

A Press Bench That Doubles as a Storage Box

1 Assembling the base. Construct an open-bottomed box of 2-by-2 uprights with ¾-inch plywood sides and ends. Tailor the dimensions of the box to size if the person who will use it is unusually large or small. Otherwise, for most adults of average build, the recommended dimensions are 18-inch uprights, 18-inch-square ends and 44½-by-18-inch sides. Drill pilot holes, and screw the plywood ends to pairs of uprights. Then turn the box on its side and, while a helper steadies one end assembly, set a plywood side over two end assemblies, drill pilot holes and screw the side to the uprights. Flip the box, and screw the other side to the other uprights.

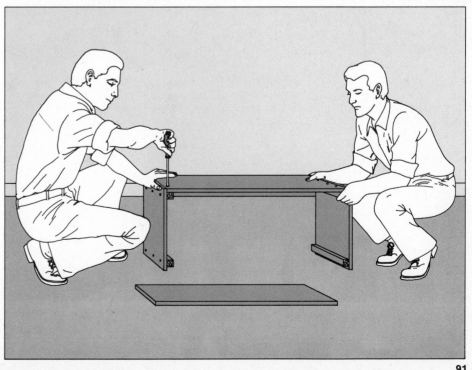

2 **Attaching cleats and padding.** Make the bench top of ¾-inch plywood with 1-by-2 cleats, padding it with either foam rubber or polyurethane foam topped with heavy-gauge, fabric-backed vinyl. First cut notches 4½ inches long and 1 inch wide into both corners on one end of a piece of plywood 2 inches longer and 2 inches wider than the outside length and width of the base. Center the base on it, and outline the uprights and the inside ends. Cut cleats to fit this outline, and screw them to the plywood.

With scissors, cut out a slab of 1-inch foam the size of the bench top. Cut some vinyl roughly 8 inches longer and wider. Center the foam on the vinyl, the plywood on the foam. Wrap the vinyl over the plywood, stapling it to the underside of the top at ½-inch intervals with 9/16-inch staples. Fold but do not cut the corners. Finish the edges with duct tape or vinyl upholstery trim.

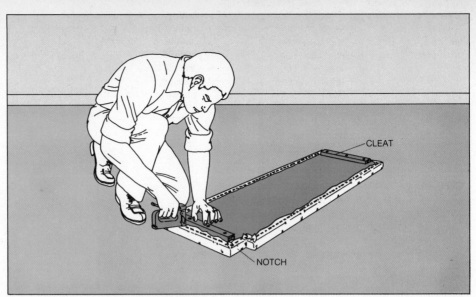

3 **Adding weight rests.** With a saber saw or coping saw, cut rounded notches, roughly 2 inches wide and 1½ inches deep, into the centers of one end of two 2-by-4s that are long enough to extend 13 inches above the top of the bench. Stand the 2-by-4s against opposite sides of one end of the base, and screw through them into the uprights. Be sure the screws miss the screws that hold the plywood sides to the uprights.

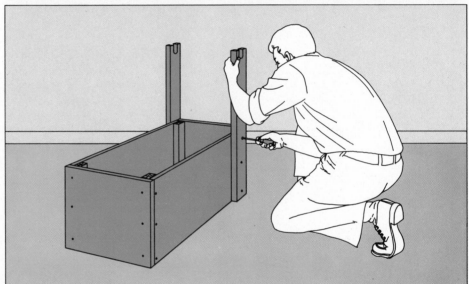

Stall Bars for Building Suppleness and Strength

1 **Preparing the uprights.** With a chalk line or a combination square, mark a line 2¾ inches in from what will be the back edge of a 2-by-8 upright that is 6 inches shorter than the height of the ceiling. Then use a combination square to make marks that cross the first line, spacing them 8 inches apart and beginning at the end that is going to rest on the floor. Make an additional cross mark 1 inch from the front edge and 8 inches from the top. Mark a second 2-by-8 upright in the same way and then, at each cross mark, use a 1⅝-inch spade bit to drill a hole through the board. If necessary, have a helper watch the drill bit from the side as you drill, to make sure that the drill remains perpendicular to the board face while you work.

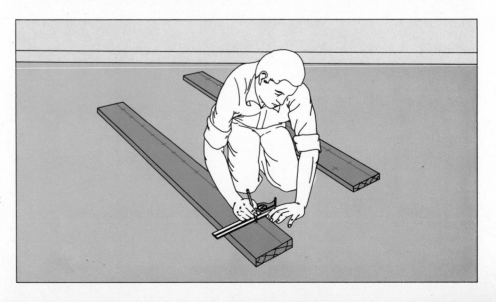

2 **Fastening the bars.** Insert 35-inch lengths of 1⅜-inch dowel into all the holes of one upright, then into corresponding holes of the second upright, using a rubber mallet, if necessary, to force the second upright toward the first until the dowels are completely seated. Check to make sure the dowels are perpendicular to the faces of the uprights, then drive tenpenny finishing nails through the back edge of the uprights and into each dowel. Similarly, drive nails through the front edges of the two uprights into the dowel nearest the top of the uprights.

Sand the assembly; finish as desired. At the site chosen for the stall bars, mark the outer edges of two wall studs whose centers are 32 inches apart. Finally, notch the bottoms of the uprights to fit around the baseboard, or remove a section of baseboard to accommodate the piece.

3 **Fastening the assembly to the wall.** Set the assembled stall bars in position against the wall so that the inside edges of the uprights are aligned with the marks that indicate the outer edges of the studs. Have a helper hold a level against one upright to check the assembly for plumb, while you shim both uprights if nec-essary. Then, while the helper steadies the as-sembly, fasten each upright to its corre-sponding stud with three 1½-inch corner braces. Use screws that are long enough to penetrate the uprights ½ inch and the studs at least 1 inch. If you are fastening the stall-bar assembly to a masonry wall, use lead anchors.

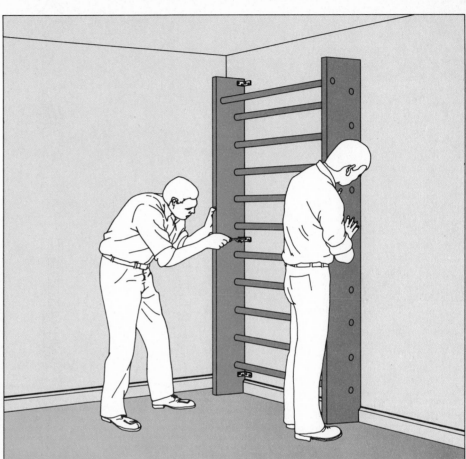

4 **Constructing a slant board.** Butt together two 7-foot lengths of 2-by-10 lumber, and join them with two 1-by-2 cleats 16 inches long. Center the cleats across the 2-by-10s, 18 inches in from each end, and screw them in place. Attach a third cleat, of 2-by-2 lumber cut 18 inches long, 1 inch from one end of the slant board, to serve as a catch for holding it over a dowel.

Measure in 4 feet from the end of the slant board opposite the 2-by-2 cleat, and pad that end of the board with foam and vinyl, as described in Step 2, opposite. Cut a 32-inch piece of leath-er or woven webbing for a foot strap (rubber up-holstery webbing or cotton belt webbing, avail-able in army-surplus stores, is equally good). Lap the webbing to the underside of the board and fasten it, 1 inch in from the edge, with scraps of plywood, screwing through the plywood and webbing into the boards beneath. Tack down the raw ends of the webbing with staples.

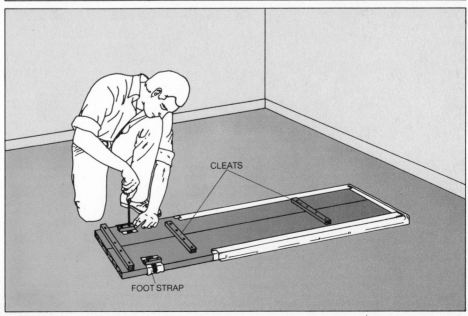

CLEATS

FOOT STRAP

Creating a Playroom to Please the Children

In a house designed by, scaled to and run by adults, a child's playroom is a home within a home, specially suited to the wide-ranging, constantly changing interests and activities of childhood. In the best playrooms the equipment challenges a child's imagination, intellect and physical skills at every stage of development. A climbing gym, for instance, can become a fort, a castle or a hideout; a chalkboard encourages artistic expression as well as practice in spelling and writing. The equipment must also be tailored to the available space, and it should be easy to care for and dismantle.

Safety involves such basics as rounding and smoothing sharp corners on all wood surfaces. If you are installing gymnastic equipment—such as an indoor swing or a climbing tower—locate it a reasonable distance from walls and, if the children are young, put a tumbling mat on the floor below. Swings have to be solidly anchored and should hang on twisted-nylon rope at least ½ inch in diameter. For the seat, the rubber-belt type is less dangerous when swinging empty than the more traditional wooden seat. The swing's metal hardware should be lubricated frequently with hard cup grease to prevent excessive wear.

To simplify playroom upkeep, use high-gloss paint so that surfaces can be wiped clean. Since children often play on the floor, choose a covering that is durable and smooth but also comparatively soft and warm. Vinyl, linoleum and sealed cork all are good choices; hard-wearing, sound-muffling carpet also has advantages, though it is harder to keep clean and makes a less successful surface for racing toy cars.

To encourage children to pick up their toys, there should be storage bins, drawers and shelves at a height that children can reach. An all-purpose plywood cube mounted on casters can serve as a cart during play hours, and afterward as a storage bin that tucks under a shelf. Limit the depth of such bins to 12 inches; anything deeper makes objects on the bottom difficult for a toddler to retrieve.

Finally, if you are building large structures, such as the climbing tower below, use materials and joinery that make the structure easy to take apart. Childhood does not last forever.

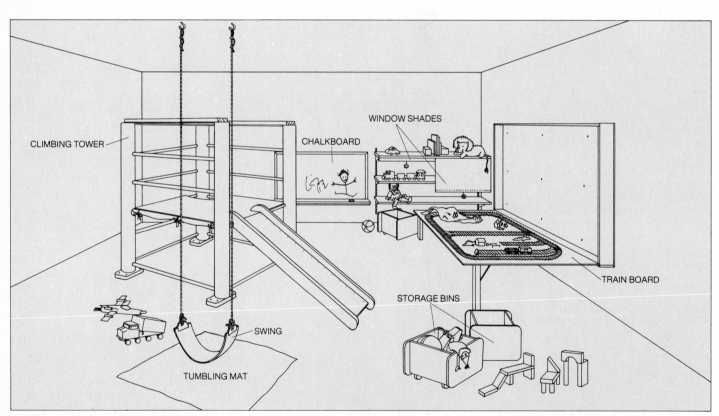

CLIMBING TOWER — WINDOW SHADES — CHALKBOARD — TRAIN BOARD — STORAGE BINS — SWING — TUMBLING MAT

An ideal playroom. The components of this well-equipped playroom for young children provide versatility, convenience and safety. A custom-built chalkboard and a fold-down train board make good use of wall space; the train board doubles as a bulletin board when it is folded against the wall. Plywood storage bins on casters simplify cleanup and can be used as wagons when empty, and window shades mounted on the storage shelves can be pulled to conceal clutter and keep out dust. Wooden blocks, made of scrap lumber, have rounded edges and are sanded smooth. Since the climbing tower and the swing encourage vigorous physical activity, they are sturdily made and solidly anchored, with generous clearances around them; a tumbling mat strategically placed beneath the swing serves to cushion falls.

As the child matures, the swing can be exchanged for a climbing rope or a trapeze, hung from the same joist-mounted eyebolts. If the Lilliputian train world loses its appeal, the foldaway train board can become a worktable for arts and crafts.

A Custom-made Chalkboard

1 **Cutting the frame sections.** Using a miter box to make the pieces fit precisely, cut two lengths of backband molding with a ¾-inch rabbet for the sides of the frame and one length for the top. Make the outer length of these sections ¼ inch greater than the dimensions of the planned chalkboard. Set the molding on edge in the box, with its back against the side of the box. For the top, cut both ends at a 45° angle; for the sides, cut one end at a 45° angle, the other end square. Reverse the direction of the angles on the two frame sides and on the two ends of the top.

For the chalk tray framing the bottom of the chalkboard, cut a 1-by-4 and a piece of half-round molding to the width of the chalkboard. Nail the molding to one edge of the 1-by-4, creating a lip to hold the chalk (*inset*).

2 **Assembling the frame.** Using yellow glue, join the mitered ends of the frame top and one frame side, holding them together with a corner clamp; reinforce the joint with 1-inch brads. Repeat for the other top corner. Then glue and nail the chalk tray to the bottom of the frame, driving the nails up through the bottom of the 1-by-4 into the square ends of the frame sides.

Cut a piece of ¼-inch hardboard and a piece of ¼-inch plywood to fit into the rabbeted back of the backband frame. Apply two coats of chalkboard paint, available at hardware stores, to the hardboard. When the paint is dry, lower the chalkboard, face down, and the plywood into the back of the frame. Secure both by using a screwdriver to drive glaziers' push points into the rabbeted edges of the frame at 4-inch intervals (*inset*). Drive 1-inch brads through the tray and into the plywood, also at 4-inch intervals.

Hanging an Indoor Swing

A safe support system. To anchor a swing, locate a ceiling joist and screw two 4-inch-long ⁵/₁₆-inch eyebolts into ¼-inch pilot holes drilled into the joist. Space the eyebolts about 16 inches apart. If the swing arc will parallel the joists, put the eyebolts in adjacent joists. Suspend the swing seat on ½-inch nylon rope. Place a metal loop—a thimble—beneath the rope where it passes through the eyebolt (*inset, right*), and secure the rope ends with rope clips. Bring each rope through an end of the swing, and secure with a bowline knot (*inset, left*). Lash the loose end to the length of rope with dental floss. Singe the end of the rope to retard fraying.

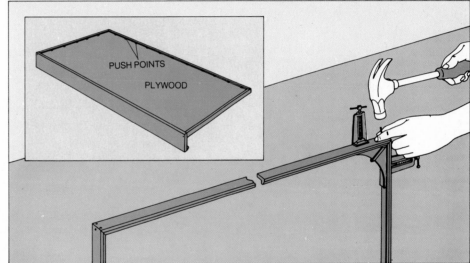

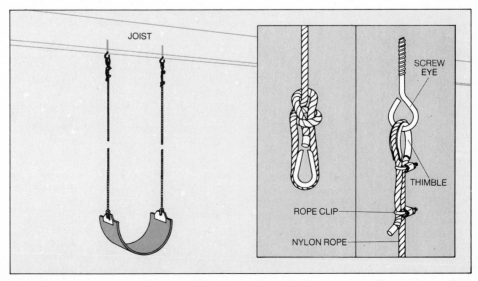

Building Toy-Storage Bins

1 Rounding the sides. Cut two sidepieces and two endpieces for the storage bin from ¾-inch plywood, making the sidepieces 5½ inches longer than the planned inside length of the bin. Using a compass, scribe an arc at each of the four corners of one sidepiece. Clamp the piece against a work surface, and round all four corners with a saber saw or a keyhole saw. Using this sidepiece as a pattern, round the corners of the other side in the same way; then smooth these corners and round the edges of all plywood pieces with a plane and sandpaper (*inset*). With a framing square and a pencil, mark a vertical guideline 2 inches in from each end of both sidepieces.

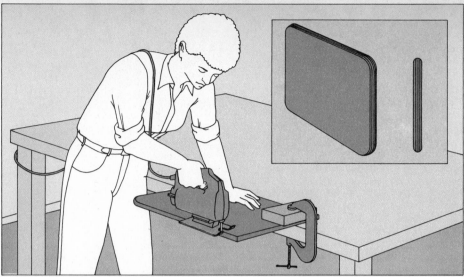

2 Joining the pieces. Clamp one endpiece into a woodworking vise, positioning it so that one vertical edge faces up. Spread yellow glue on this edge, and place a sidepiece over it, aligning the guideline on the sidepiece with the edge of the endpiece. Drive sixpenny finishing nails through the two pieces to secure the joint. Turn the assembly, rest it on the top of the workbench, and secure the second sidepiece to the opposite edge of the endpiece.

Cut a ¾-inch plywood bottom to fit into the three-sided assembly, sizing it to fall ¾ inches in from the guidelines at the unattached ends of the two sidepieces. Glue and nail the bottom in place, flush with the bottom edges of the three-sided assembly; then glue and nail the second endpiece in place to complete the bin.

Countersink all nails, fill the holes with wood putty, and sand all the surfaces smooth. Apply primer and enamel to all interior and exterior surfaces, or finish the bin with three coats of polyurethane varnish. Screw plate-mounted casters to the bottom of the bin (*inset*).

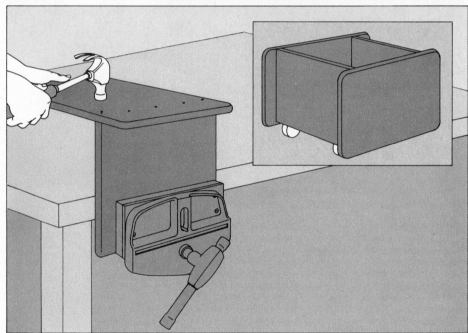

Creating Building Blocks from Scrap Lumber

An assortment of shapes and sizes. Geometric shapes cut from close-grained hardwood, such as maple or birch, make inexpensive but durable building blocks. The shapes shown here can be cut from standard lumber sizes, such as 1-by-1, 1-by-2, 2-by-4 and 4-by-4, and from dowels 1 inch or more in diameter. Be sure to cut all pieces large enough so that they do not end up in your child's mouth. As a further safety measure, round all edges and corners, and smooth all surfaces with sandpaper. Paint the blocks with two or more coats of polyurethane or enamel.

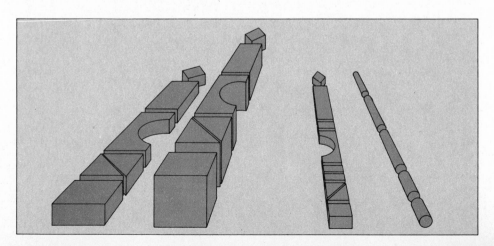

A Train Board That Folds against the Wall

1 Constructing the wall frame. Cut two 8-foot lengths and two 46½-inch lengths of 1-by-6 lumber. Join the four pieces, using yellow glue and eightpenny nails, to create a frame whose outer dimensions are 4 by 8 feet. Spread glue around one edge of the frame, lay a 4-by-8 sheet of ½-inch plywood over it, and nail the plywood

in place with eightpenny finishing nails at 8-inch intervals. Allow the glue to dry thoroughly.

Locate and mark the studs in the area where you plan to install the wall frame for the train board. Then mark the eventual position of the frame on the wall, keeping in mind that the train

board should be no more than waist-high to the child using it. Have a helper hold the wall frame in place while you drill pilot holes for 3-inch flat-head screws, No. 12, through the frame's plywood back and into the studs; drill at least three pilot holes in each stud. Drive in the screws to secure the frame to the wall.

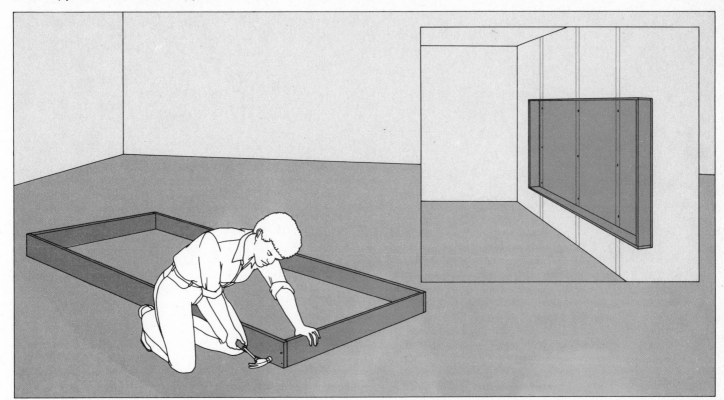

2 Bracing the train board. Use a second 4-by-8 sheet of ½-inch plywood as the train board; brace it with four pieces of 1-by-2 lumber. Glue and nail these pieces to one side of the plywood, forming a flat, rectangular support frame. Position the support frame in such a way that its outer edges are about 8 inches in from the edges of the plywood sheet on all sides.

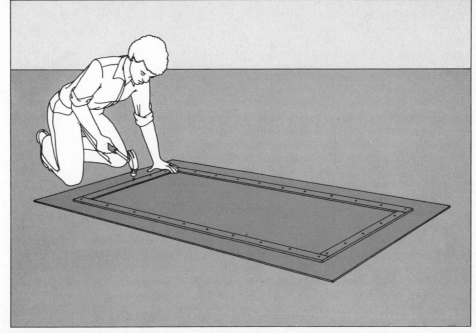

3 **Attaching folding legs.** Using 2-by-2 lumber, cut two legs ½ inch shorter than the distance from the floor to the underside of the wall frame. Attach each leg to the underside of the train board with a 3-inch T hinge, positioning the legs 2 inches outside the sides of the support frame and aligning the front of the legs with the front of the support frame. Screw the long strap leaf of each hinge to a leg, and the short rectangular leaf to the plywood, so that the legs will drop down against the underside of the board (the exposed side) when it is closed. Screw a folding brace to the inside of each leg and the underside of the plywood.

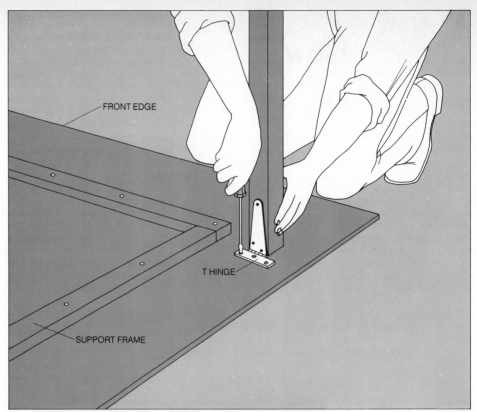

FRONT EDGE

T HINGE

SUPPORT FRAME

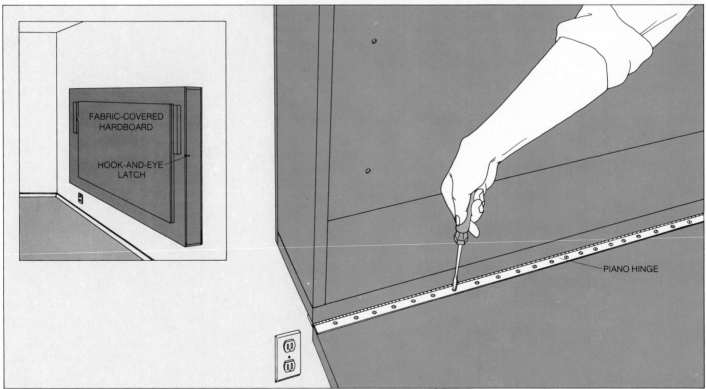

FABRIC-COVERED HARDBOARD

HOOK-AND-EYE LATCH

PIANO HINGE

4 **Mounting the train board.** Install a piano hinge to secure the back of the train board to the lower edge of the wall frame. Screw one hinge leaf to the outside bottom edge of the frame and the other to the top of the train board, so that the train board will cover the wall frame when it is closed. Mount train tracks and accessories on the board, and attach wiring to the underside, locating it within the rectangle formed by the support frame. Install hook-and-eye latches on both sides of the assembly to hold the board in its closed position. Nail a fabric-covered piece of hardboard over the 1-by-2 support frame to conceal the wiring and serve as a bulletin board when the train board is closed *(inset)*.

An Indoor Climbing Tower

The urge to conquer heights seems unquenchable in young children; they are constantly scaling cabinets, dressers, bedposts and refrigerator doors. To provide a more appropriate outlet for this energy, you can add a simple but challenging climbing tower to the equipment you make for the playroom.

The pleasantly rustic-looking structure shown at right is built with dowels and hefty posts 4½ inches in diameter, the latter sold for stockade fencing by lumber dealers. By substituting ordinary 4-by-4s for the stockade posts, you can simplify the measuring and drilling steps in the tower's construction, but you will sacrifice the rustic look and you may increase the cost as well.

You can expand or modify many details in the basic design according to your whim and the space available, but certain features in the tower's construction are essential for safety. In planning the layout, allow at least 4 feet of clear space on each side. Before assembly, prepare all posts by sanding their surfaces smooth and rounding off any sharp edges. Fill large cracks in the posts with wood putty to avoid pinched fingers, and seal the wood with two or three coats of polyurethane to reduce splintering.

To reinforce the tower, stabilize each post with a 2-by-6 base that can be screwed to the floor and subfloor. Also, plot the location of dowels according to the general design rules described at right, above, to ensure that they function as structural supports as well as climbing aids. Finally, it is always a good idea to keep an eye on very young children while they climb.

A Basic Framework of Stockade Posts and Thick Dowels

A sturdy tower. Stockade posts, 4½ to 6 feet tall and cut square at the ends, are set inside the corners of a 4-foot square to provide the frame for this climbing tower. Bases, lag-screwed to the post bottoms, are screwed to the floor.

For rigidity, four 1½-inch dowels connect the posts near their bases, three 2-by-4s form a railing between the tops, and a dowel extends diagonally between posts beneath the platform; all are screwed in. Other dowels are set at least 1 foot apart for safety. The platform rests on four dowels, 3 feet above the floor, and has a quarter-circle cut from one corner for a child to climb through. A slide is bolted on, and fabric unfurls from beneath the platform to form a tentlike hideout. The flaps, with 2-inch pockets stitched into their top edges, are slid over the dowels as the tower is assembled. Ribbons stitched to the flap hems lash them to the dowel.

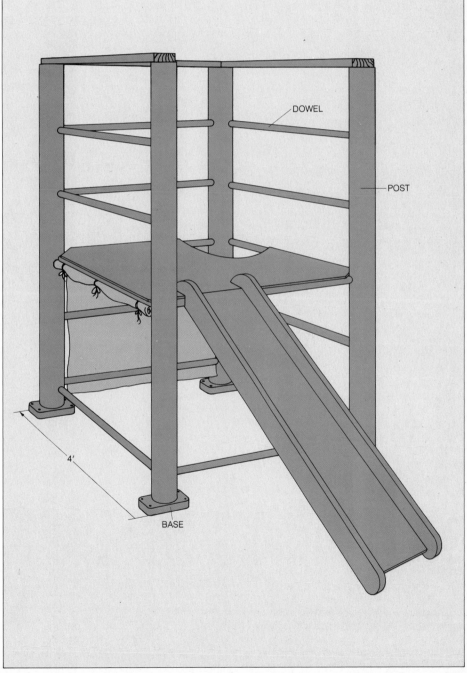

DOWEL

POST

4'

BASE

Assembling the Tower

1 **Attaching bases to the posts.** Cut each post for the tower to its proper length, sand it smooth, and round the edges of its top end. From 2-by-6 lumber, cut a post base 8 inches longer than the diameter of the post, center it over the bottom of the post, and drive two nails to hold it in position temporarily. Then drill two pilot holes for 3-inch-long lag screws, through the base and into the end of the post, providing the holes with countersink wells for the screwheads. Drive the lag screws into the holes to secure the base to the post. Attach similar bases to all of the remaining posts in the same way.

2 **Locating positions for dowel holes.** Outline a 4-foot square on the floor, and stand a post in each corner, with the posts' outside edges touching the lines. Draw a second set of lines, joining the midpoints of the four bases; mark the points where these guidelines intersect the bottoms of the posts. Then snap a chalked plumb line from the center top of each post to each of the two marks at the bottom; these vertical lines establish the positions for the dowels that connect the posts.

To establish the positions for the diagonal bracing dowel on two posts, place a protractor on the top of each of these posts *(inset)*, lining up the two previously chalked lines with the 0° and 90° marks, and snap a third chalk line down the inside of the post at the 45° mark.

Measure up from the bottom of each post to mark the locations of dowel holes, lining up the holes so that each connecting dowel is level. Make sure the supports for the platform lie in one plane, and stagger the position of the diagonal bracing dowel, to avoid having three dowel holes at the same level. Measure the spans between the posts, add 3 inches, and cut the required number of 1½-inch dowels to this length. Measure and cut a dowel for the diagonal brace in the same way.

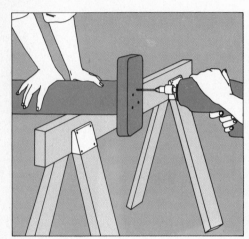

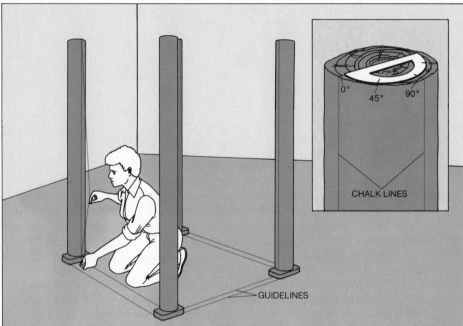

CHALK LINES

GUIDELINES

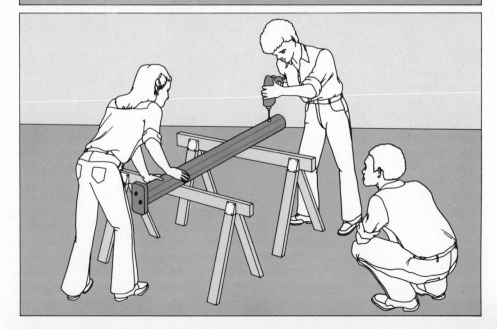

3 **Drilling dowel holes.** Rest a post on two sawhorses and, with the aid of two helpers, drill a 1½-inch-wide hole at each dowel location. Have one helper sight along the length of the post, and the other across its width, to make sure you are holding the spade bit perpendicular to the post. Mark the shank of the bit with tape to guide yourself in drilling each hole 1½ inches deep. Do the same with the other posts. Test-fit the dowels in their holes, beveling and sanding down the dowel ends if necessary.

4 **Fitting the dowels.** Use a mallet to hammer in all the dowels on one post. Then reposition the post in its corner, and have a helper brace it while you hammer an adjacent post onto the free ends of the dowel. Fit more dowels into the empty holes on the second post, including the interior bracing dowel. Use the same techniques to join the third and fourth posts, first to each other, then to the free dowels on the first and second posts. Add three 2-by-4s, mitered where they meet, to the four post tops.

Anchor each dowel end by drilling a pilot hole for a 3-inch screw through the post and into the dowel at a 90° angle to the dowel. Add a countersink well, and then drive the screws into place. Finally, drill pilot holes for 3-inch screws down through the extending lips of each rectangular base, and countersink the screws to secure the posts to the floor.

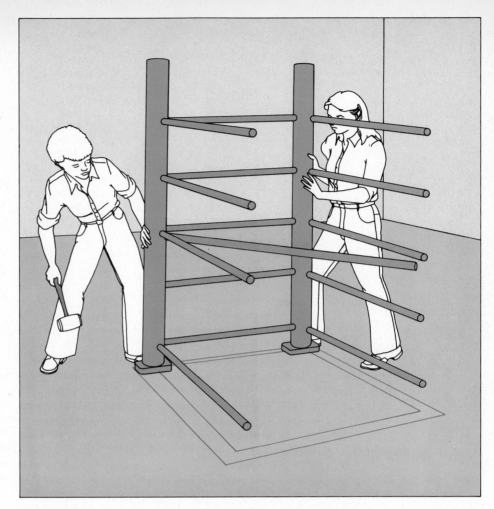

Attachments for the Tower

A platform and a slide. A strong platform of ¾-inch plywood is trimmed at the corners to fit against the posts and is supported by dowels set at the same level. Parallel 1-by-3 cleats, attached to the underside, fit snugly against the insides of the dowels to keep the platform in place. A quarter-circle is cut at one corner, large enough so that a child can climb through.

The simple slide slants to the floor at a 20° angle. Sides are cut from well-sanded 1-by-4s, with rounded ends and edges; notches near the top ends rest on the platform, and two bolts driven vertically through the notched ends fasten the slide to the platform. A layer of ¾-inch plywood covered by a layer of ⅛-inch tempered hardboard forms the sliding surface; it is supported by 1-by-2 cleats nailed to the inside faces of the sides and fastened to those supports by countersunk finishing nails whose heads are then covered with wood putty. All surfaces on the slide are sanded smooth before assembly and coated with polyurethane on completion.

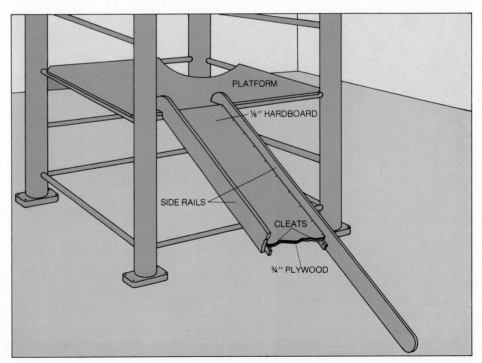

PLATFORM

⅛" HARDBOARD

SIDE RAILS

CLEATS

¾" PLYWOOD

Rec Room or Rumpus Room, the Room for All Ages

Space where the family relaxes together—in shared activities or individual pursuits—has evolved from a simple bench by the hearth to a sophisticated entertainment center that may contain games, a home theater, and space for preparing refreshments.

If you are starting with an empty space, plan the room from the floor up, using graph paper to plot space requirements. Floor games such as shuffleboard and hopscotch require long stretches of floor space—enough to accommodate the game itself as well as the movement of players around the playing surface. Table-tennis and pool tables take up width as well as length, and a dart game

needs a minimum of 8 feet between the dart board and the base line. For a home theater, allow at least 7 feet between the projector and the screen for the best combination of image size and brightness. And if you intend to install a wet bar, try to locate it near existing plumbing lines to avoid long extensions.

Vinyl tiles provide a durable, easily maintained floor covering. Colorful border strips, designs, numbers and game inserts, available by special order through most flooring suppliers, can add a custom touch. Game-insert tiles may be thicker than household floor tiles, so be sure to match the thickness of the field tiles—those used for the rest of the floor—with

that of the insert. Lay the tiles on the same sort of base used for ordinary tile installations. For even more variety in games or graphics, you can paint the outlines for the game directly onto the floor. Use wide masking tape to lay out the lines; for patterns or numbers, cut stencils from heavy paper or cardboard.

A home theater, for showing films and slides and for projecting television on a large screen, can fit into any quiet corner of a room. You can convert a good-quality 12-inch or 15-inch television set into a projector with a little rewiring and an added lens. The rewiring, which should be done by a television repair technician, consists of reversing the yoke

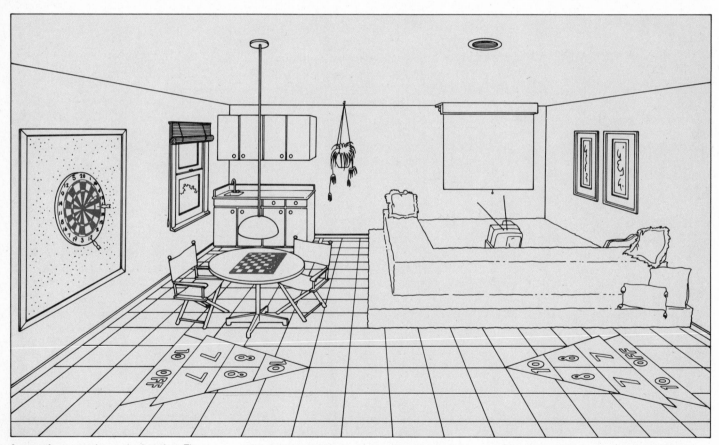

A room for recreation and relaxation. The family room pictured here is designed to be versatile and to adapt to almost anyone's idea of fun. The space is divided visually and physically to allow several different activities to be carried on at once. A raised platform and bench, both carpeted, provide seating for a theater area outfitted for viewing wide-screen television or home movies. A movie screen, mounted on

the ceiling behind a cornice, can be rolled up out of sight when the area is used for other purposes, and the bench can also function as a gallery for spectators cheering on a rousing game of darts or shuffleboard.

Cork sheeting, mounted on the wall behind the dart board, protects the wood paneling or wallboard from errant darts. The shuffleboard court

consists of numbered and shaped tiles, which come in kit form and are meant to be surrounded by conventional tile flooring. A wet bar, fashioned from prefabricated cabinets and outfitted with a bar sink and a half-sized refrigerator, provides a place for the preparation of refreshments, as well as storage space for liquor and snack supplies. The game table can be used as easily for a buffet as for checkers or poker.

leads of the picture tube so that the image on the screen appears upside down and backward. But you can build a hood for attaching the special lens, which is designed for home-projection television and is available from camera or movie-equipment suppliers.

For the greatest brightness, get a lens with a speed no slower than f/2 and a diameter of at least 6 inches. With the lens, purchase an 8-inch-square flange plate to mount on the hood and hold the lens in place. A low, rolling projector base with an inclined top allows proper positioning of any type of projection equipment—film, slides, or television—at the same time making it easy to move the equipment out of the way when it is not in use. The base shown on page 106 includes a large sliding shelf for a video-cassette player or other accessories.

The best screen for projected television is one with an ultrabright, paraboloid surface with a brightness rating of 17- or 20-over-white. This superscreen is available from makers of projection-television systems and can be hung on a wall with brackets or placed in a floor stand. Flat movie screens are less expensive and less obtrusive, especially when ceiling-mounted in a cornice, as shown here. Although the image brightness is slightly less than it would be on the ultrabright screen, a high-quality movie screen, with at least a 14-over-white rating, will nevertheless yield a satisfactory image as large as 50 inches square in low light. In some rooms you may need to add dark draperies and dimmer switches for overhead lights, to reduce light for viewing.

A wet bar outfitted with a bar sink and a half-sized refrigerator is a useful addition to the family room, especially if the kitchen is some distance away. You can make it from prefabricated cabinets, adding doors, adjustable shelving, countertop and sink for a custom installation. Traditionally a bar sink provides only cold water—for mixing drinks and filling ice trays—but a hot-water supply line can be added if desired. Choose a bar faucet, with a gooseneck spout, for ease in filling pitchers and tall glasses.

If the faucet comes equipped with two handles, use a cap fitting to block off the hot-water side underneath the sink. And make sure that you anchor any hanging cabinets securely on the wall—a fully stocked liquor cabinet may weigh hundreds of pounds.

Tile Graphics of a Floor Game

1 **Laying out the court.** Measure and mark off the dimensions of the court (in this example a shuffleboard court), lining up the base lines parallel with a wall and outlining the game inserts on the floor. Then snap two intersecting chalk lines to locate the court center. Using the lines as guides, set the game-insert tiles with adhesive, according to the requirements of the game.

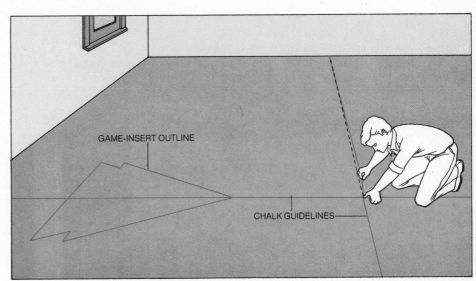

GAME-INSERT OUTLINE

CHALK GUIDELINES

2 **Positioning the field tiles.** Lay rows of field tiles around the insert and toward the walls, to check for position. Start at the center of the court, using the intersecting chalk lines as a guide, and work to the walls or to the edge of the area being tiled. If the space remaining at a wall is less than half a tile, reposition the entire row of tiles. Using this initial row of tiles as a guide, position a second row of tiles perpendicular to the first and as close to the game insert as possible. Continue to place field tiles around the insert, checking to make sure that none of the irregular spaces left between the field tiles and the insert will be too small to tile successfully. If such spaces do occur, move the chalk lines and the field tiles as necessary.

When you have arrived at a proper arrangement of field tiles, snap new intersecting guidelines for final placement. Set all of the whole field tiles, using the recommended adhesive.

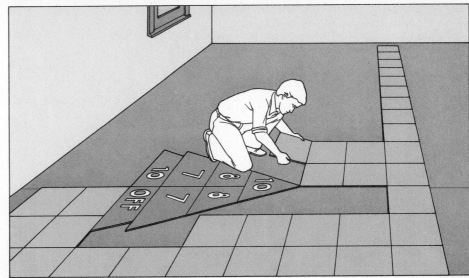

3 **Cutting the border tiles.** To fill the gap between a wall and the last whole tile in a row, rest two loose tiles squarely on top of the last complete tile, then slide the upper tile across the gap until it touches the wall. Using the edge of the upper tile as a guide, score the lower tile with a utility knife. Snap or cut the tile along the scored line, and fit the section not covered by the guide tile into the gap, securing it with tile adhesive. Continue in this fashion until all the gaps at the edge of the tiled area are filled.

4 **Framing the game insert.** To fill an irregular gap between a whole field tile and the game insert, lay a loose tile in the gap with one edge touching the adjacent field tile and the opposite side overlapping the insert. Place a metal straightedge on top of the overlapping tile, lining up the straightedge with the edge of the insert, and score the overlapping tile along this line with a utility knife. Snap or cut the tile along the scored line, and set the cut tile into the gap with tile adhesive.

If the shape of the game insert requires the framing tile to be cut in two directions, use two straightedges to follow the angles of the game insert. Score the overlapping tile, using the lines of the two straightedges as guidelines.

A TV Projection Hood

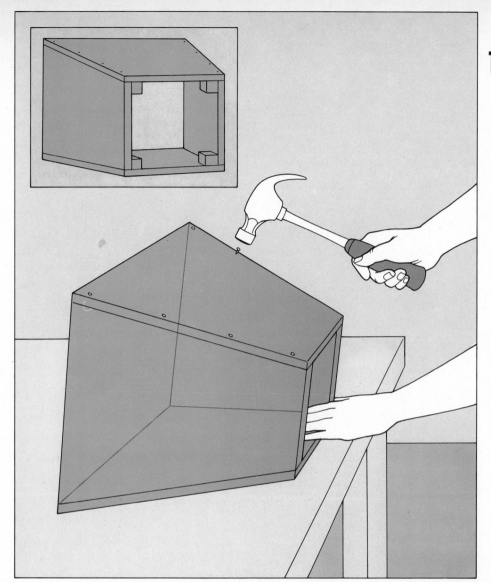

1 Assembling the hood. Cut four pieces of ½-inch plywood, tapering them to fit the television screen at one end and an 8-inch-square lens flange plate at the other; make the depth of the hood equal to the diagonal measurement of the screen. Cut the wide end of the hood sides equal to the height of the lip around the television screen, and the two narrow lens ends 7 inches long. Cut the wide ends of the hood top and bottom 1 inch longer than the width of the television lip, and the narrow lens ends 8 inches long. Bevel the edges so that the wide end of the hood will fit flush against the console and the lens flange will fit flush against the narrow end of the hood. Spread a thin layer of glue along the upper edges of the hood sides, and drive 1¼-inch finishing nails through the hood top into the edges of the sides. Turn the hood upside down and attach the hood bottom in the same way.

Glue and screw four ½-inch-square blocks of wood, cut from 1-inch stock, into the inside corners of the narrow end of the hood. Screw the lens flange plate, which comes with the lens, to the corner blocks, and install the lens according to the manufacturer's instructions.

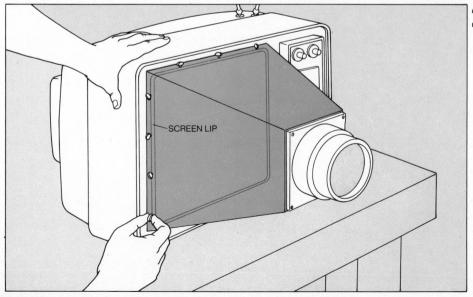

SCREEN LIP

2 Attaching the hood. Drill ⅛-inch holes at 3-inch intervals around the screen end of the hood, positioning the holes at a distance from the edge equal to half the depth of the lip on the television screen. Screw a ¾-inch No. 4 thumbscrew into each hole, set the hood over the lip and tighten the thumbscrews against the lip, to hold the hood in place.

If the front of the television console is curved or the controls lie close to the lip, use a rasp to taper the edges of the hood to fit snugly against the outside of the lip. Use foam weather stripping to plug any light leaks that remain.

A TV Projection Cabinet

Enclosing the console. If your television set lacks a lip against which to fasten a lens hood, mount the hood in a plywood cabinet large enough to accept the television set. Make the cabinet (a simple box with a removable back panel) slightly larger than the television set, and cut openings into its front for the screen and controls. Then cut 3-inch-long ventilation slots into the sides, back and top.

Construct a lens hood identical to the one shown on page 105, and attach it to the cabinet with 2-inch corner brackets, bent to fit the angled sides of the hood. Screw the brackets to the inside surface of the cabinet and the hood.

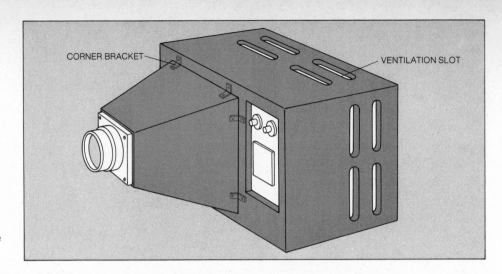

A Versatile Projector Base

1 Assembling the frame. Construct a box of ¾-inch plywood, canting the top 15 degrees. For the back of the box, cut a piece 9 inches high and 20 inches wide. Cut two sidepieces 22 inches long, tapering one long edge upward at an angle of 15 degrees, back to front, beginning from a height equal to the height of the back of the box. Glue and screw the sides to the back.

Cut a top for the box, making it 1½ inches wider than the width of the back piece and slightly longer than the slanting edge of the sides. Bevel the front and back edges of the top piece at a 15° angle, so that they line up exactly with the front and back edges of the sides. Glue and screw the top into place. Then measure and cut a bottom, and secure it in the same way.

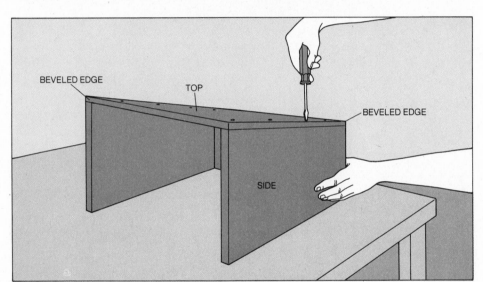

2 Installing a sliding shelf. Using ½-inch plywood, construct a shelf to hold auxiliary equipment. Make the shelf ¾ inch shallower and 1 inch narrower than the inside measurements of the bottom of the projector base. Secure the shelf to a 3-inch-high frame that has the same outer dimensions as the shelf. Nail the framing strips together, then nail the shelf to the frame.

Finish the front of the shelf with a 1-by-6 board cut 1½ inches longer than the width of the shelf; screw the shelf to the board, aligning their bottom edges to create a 2½-inch lip at the front of the shelf. Mount the shelf on drawer glides (*page 13*), and add four casters to the bottom of the base (*page 17*).

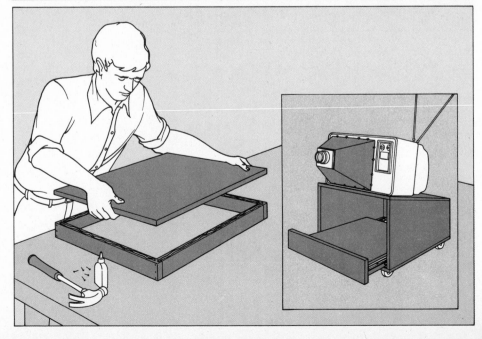

A Concealed Projection Screen

Mounting a screen behind a cornice. Cut a mounting board from 1-inch lumber, slightly wider and longer than the projection-screen case. Cut a 1-by-6 cornice board of the same length. Clamp the cornice board to the front of the mounting board, using scrap wood to prop up its unsupported side, and drill ⅛-inch pilot holes through the cornice board into the mounting board at 6-inch intervals. Use 2-inch flat-head screws to join the two boards, countersinking the heads and covering them with wood putty.

Install a screw hook near each end of the mounting board, making the distance between the hooks equal to the distance between the mounting rings on the screen case. Have a helper hold the cornice assembly against the ceiling while you drill pilot holes through the mounting board into the ceiling joists. Secure the assembly with 3-inch screws. Paint the assembly to match the ceiling or the wall, then hang the screen from the screw hooks *(inset)*.

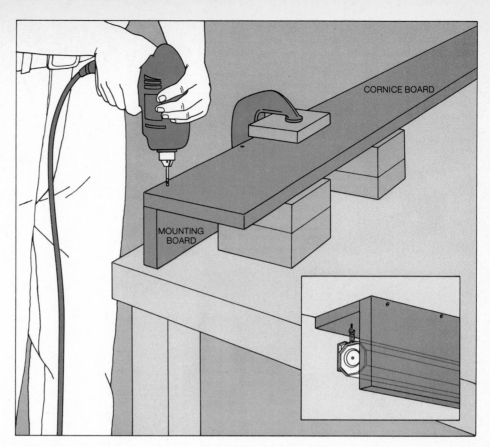

CORNICE BOARD

MOUNTING BOARD

From Prefabricated Cabinet to Customized Wet Bar

1 Hanging a wall cabinet. To position a hanging cabinet for attaching to the wall, rest it on a temporary 1-by-3 ledge nailed to the wall studs at the planned height of the bottom of the cabinet. Have helpers support the weight of the cabinet while you check the front for plumb, sliding thin strips of wood behind the cabinet, if necessary, to correct its vertical alignment. Drill pilot holes through the hanger bar at the back of the cabinet into the studs. Fasten the cabinet to the wall with 3-inch No. 8 screws or wall anchors, if necessary; then remove the ledge and install the cabinet doors *(page 74)* and adjustable shelving *(page 15)*.

If you are hanging several adjacent cabinets, plumb and level each one as you install it, making sure that all the cabinet faces are flush. Clamp the adjoining sides of the cabinets together, and connect them with wood screws after they have been mounted on the wall.

HANGER BAR

2 Installing the floor cabinets. Position the double base cabinet, using the vertical edges of the wall cabinets as guides, and drive shims between the floor and the base until the top of the cabinet is level (*below, left*). Use a block of wood between the shim and the hammer, to protect the cabinet and the floor from stray blows.

Drive shims down between the wall and the cabinet at stud locations behind the cabinet, to make the cabinet plumb (*below, right*). Then drill pilot holes and drive screws through the back of the cabinet and through the shims, into the studs. Use a dovetail saw to trim off any shim ends that can still be seen, and cover the gap

between the cabinet base and the floor with a length of vinyl cove molding.

If you are installing several base cabinets, plumb and level each with shims if necessary. Then fasten the cabinets together after they are installed, as in Step 1, page 107.

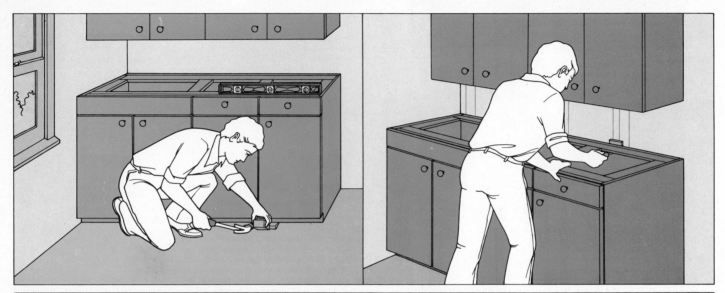

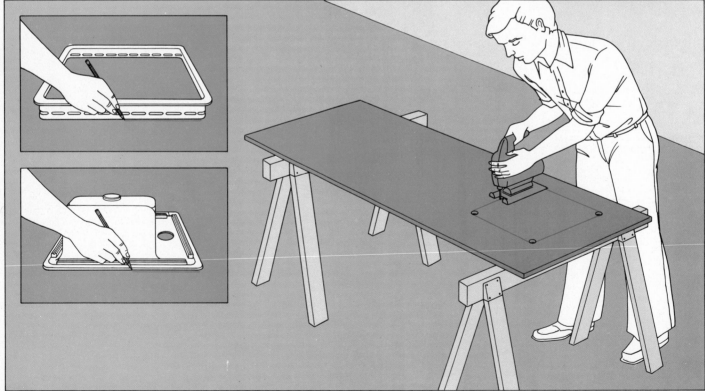

3 Preparing a countertop for a sink. Cut a ¾-inch plywood countertop for the base cabinet. Make the countertop with a 1-inch overhang at the front and at any side that does not abut a wall. Set the countertop on sawhorses, and draw the outline of the sink bowl, positioning it in

the center of the sink side of the cabinet. Drill a pilot hole at each corner just inside the outline and, using a saber saw, cut along the line.

For a sink supported by a separate steel frame, use the frame as a template for marking

the sink cutout (*inset, top*). For a one-piece sink, first turn the sink upside down on the countertop and trace around the rim (*inset, bottom*); then draw a second outline inside the first, separated from it by the width of the sink rim, and use this as the cutting line.

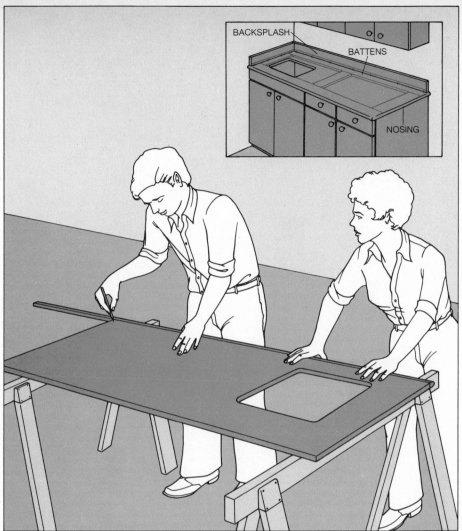

4 **Finishing a wooden countertop.** Trim the countertop's front edge with a strip of ¾-inch wooden nosing, marking the nosing for a 45° miter cut at outside corners or for a square cut where the countertop meets a wall. Glue and nail the nosing in place, using 1½-inch finishing nails. Install similar nosing on all of the exposed counter edges.

To install a backsplash, drill pilot holes at 8-inch intervals along the back of the countertop, ⅜ inch in from the edge, and along any side that abuts a wall (*inset*). Cut the backsplash from a length of 1-by-4 lumber, butt-joining the side section or sections into the back. Lay a bead of caulking along the line of holes and in the joint; then, working from the underside of the countertop, attach the backsplash to the countertop with 2½-inch No. 10 screws.

Position the countertop on the base cabinet, setting it flush with the back wall. Drill pilot holes up through the cabinet battens, and drive 1½-inch No. 8 screws through the battens, and into the countertop at 6-inch intervals. Finish the counter with two coats of polyurethane varnish.

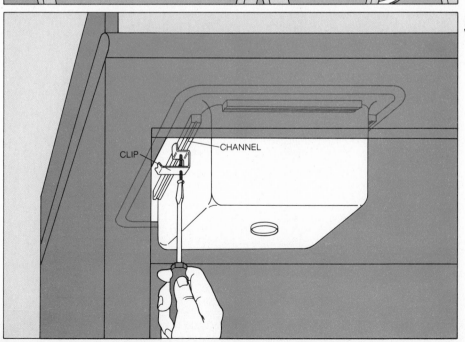

5 **Setting in the sink.** Apply a ½-inch bead of plumber's putty around the lip of the sink opening in the countertop. Lower a one-piece sink into the cabinet (shown here with door removed, for clarity), securing it to the underside of the lip with the clips provided by the manufacturer. Slide two clips onto the channels under each side of the sink, and adjust them to grip the underside of the countertop. Tighten the clips with a screwdriver to pull the sink rim downward and to eliminate gaps between the rim and the countertop.

To install a sink that has a separate frame, first drop the frame into the sink hole over a bead of caulk, and then lower the sink into position over the frame.

Install the faucet, inserting the water-supply tubes and threaded mounting studs through the fixture holes. Cap the hot-water valve, if there is one that is not to be used. Finally, attach the sink to a ½-inch cold-water supply line (*page 128*) and a drain line (*page 124*).

4

Basic Techniques of Adaptation

A handy hookup. A plumbing connection station is fitted with all the links needed to operate a washing machine and dryer. A single-lever valve turns the water supply off and on. The large opening in the bottom of the station box is for a standpipe drain. Electric cables will be routed to the station's two outlet boxes—a 120-volt circuit for the washing machine, a 240-volt circuit for a dryer—and their receptacles wired to the cables. Finally, wallboard will cover the rest of the wall, and faceplate will be added.

One of the challenges of putting an existing room to new use is that the room may not be ready for it. An artist's studio may need more windows and lighting fixtures than an average room is likely to have. Setting up a darkroom in the corner of an existing room requires the construction of walls. A laundry room must have plumbing connections for a clothes washer and 240-volt power for an electric dryer. Using the techniques described in this chapter, you can add new walls, windows, doors, plumbing, electric outlets and lights as you need them. The trick, however, is to choose a location for the new facility where you will need to add or change as little as possible.

Given a specific space for the new function, plan the modifications and the arrangement of new features so that the conversion is as easy as you can make it. If, for example, a new sink is needed, put it where the drain line can run in a direct path to an existing drain. If there is more than one possible location for the new facility, consider how well each location will adapt to the modifications and special features needed; then balance the relative ease with which these changes can be made in the different locations.

One of the things to consider in preparing your evaluation is the location of the space relative to other areas of the house. Should the new facility ideally be near the front door? Away from the bedrooms? Handy to the kitchen? What about temperature and humidity, both of which may affect the desirability of a site? A room that stays below 75° in summer is excellent for photographic work; the air of a garden room should not be dry. Then there is the question of the floor. If you choose a room where the existing floor is compatible with the new activity, you save the work of installing one. Concrete, for example, is desirable for some activities, but not for others. In a children's playroom the relative softness of a resilient floor covering is often desirable; in a sewing room, removing snippets of thread from a carpet could be a full-time job.

Sometimes the deciding factor in the choice of a room for a special purpose will be the ease with which you can add equipment that will make it usable. Heaters, dehumidifiers and sound-absorbing mats can compensate for the shortcomings of a room and make what would appear to be a difficult or an impossible conversion relatively simple. A small window air conditioner, for instance, may be all you need to keep a room on the sunny side of the house cool enough in summer to maintain darkroom chemicals at the correct temperature.

Of course, in some cases you may think it necessary or desirable to go beyond the basic modifications described on the following pages. If so—unless you have expertise in wiring, plumbing and construction—it is best to get professional help.

111

Structural Changes to Create New Spaces

Few houses have a spare room that can be used for a specialized activity or hobby. More often than not, making space for a special purpose—without enlarging the house—means dividing up an existing room. In a couple of weekends, you can frame and cover a partition wall, hang a door and install its latch.

Before you carve up a room, however, determine how the new barrier will affect the present use of the space. If the new wall will block a window, the room will be darker. And if you block a thoroughfare, traffic may not flow smoothly.

Much of the new wall's construction takes place on the floor. Here wall studs are nailed to the top plate and the rough frame for a doorway is built.

The simplest wall, one without a door, requires little more than accurate measuring, marking and sawing. Such a wall can extend out from an existing wall, or it can be fastened flat against a masonry wall to provide a nailing surface for wallboard or other finishing material.

A wall containing a rough frame for a door requires more measuring steps. Buy a prehung door before you begin the

wall, and follow the manufacturer's instructions concerning the clearances to allow within the rough frame for the door and its jamb (the finished frame).

To attach a wall to wood framing, find studs and joists hidden behind wallboard. To do this, tap until you hear a solid sound; then drill a tiny hole in this location to verify the position.

In a masonry basement, attach the new wall with fluted masonry nails or hardened cut nails. These can be driven with a hammer or a small sledge, but the job is easier if you rent a stud driver—a special gun powered by .22-caliber blank cartridges that drives nails into mortar, brick, cinder block or poured concrete.

After the studs are in place and you have added necessary plumbing or electrical connections *(pages 124-133)*, cover the framing with wallboard. Depending on the intended use of the new space, you may want to use a fire-retardant (Type X) wallboard. Otherwise, using standard ½-inch gypsum wallboard is the easiest way to do the job.

Wallboard comes in 8-, 10- and 12-foot lengths and 4-foot widths; it can be in-

stalled horizontally or vertically, whichever requires fewer cuts. If you have measured the framing carefully, the parallel edges of a standard sheet will fall at the centers of two studs, where they must be fastened. But you almost always have to trim a sheet at the end of a wall or where you must patch a hole cut for nailing blocks *(page 113)*. To trim wallboard, score the paper covering with a utility knife, snap the core along the score, and cut through the paper on the other side. Holes can be cut with a wallboard or keyhole saw. Cut pieces large enough so that the parallel edges will lie at stud or joist centers for nailing.

To fasten the sheets to wood framing, use wallboard adhesive and wallboard nails. To cover nailheads and seams, use joint compound—the premixed type is easiest to use—and two joint knives, 6 and 10 inches wide. You will also need perforated joint tape and, for outside corners, strips of metal corner bead.

Each coat of joint compound takes about 24 hours to dry, then the third coat must be sanded smooth. Always wear a respirator and goggles for this dusty job.

Techniques for Erecting a Stud-wall Partition

1 Marking the top and sole plates. Cut a pair of 2-by-4s to the length of the planned wall and place them flat on the floor, side by side, with their ends aligned. These will be the top plate and the sole plate of the partition. Using a steel square, pencil pairs of parallel lines 1½ inches apart (the same width as the shorter arm of a steel square—and the width of a 2-by-4) across both plates simultaneously, to indicate stud positions. Pencil an X in each of these rectangles to mark its center. Mark the first stud position flush with one end of the plates; place a mark for the center of the second stud 16 inches in from the end of the plates, and continue marking at 16-inch intervals. Mark the last stud position flush with the opposite end of the plates, no matter how close it is to the next-to-last stud.

Since the partition will be bearing no weight but its own, your building code may permit the economy of spacing studs at 24-inch intervals, center to center. Either 16- or 24-inch spacing will permit the use of standard 4-by-8-foot sheets of wallboard with a minimum of cutting.

2 **Marking the position of the wall.** For a wall
that will run perpendicular to overhead joists,
snap a chalk line across the bottoms of exposed joists or across the finished ceiling, to indicate an edge (inner or outer) of the top plate.
Then drop a plumb line from several points along
the line so that a helper can mark where the
plumb bob touches the floor. Then snap a chalk
line connecting the floor marks, to establish a
matching position for the sole plate.

If the new wall will parallel the joists, try to position it directly under a joist so that the top
plate can be nailed to it. If this cannot be done,
cut away any ceiling covering between the
joists on either side of the plate so that you can
toenail blocks at 16-inch intervals between the
joists to support the top plate (*inset, near right*).
Snap a chalk line across these nailing blocks
to establish a position for the top plate. If the new
wall will meet an existing stud wall at a point
between studs, cut two holes in the old wall and
install 2-by-4 nailing blocks at one third and
two thirds of the distance from floor to ceiling (*inset, far right*). To patch holes you have cut
in the wall or ceiling, nail pieces of wallboard to
the exposed studs or joists and to the nailing blocks after the new wall has been erected
but before it is covered with wallboard.

To find the length of the new studs, measure
the distance between the floor and ceiling chalk
lines at three or more points along the wall
span. If these measurements vary by less than
¾ inch, subtract 3 inches from the shortest
measurement (to allow for the combined thick-
nesses of the plates) and cut all the studs to
this length. But if the variation in measurements is
greater than ¾ inch, you will have to measure
and cut each individual stud after the sole plate
has been installed (*Step 3*).

JOISTS

NAILING BLOCKS

STUDS

NAILING BLOCKS

3 **Assembling the top plate and studs.** With the
top plate on edge on the floor, hold each stud end
against its marked position and drive two 16-
penny nails through the top of the plate into the
end of the stud.

At the point where the new wall will meet the
old, drop a plumb line from the ceiling corner to
the floor. If the plumb bob hangs slightly away
from the wall, mark its position on the chalk line
on the floor to indicate where the end of the
sole plate should fall.

Lay the sole plate flat, its end butted against the
existing wall or even with the plumb mark if
there is one, its edge even with the chalk line.
Drive 12-penny nails at 1-foot intervals through
the plate and into the floor; for a concrete
floor, use masonry nails or hardened cut nails.

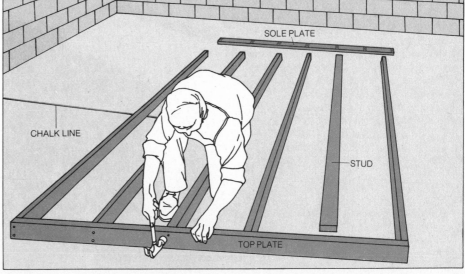

SOLE PLATE

CHALK LINE

STUD

TOP PLATE

4 **Erecting the wall.** With the aid of a helper, lift the wall frame onto the sole plate, and set the edge of the top plate even with its chalk line. Check to be sure the stud nearest the existing wall is plumb, then fasten the ends of the top plate directly to the joists or to nailing blocks with 16-penny nails, shimming small gaps with thin wedges as necessary. Nail the end stud to a masonry wall with masonry nails, to a stud or to nailing blocks with 12-penny nails; shim if necessary. Then nail the rest of the top plate.

Center the bottom of each stud over its mark on the sole plate, check to be sure it is plumb, and toenail the stud to the plate with three tenpenny nails—two on one side and the third centered on the other side.

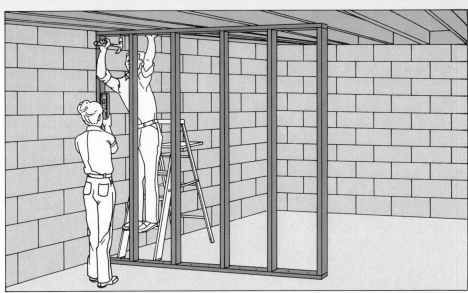

5 **Constructing a corner assembly.** To reinforce the wall at a corner, toenail an extra stud to the top and sole plates of the first wall, 1½ inches in from the last stud. Cut three 10-inch nailing blocks from 2-by-4s, sandwich them between these last two studs at the top, middle and bottom of the wall, and fasten each block with four tenpenny nails.

Construct the second wall as you did the first one (*Steps 1-4*). Nail its end stud to the corner nailing blocks with 16-penny nails (*inset*).

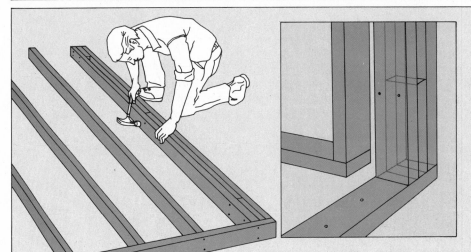

Building a Frame for a Door

1 **Forming the sides of the opening.** To prepare a rough doorframe, mark all stud positions on a top and sole plate as you would for a solid wall (*Step 1, page 112*). Then add marks to position the outer studs and the shorter jack studs that will form the sides of the rough door opening.

Cut the two outer studs to the same length as the other studs, and the two jack studs 1½ inches shorter than the planned height of the rough opening, to allow for the thickness of the sole plate. Lay a jack stud on top of an outer stud, with bottom ends aligned, and fasten the two together by driving a pair of 12-penny nails into each end of the assembly. Stagger more nails at 1-foot intervals in a zigzag pattern to forestall warping. Do the same with the other pair of door-framing studs. Then nail the full-length studs to the top plate as in Step 3, page 113.

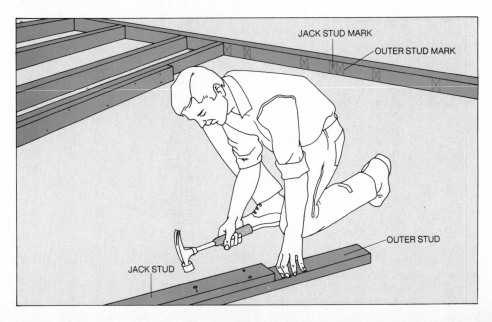

JACK STUD MARK

OUTER STUD MARK

OUTER STUD

JACK STUD

2 **Adding a header and cripple studs.** Cut a 2-by-4 header to fit horizontally between the outer studs of the door opening, lay the header flat across the tops of the jack studs, and drive two 16-penny nails through each outer stud into an end of the header. Cut 2-by-4 cripple studs to fit between the top plate and header. Check with a square to make sure they will be vertical; then fasten each one at the position marked for it, using pairs of 16-penny nails driven through the top plate and the header (inset, near right).

Turn the marked sole plate face down, and saw three fourths of the way through it at the inside edge of each jack-stud mark. Then install the sole plate and wall as in Step 3, page 113, and Step 4, page 114. With the frame upright and all studs nailed in place, use a handsaw to cut away the section of sole plate within the door opening, sawing down to meet the cuts on the underside of the plate (inset, far right).

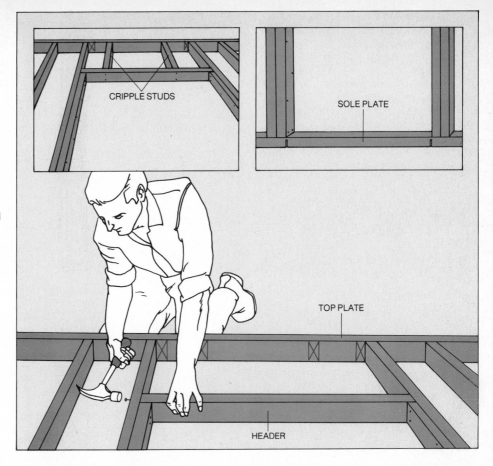

CRIPPLE STUDS

SOLE PLATE

TOP PLATE

HEADER

Covering the Framing with Wallboard

1 **Fastening wallboard to ceiling joists.** Measure and trim the first wallboard panel for a ceiling so that one narrow end fits into a corner and the opposite end falls directly at the midpoint of a joist. Use a caulking gun to apply beads of wallboard adhesive to the joists within the panel area. Then, with the aid of a helper or two, press the panel into place and drive a wallboard nail into each joist where it crosses the lengthwise center of the panel. Drive each nail flush, then dimple it by tapping the head lightly to set it slightly below the surface; take care not to break the paper covering. Drive a second row of nails into the joists, 8 inches in from the wall edge of the panel, then a third row ½ inch in from the outer edge. Fasten each end of the panel with a row of nails spaced 16 inches apart.

Butt the end of the next panel against the free end of the first, glue and nail it to the joists, then continue butting panels end to end until you reach the opposite wall. Cut the last panel as necessary to fit into the remaining space. Continue fastening subsequent rows of panels in the same manner until the ceiling is covered.

2 **Fastening wallboard to studs.** Mark the stud-center locations on both ceiling and floor, apply adhesive to studs that will be covered by the first section of wallboard, and lift the panel into place. Rest its bottom end on a foot lever made from two scraps of wood, and press down on the lever to push the top of the panel snug against the ceiling. Using the ceiling marks to locate stud centers, drive a wallboard nail into each stud 8 inches from the ceiling. Release the lever, and drive nails along each stud at 18-inch intervals, ending with a row 1 inch from the bottom edge of the panel. Dimple the nails as in Step 1. Install succeeding wallboard sections in the same way, butting the edges at stud centers.

For a wallboard section that will border a door or window, measure from the ceiling to the top of the opening (before you put on the interior casings or with the casings removed) and, on each side, from the nearest wallboard edge to the edge of the opening. Outline the opening in a corresponding position on the wallboard, and cut out the section with a keyhole or wallboard saw. Install the wallboard as before; the window casings will cover the cut edges.

3 **Concealing the joints.** Using a 6-inch joint knife, spread compound evenly over the wallboard joint. Press the end of a roll of perforated tape into the compound at one end of the joint; then guide the tape with one hand as you run the blade of the knife over it along the joint to press the tape into the compound. Finally, run the knife down each side of the joint, pressing hardest on the outside edge of the knife to spread the compound into a very thin, feathered edge. Let the compound dry for 24 hours and apply a second coat with a 10-inch knife, feathering the compound out 10 inches on either side of the joint. After another 24 hours apply a third coat, feathering again.

To conceal an inside corner joint, spread compound along one side of the joint, then along the other side. Crease a length of tape down the middle, press it into the corner with your fingers and run the knife over the tape on each side of the crease. Then coat the tape with two more layers of compound applied at 24-hour intervals. At an outside corner, nail a strip of metal corner bead over the joint and coat it with compound one side at a time, in layers as for an inside corner. Cover nail dimples with two perpendicular strokes of the knife; apply three coats of compound at 24-hour intervals.

Wearing a respirator and goggles, sand all the dry compound lightly with 100-grit garnet sandpaper on a sanding block. Be careful that you do not roughen the adjacent paper covering.

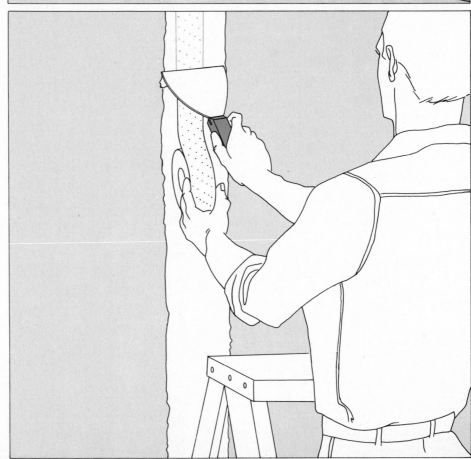

Installing a Prehung Interior Door

1 **Fitting the door into place.** Working with a split-jamb unit, push the jamb section that contains the door into the rough-framed opening, until the casing is flat against the wall. From the opposite side of the door, insert pairs of blunt but wedge-shaped shims (*inset*) between the side jambs and the jack studs on both sides at the heights of the hinges; rest the door temporarily on two additional pairs of shims. Adjust the shims behind the jamb on the hinge side until both the side and the front of that jamb are plumb, then have a helper on the opposite side of the door nail the hinge-side casing to the rough frame with eightpenny finishing nails at 12-inch intervals. Then, working on the casing side, adjust the top casing so that there is an even ⅛-inch gap between the head jamb and the top of the door, then nail the top casing onto the header. Adjust the shims at the jamb on the lock side in the same way, and nail on the lock-side casing. From the other side of the door, insert two pairs of shims above the head jamb and one more pair at the middle of each side jamb. Drive two 16-penny finishing nails through each pair of side and top shims; cut off protruding shim ends.

2 **Installing the back jamb.** Slip the tongue of the back jamb into the groove of the first jamb; push the back casing flat against the wall. Fasten the casing with eightpenny finishing nails, and then drive 16-penny finishing nails through the jambs into the rough frame at 12-inch intervals.

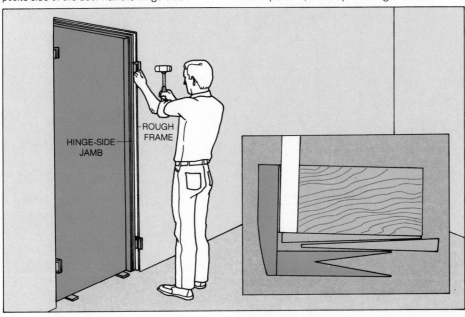

A Doorknob That Locks from the Inside

Installing a privacy lock. If you buy a ready-made prehung door, choose a lockset to fit the predrilled holes. The set shown can be locked from the inside with a push button. To install it, slip the latch bolt into its hole in the door, the beveled side of the bolt facing the strike-plate position as the door closes. Cut a mortise for the latch-bolt plate; screw the plate to the door. Push the latch bolt in ⅛ inch and insert the outside-knob unit, sliding the screw posts, spindle tongue and locking bar through their corresponding holes in the latch bolt. Push the inside-knob unit onto the spindle tongue and locking bar, align its holes with the screw posts and fasten the knob units together, using the machine screws provided. Cut a mortise in the side jamb, positioned to receive the strike plate and the latch bolt, and install the strike plate.

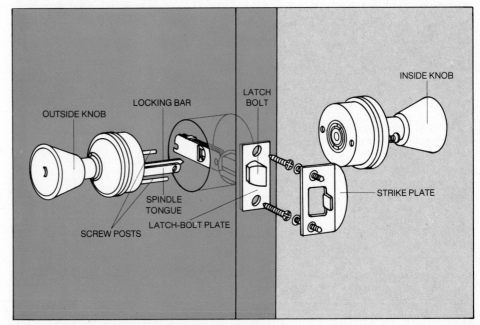

Brightening a Studio with a Wall of Windows

In many special purpose rooms natural light, and lots of it, is essential. Painters, sculptors, weavers and people who work with fabrics need it to see true colors and textures, and indoor gardeners need it for their plants. Letting in more daylight can be costly, messy and time-consuming if it involves breaking through large expanses of wall and rerouting wiring, ductwork and plumbing. But in a wood-frame house you can often create a window wall without major structural changes.

Sometimes you can simply lengthen existing windows. Where there are no windows, you may create them by removing narrow sections of wall between studs and inserting fixed glass panels in the openings. It is easy to saw through wood or aluminum siding, but more elaborate techniques are needed for stucco or brick veneer. As many as three adjoining spaces between studs can be opened in this way without affecting structural soundness, and usually without interfering with utility lines.

The windows can be made either of plate glass or of more expensive insulating glass—two layers of glass sealed with a space between them. The latter conserves energy and adds comfort if you live in a climate with extreme temperature ranges. To save money, you can buy either type of glass and build the frame yourself. But a factory-made unit meeting your specifications has the advantage of being guaranteed against leakage. You may pay as much as double, however, for this advantage.

The new windows, whether homemade or factor-built, should be ½ inch shorter than the height of the rough opening and ½ inch narrower than the distance between the studs, to allow clearance for easy installation.

If you are ordering factory-built windows, specify the wall thickness—the distance from the surface of the exterior sheathing to the surface of the interior wall—so that the manufacturer can provide window jambs of the correct depth. Order windows without the exterior trim, called brickmold, attached. The windows should have slanted sills to allow rain water to run off, but you may have to trim down the sill extensions, called horns, to create a single, continuous sill

under the entire set of windows. Be sure not to cut through the exterior wall until the windows arrive: It sometimes takes as long as eight weeks to get delivery of a factory-built unit—a long time to keep out the elements.

Finally, before you open a wall for new windows, give some thought to its exposure. For painters and other people who work with color, north light is preferred because it tends to be even and diffuse throughout the day; it does not distort colors or fade fabrics. But a southern exposure will provide a higher level of light intensity and help to warm the house. Sometimes you can have the best of both exposures by opening a south wall, then controlling the sun with a translucent awning or sun screen, or with a tinted-plastic filter applied directly to the glass.

Installing Glass Between Studs

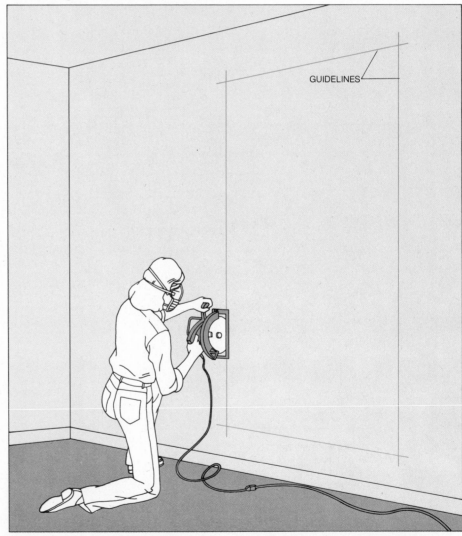

GUIDELINES

1 Cutting through the interior wall. After locating and marking the stud positions, plot a single large opening for the set of windows, making it ½ inch taller than the window units and locating the sides of the opening along the inner edges of two studs. Cut along the plotted lines with a circular saw set to cut through the wallboard but not into the studs. Wear a respirator and goggles for dust protection. Pull off the wallboard, exposing the intermediate studs, and remove any insulation. Drive a nail through to the outside at each of the four corners. Snap chalk lines on the outside wall, from nail to nail, to mark the exterior cut line.

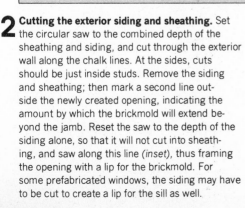

STUD
SHEATHING
WALLBOARD
SIDING

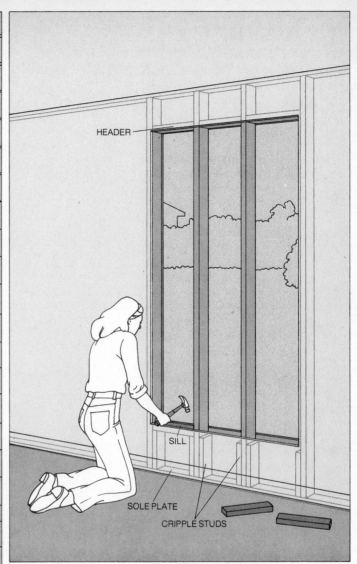

HEADER

SILL

SOLE PLATE

CRIPPLE STUDS

2 **Cutting the exterior siding and sheathing.** Set the circular saw to the combined depth of the sheathing and siding, and cut through the exterior wall along the chalk lines. At the sides, cuts should be just inside studs. Remove the siding and sheathing; then mark a second line outside the newly created opening, indicating the amount by which the brickmold will extend beyond the jamb. Reset the saw to the depth of the siding alone, so that it will not cut into sheathing, and saw along this line (*inset*), thus framing the opening with a lip for the brickmold. For some prefabricated windows, the siding may have to be cut to create a lip for the sill as well.

3 **Adding headers and rough sills.** Frame the top of the opening with 2-by-4 headers cut to fit snugly in each opening between studs, and nail them in place at each end with three tenpenny nails. Begin with the center header; then add the headers at each side, face-nailing them when possible, toenailing them when necessary. Position each header so that it is level, and align its lower edge with the cut wallboard.

Insert a ruler into the opening between the wallboard and sheathing, and measure the distance between the sole plate and the lower edge of the cut wallboard. Subtract 1½ inches from this measurement, and cut 2-by-4s to this length, two for each opening between studs. Slide the 2-by-4s, called cripple studs, into the opening between the wallboard and sheathing, and nail them to the studs. Then cut a 2-by-4 rough sill to fit snugly between each pair of full-length studs, and nail each sill to the top of two cripple studs. Be sure that each sill is level and flush with the edge of the wallboard.

4 **Cutting and installing the drip cap.** Measure the width of the opening in the siding, and cut a drip cap from prebent aluminum flashing to fit it (*right*). Pry up the edge of the siding at the top of the opening, and use a hacksaw to cut the nails holding it to the sheathing. With the nails out of the way, slide the wider edge of the drip cap up between the siding and the sheathing. Then renail the lower piece of siding through the drip cap, using galvanized nails.

5 **Adjusting the sill.** Working from the outside, tilt one of the center windows into place in its opening, resting it against temporary braces nailed across the top and bottom of the studs on the inside of the opening. If the horns of the window sill extend beyond the midpoint of the studs framing the opening, mark and trim off the excess with a fine-toothed saw. Mark and remove excess horn from all the other adjoining sills in the same way, so that the windows, when installed, will have one continuous line of sill. Then remove the temporary braces.

6 **Leveling and securing the windows.** While a helper holds the window in place on the outside, insert shims between the side jambs and studs on the inside. Then wedge shims between the sill and the bottom jamb, checking that the window is plumb and level. Fill spaces with scraps of fiberglass insulation. Then drive tenpenny finishing nails through the jambs and shims into the studs at 12-inch intervals, and add a single nail at the center of the sill and one at the center of the header. Countersink the nails and fill the holes with wood putty. Repeat for each window.

7 **Trimming the exterior.** Cut and install a section of brickmold to trim the top of the window; cut the ends square for butt joints, or miter them as in Step 8. Use a T bevel to measure and transfer the slope of the sill to the bottom edge of the two pieces of brickmold that will trim the sides of the window. Cut along the marked line, using a miter box and backsaw *(inset)*. Miter or square-cut the top of each sidepiece to fit against the top brickmold section.

Cut a trim strip of ½-inch-thick wood to cover the combined width of the stud and jambs framing each window. Bevel the bottom end of the strips to fit the slope of the sill, and attach them with fourpenny finishing nails 8 inches apart. Caulk the space between brickmold and siding and between the sill sections. Nail one strip of molding across the front edge of the sills, countersink the nails, and fill the holes with wood putty.

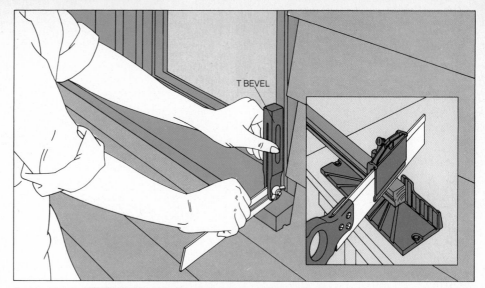

8 **Cutting the inside trim.** Select preshaped window casing to match the other trim in the room, and cut four lengths to frame the new window. Make each section long enough to span one side of the opening, plus enough for a miter at each end—usually 10 to 12 inches, depending on the casing width. Mark the distance between the two outer jambs on the inner edges of the top and bottom sections of frame, centering this measurement on each length of casing. Place a casing strip flat side down in a miter box, and cut the casing at a 45° angle outward from this mark; then do the same with the other length. Reverse the direction of the miter cut at the other end of each piece.

Cut casing for the sides in the same way, using the distance between the inner edges of the top and bottom jambs to establish the inside measurement for these two sections of frame.

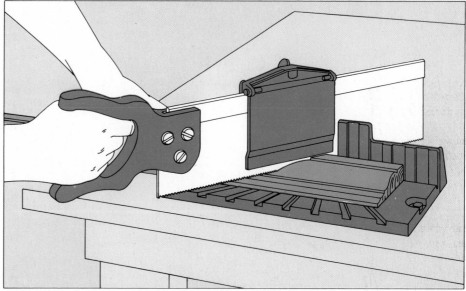

9 **Attaching the trim.** Nail the mitered sections of casing to the wall around the opening, inner edges of the casing strips flush with the inner edges of the window jambs. Use fourpenny finishing nails through the narrow part of the casing, sixpenny nails through the wide part, placing the nails 8 inches apart. Lock-nail each mitered corner with two fourpenny finishing nails—one placed vertically, the other horizontally, through the wide edges of the casing *(inset)*.

Nail a strip of wood over each intermediate stud, to make the surface flush with the window jambs. Then cover each vertical separation, including the jambs, with a strip of wood ½ inch thick. Round the ends of the strips so that they will blend into the top and bottom casings, and nail them in place with threepenny finishing nails, driven into the studs at 8-inch intervals. Countersink the nails; fill the holes with wood putty.

Lengthening an Existing Window for More Light

1 **Removing the casing.** Using a nail set, drive corner-locking nails completely through to free each mitered corner and, with a utility knife, cut through the paint at the seam between the casing and the wall. Then pry off the casing with a pry bar braced against a wooden block. If the window has an inner sill (the stool) with an apron below, pry these off, too, and set them aside for use with the new window.

On the outside wall, use a cold chisel to break the caulking seal between the brickmold and the siding. Pry off one section of brickmold to see if the window jamb is nailed to the studs. If it is, pry off all the brickmold, and fit a hacksaw into the crack between the jamb and the studs and header to cut through the nails.

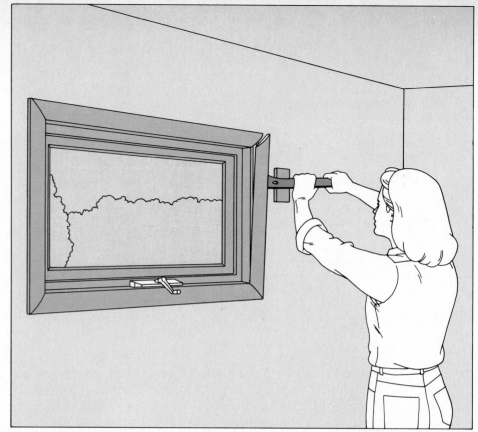

2 **Taking out the old window.** Working inside, place a wood block against one corner of the window jamb; strike it sharply with a four-pound maul to loosen the window, forcing it toward the outside. Repeat at each corner, then move outside and pry the window out of its opening. Leave the drip cap in place, but pull the cut nails out of the old frame and the studs with pliers or a nail puller.

To establish a cutting line for the new opening, measure the height of the new window from the bottom of the sill to the top of the jamb. Add 2 inches to this measurement for a new rough sill plus clearance, and draw a line from the sides of the existing opening downward to equal this amount, measuring from the bottom of the window header. Draw a level line to mark the bottom of the new hole; cut along all three lines with a circular saw as in Step 1, page 119.

Using the techniques described in Step 2, page 119, transfer the dimensions of the new opening to the outside wall. Cut both the main window opening and the inset for the brickmold.

3 **Preparing the opening.** Using a handsaw, cut off the existing cripple studs even with the bottom edge of the new opening, and cut the old rough sill in half. Pull both of these sections away from the jack studs that frame the sides of the opening. Nail a new 2-by-4 rough sill to the tops of the just-cut cripple studs, using two tenpenny nails (inset); toenail the outer ends of the sill to the jack studs with three tenpenny nails.

Lift the window into the opening from outside, and have a helper hold it in place while you adjust its position. Working inside, drive shims between the window and the rough sill and between the window and the jack studs, until the window is plumb and level. Also make sure the brickmold on the outside is flush against the sheathing and that it butts against the cut edge of the siding (page 119). When the window is in position, anchor it temporarily by driving a tenpenny nail through the top corner of the brickmold.

OLD ROUGH SILL

CRIPPLE STUDS

NEW ROUGH SILL

4 **Adding a jamb extension.** With the window snug in its opening, check to see that the inside edge of the jamb is flush with the inside wall surface. If it is not, extend the jamb by nailing on strips of ¾-inch-wide wood, cut to the necessary thickness. (Some manufacturers supply precut jamb extensions if you include the wall depth when ordering a window.) Nail the extension to the jamb, using sixpenny nails spaced at 8-inch intervals.

Fill the space between the window frame and jack studs with scraps of insulation. Then secure the window by driving tenpenny finishing nails through the jambs into the jack studs and the header, setting the nails 8 inches apart.

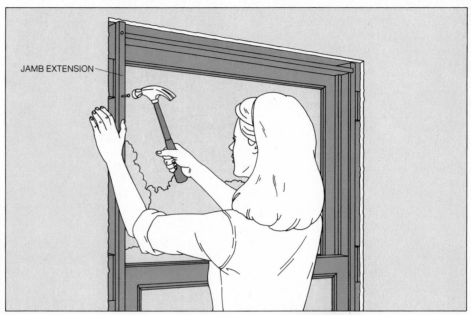

JAMB EXTENSION

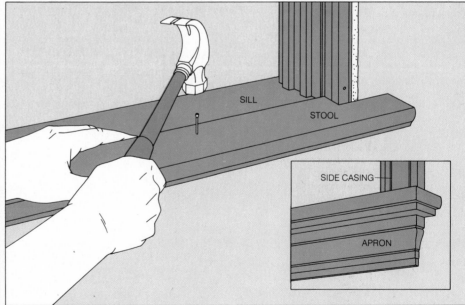

SILL

STOOL

SIDE CASING

APRON

5 **Attaching the trim.** Make a level base for the apron and stool by patching the lower edge of the opening to bring it flush with the wall. Replace the apron and stool from the original window if available, or cut new ones. Matching the other window trim in the house, cut the stool long enough that it will overlap the casing at the sides of the window. Mark and cut notches on the stool where it extends beyond the jamb. Then secure the stool to the sill with sixpenny nails, and drive eightpenny nails through the horn into the jamb and stud.

Frame the top and sides with casing as in Steps 7 and 8, page 121, but make square cuts at the bottoms of both sidepieces. Cut an apron to reach the outside edges of the sidepieces; nail it to the studs. Countersink all nails and fill the holes with wood putty. On the outside, caulk between the brickmold and the siding.

123

Extending Plumbing for Special Uses

Adapting a room for a special purpose may require the addition of plumbing or wiring to serve the special activity. Usually you can tap into existing electric and plumbing lines with a few basic tools and techniques, and in many cases no major structural work is needed. Sometimes, however, the job may be complicated by the need to cut holes through walls, floors, studs or joists. If such alterations are extensive, you may prefer to have the new line installed by a professional, reserving for yourself only the job of connecting the new fixture.

The more complicated extensions are those involving plumbing. In some localities, a plumbing system cannot be extended without a permit from local building authorities. They may require a sketch of the existing plumbing and your proposed addition—a useful planning aid even when it is not required. The plumbing inspector may be able to suggest improvements, along with specifying the size and kind of pipe required.

Whenever the local code allows it, use plastic pipe; it is inexpensive, lightweight and easily joined with quick-drying solvent cement. If your local code requires metal pipe, choose copper, which is lighter and easier to install than cast-iron or steel pipe. For copper pipe, you will need solid-wire solder, half tin and half lead, to seal the joints. If the new plumbing is being connected to a threaded fitting, you will also need an adapter. Usually this is made of the same material as the new pipe, threaded at one end to screw directly onto the fitting, with a collar at the other end for cementing or soldering onto the new pipe.

Plastic, copper and small steel pipe can be cut with a hacksaw; use a miter box for loose pipe to ensure a precise cut. After cutting plastic pipe, remove any frayed plastic with a knife, and bevel the outside of the cut for ease in joining one section to another. Use a file to remove burrs from the cut end of copper pipe. Cutting into cast-iron or steel drainpipe usually requires an appropriate pipe cutter, available from tool-rental companies.

All plumbing lines, whether for water supply or for drainage, take the same basic installation techniques. But drain lines require greater precision in the placing of pipes because waste water is not under pressure and is only gravity-propelled.

All horizontal drainage runs must slope at an angle of ¼ inch per foot; downward runs must be within 45° of vertical. In addition, each inlet into the drain system must be sealed with a trap—a U-shaped section of pipe that fills with water to keep sewer gases from escaping into the house. Each trap must be vented just past this water seal to prevent the water in the trap from being siphoned out by movement of water and waste elsewhere in the system. Usually, the vent is a pipe leading upward, joined eventually to a larger open-ended pipe protruding through the roof. Where such a vent is difficult to install, your plumbing inspector may allow you to substitute an automatic venting device (page 127).

To find a drainpipe suitable for tapping, look for a pipe at least 2 inches in diameter, running down from a trap. If no trap is visible and you find two virtually identical vertical pipes, side by side, either of which may be a drain, try running the hot water at a nearby fixture. The pipe that gets warm to the touch is the drain; the other is a vent pipe.

When connecting into an existing line, remember that drainpipe dimensions differ, depending on their use, and that the existing line must be larger than the proposed extension unless an inspector says otherwise. A washing-machine standpipe drain, which works best if made of 2-inch (inner diameter) pipe, should feed into a 3- to 4-inch line; a sink, which needs only 1½-inch pipe, can feed into a drain 2 inches in diameter.

To fasten runs of new pipe directly to framing members or walls, use rigid pipe straps in the appropriate size, placing them 4 to 8 feet apart. To fasten the sloping horizontal runs of drainpipe underneath joists, use flexible iron straps, perforated at ½-inch intervals for nailing; space them about 3 or 4 feet apart.

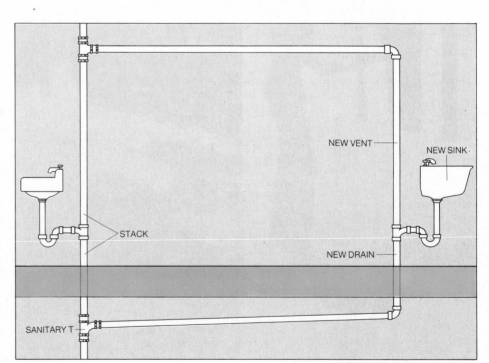

A simple branch drain. In this typical branch line for a new plumbing fixture, a new horizontal drainpipe slopes upward from an existing vertical drain—a stack—that functions as both drain and vent. The new drainpipe is joined to the stack (at a point below the highest existing drain inlet) by a fitting called a sanitary T, which has a curved throat to steer waste water down into the stack. An elbow fitting carries the branch line up to a second sanitary T, which connects to a trap under the new fixture. A new vent pipe, joined to the top of this second T fitting, returns the line to the stack, meeting it at a point above the highest existing drain inlet.

Joining Plastic or Copper Pipe

Cementing a plastic joint. After you dry-fit the parts for the entire branch line, mark each joint for later alignment by scratching a line across the pipe and its elbow or T fitting. Then disassemble each joint, one by one, and spread a layer of solvent cement inside the collar of the fitting and around the beveled end of the pipe. Press the parts together, twisting the joint to spread the cement, and line up the scratched alignment marks. Do not put pressure on the joint until the cement has dried for at least an hour.

Soldering a copper joint. First dry-fit the parts for the entire branch line; then disassemble the parts at each fitting, one at a time, and burnish the end of each piece of pipe and the inside ends of every fitting with emery cloth. Wearing rubber dishwashing gloves to keep the irritating flux off your hands, brush noncorrosive solder flux onto the end of the pipe and the inside of the fitting. Then reassemble the parts, twisting the pieces so that the flux will be distributed over the surfaces to be joined.

Direct the flame of a propane torch onto the joint until the copper pipe is hot enough to melt the tip of a length of wire solder held against it. Withdraw the flame, and feed the solder into the joint. When the solder circles the entire joint and begins to drip, withdraw it. Allow the solder to harden before proceeding to the next joint. If you are using the propane torch near flammable material during the soldering operation, be sure that you protect the material from the torch flame with an asbestos shield.

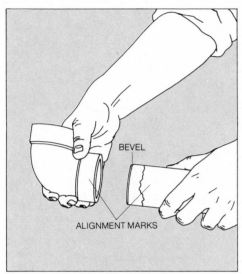

BEVEL

ALIGNMENT MARKS

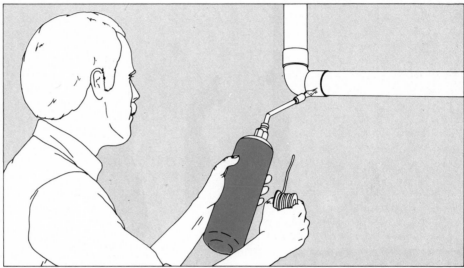

Installing a Branch Drain

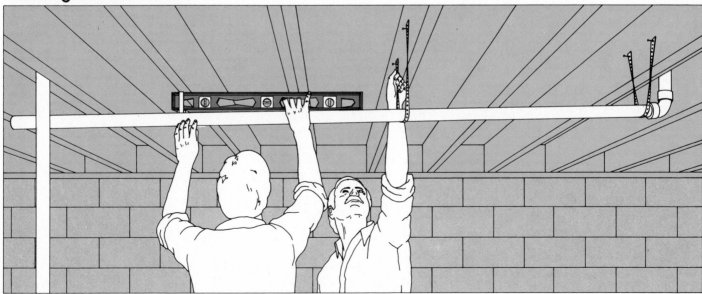

1 Positioning the new line. Using rigid pipe straps for vertical runs and flexible pipe straps for horizontal runs, attach the new drainpipe to wall surfaces and ceiling joists, beginning at the new fixture and working toward the existing drain.

Be sure to establish a downward slope of ¼ inch per foot on all horizontal runs. To get the correct slope, use a carpenter's level with a shim taped to one end to lift the level ¼ inch per foot. For instance, a 2-foot level needs a ½-inch

shim. When you reach the existing drain, hold the connecting, hubless-style, cast-iron sanitary T fitting against the drain so that the T's curved throat lines up with the new branch; mark the positions of the T ends on the existing drain.

2 **Cutting into a cast-iron or steel drain.** To remove a section of existing drainpipe to make room for the sanitary T fitting, cut the pipe ¼ inch outside each of the two marks that you made in Step 1. When cutting such a section from a vertical pipe, support the upper part of the pipe temporarily by bolting a two-part stack clamp

(inset) around the pipe as near the ceiling as possible; rest the arms of the clamp on two 2-by-4s wedged and nailed between the joists. If the pipe is cast iron, which is heavier and less self-supporting than steel, provide additional support by wedging two longer 2-by-4s between the floor and the short 2-by-4s at the ceiling.

Tapping into Copper or Plastic Pipe

Adding fittings for a sanitary T. To join a branch line to an existing plastic or copper drain, mark the position for a plastic or copper sanitary T as in Step 1, page 125, but cut the drainpipe 3 inches past these marks, removing a pipe section 6 inches longer than the length of the T. From the removed pipe cut two shorter sections, each one slightly less than 3 inches long plus the depth of the T's collar—which varies with the diameter of the T. Cement or solder these

short lengths of pipe into the ends of the T. On plastic pipe, join the extended T to the existing drain with neoprene sleeves and metal clamps as in Step 3, below. On copper pipe, burnish the cut ends of the drain, the ends of the T extensions and the interior of two copper slip rings, then apply flux to all these surfaces. Slip a ring over each drain end, place the T assembly between them, and slide the rings over the joints between T and drainpipe; solder all the joints.

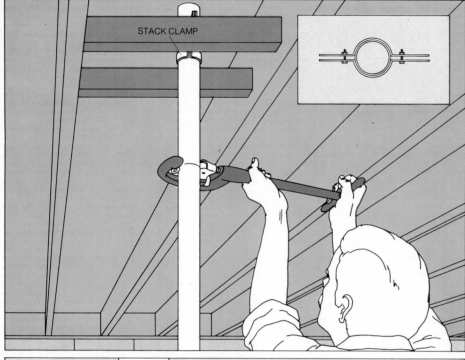

STACK CLAMP

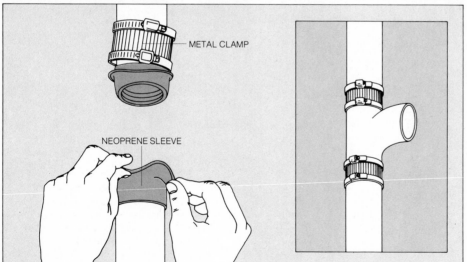

METAL CLAMP

NEOPRENE SLEEVE

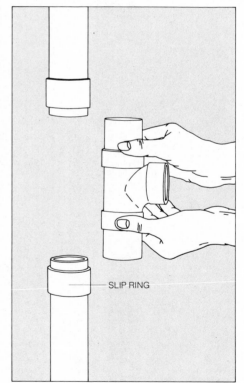

SLIP RING

3 **Inserting the sanitary T.** Fit the neoprene sleeves of two hubless pipes clamps over the cut ends of the cast-iron or steel drainpipe. Then slide a metal clamp over each of the sleeves, and fold the free end of each sleeve back over the end of the pipe. Put the sanitary T fitting in place between the pipe ends, and then unfold the sleeves over the ends of the fitting. Center the metal clamps over the sleeves *(inset)*, and tighten the screws of the clamps.

Cut a plastic branch line to end ¼ inch short of the T, and connect pipe and T with a neoprene sleeve and metal clamp, as above. To join a branch line of copper to the sanitary T, use a cast-iron T with a female-threaded opening and turn a male-threaded copper adapter into it, sealing the two by wrapping the male adapter threads with pipe-joint tape before screwing the adapter and the T together. Then cut the copper pipe and solder it to the copper adapter.

Completing the Branch Drain

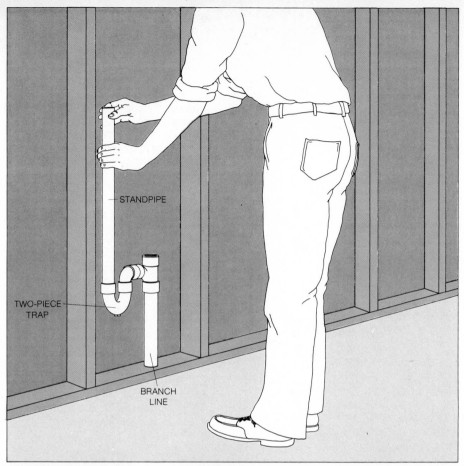

STANDPIPE

TWO-PIECE
TRAP

BRANCH
LINE

1 Adding a trap and standpipe. At the fixture
end of the branch line, install a second sanitary T.
Position the T so that its curved inlet is 6 to 18
inches above the floor, depending on what is convenient. Connect a two-piece trap to the T's
curved inlet with a very short piece of pipe, then
join a length of vertical pipe to the inlet of the
trap, to form a standpipe. Make this pipe 18 to 30
inches high and, for a washing machine, tall
enough to stand 2 to 6 inches above the machine.

For a plumbing connection station, the piece of
pipe between the sanitary T and the trap must
be long enough to position the standpipe under
the drain hole of the station. Be sure to slope
this pipe downward from trap to T, ¼ inch per
foot, and do not extend the run more than
4½ feet, to prevent siphoning of the trap. If the
station is mounted between studs, route the
pipe through holes drilled in intervening studs.

Similarly, you must extend a horizontal pipe from
the sanitary T to receive waste water from the
trap of a new sink or laundry tub. In such a situa-
tion, you can make the horizontal pipe protrude from the wall either by turning the sanitary
T so that the opening points outward or by inserting an elbow in the pipe after it has traveled
along the wall to the fixture location.

VENTING
DEVICE

STANDPIPE

2 Venting the line. To vent a new drain line
through an automatic venting device, screw the
device into a female-threaded adapter, then
join the adapter to the top of an extension pipe
leading up from the top of the second sanitary
T. Make this extension pipe at least 4 inches long
and, preferably, 2 to 6 inches higher than a
standpipe or the top of a fixture such as a sink. Do
not seal the automatic vent inside the wall, since
it may eventually need servicing or replacing.

To vent a new line through the existing stack
going through the roof, use the same procedures
as in tapping into the existing drain, but reverse directions. Install a sanitary T with its curved
inlet facing up instead of down, or use a standard T fitting without a curved inlet. Slope the
horizontal runs upward to meet the existing
vent pipe, ¼ inch per foot.

Extending Water Supply Lines

Hot- and cold-water lines are extended in much the same way as drains are, but the job is simpler. Supply pipes and fittings are smaller and therefore easier to handle and, since the water supply is pressure-fed, the slope of the pipes is unimportant.

New supply lines can be routed directly to a new fixture or to a plumbing connection station, which can be either surface-mounted or recessed in the wall. The station has a large hole for the standpipe drain and two smaller ones for the hot- and cold-water lines; these two lines should preferably be connected to a lever valve so that the water in both pipes can be shut off simultaneously.

As with drain lines, use plastic pipe for new supply lines wherever building codes permit; otherwise, use copper pipe. For hot-water lines, plastic pipe must be rated for hot-water use, indicated by markings on the pipe. Use pipe with a ½-inch inner diameter for the new run, but if you tap into a ¾-inch line you will ensure that none of the fixtures

along the line will be starved for water.

Because supply lines are lighter than drain lines, you do not need to brace them when you cut into them. But before you cut a line, be sure to turn off the inlet valve on your hot-water heater in addition to shutting off the main water-supply valve for the house. Then open all fixture taps in the system to drain the pipes. After cutting into a horizontal pipe, pull it downward gently to help drain any water that remains inside.

Join pipes and fittings using the techniques described on pages 124-125, dry-fitting them before making the final cement or solder connections. Tap into an existing supply line with a ¾-inch-to-½-inch reducing T fitting, so called because the side opening is only ½ inch and the openings at each end are ¾ inch. When you join threaded pipes and fittings, wrap the threads with pipe-joint tape to lubricate and seal the joint, and to allow easy disassembly. Support new runs of pipe, both vertical and horizontal, with rigid pipe straps about 4 feet apart.

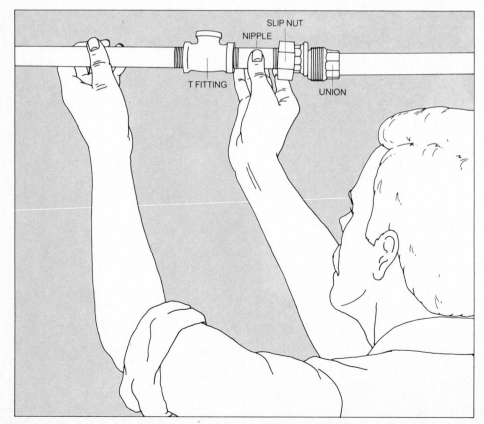

SLIP NUT

NIPPLE

T FITTING

UNION

Tapping into a supply line. If the existing line is a threaded steel pipe, cut into the pipe at the point where you want to insert a ¾-inch-to-½-inch reducing T fitting, then unscrew the two cut sections from the nearest joints. Then screw a pipe nipple and a union fitting into one arm of a threaded T, and measure the length of this assembly. Subtract ¾ inch from this length, and shorten one of the cut sections of pipe by this amount. Then have a hardware or plumbing-supply dealer thread the two cut ends.

Screw the two pipe sections back into the supply line. Remove the male-threaded part of the union from the T assembly, and attach it to one of the free ends of the supply pipe, then screw the rest of the T assembly onto the other free end. Tighten the union slip nut over the male-threaded part of the union to complete the joint, and fit a ½-inch threaded adapter into the side opening of the T to make the transition to either plastic or copper pipe.

If the existing supply line is copper or plastic, cut away enough pipe to accommodate a ¾-inch-to-½-inch reducing T fitting, and solder or cement the fitting onto the cut ends of the pipe.

Installing a Plumbing Connection Station

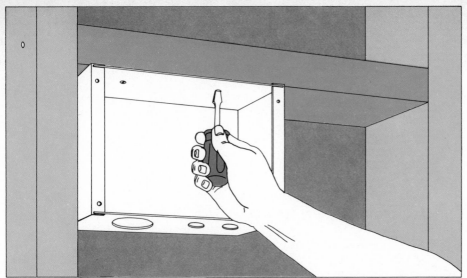

1 **Mounting the box.** Nail a supporting header between two studs (*page 115*), and then screw the connection-station box to the header. Position the box so that its drain hole will be directly above the trap outlet for the standpipe. If the wall surface is to be finished, you must also make sure that the front edge of the connection-station box will be flush with the finished wall.

VALVE ADAPTER
45° ELBOW
NIPPLE
VALVE MOUNT
LEVER VALVE
VALVE ADAPTER

2 **Mounting the valve.** Remove the adapter from one arm of a lever valve (*inset*), and screw it into a 45° elbow. Screw a threaded nipple into the other end of the elbow, and join the nipple to the valve mount supplied with the connection station. Slip this assembly into one of the small holes in the bottom of the box, and add a rubber washer, a lock washer and a nut. Assemble an identical valve connection in the other small hole. Then screw the lever valve to these adapters, and fasten the unit in place by tightening the nuts against the lock washers.

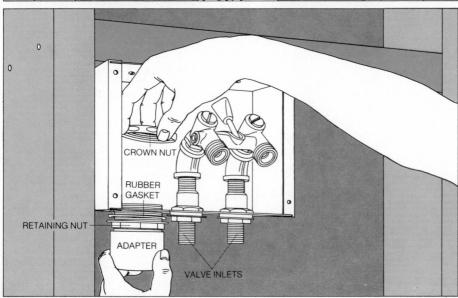

CROWN NUT
RUBBER GASKET
RETAINING NUT
ADAPTER
VALVE INLETS

3 **Connecting the pipes.** To connect a standpipe, slip a rubber gasket and a retaining nut onto one end of a male-threaded copper or plastic pipe adapter, and insert the adapter up through the large hole in the bottom of the station box. Screw a crown nut onto the top of the adapter, and tighten the retaining nut against the underside of the box. Cut a standpipe to fit between the bottom of the adapter and the inlet of the drain trap below. Cement or solder the standpipe to the adapter and to the trap (*page 127*).

To connect the supply lines, run pipes to the valve inlets, connecting them with either copper or plastic female-threaded pipe adapters or, if you are working on copper pipe, with solder; some models of connection stations have recessed inlets that allow copper pipe to be soldered directly onto the valve fitting.

Adding New Electrical Circuits

New wiring for an area devoted to a special activity can be extended from an existing circuit, or it can be a new circuit originating at the main service panel of the house. Which you use depends on how much electricity the new activity will require and on how heavily the existing circuit is used. If the additional load is not great—a few lighting fixtures, for example—you can probably extend an existing circuit by adding a new outlet.

If the added load will be heavy, however, such as that needed to operate a photographic print dryer, the cable for the new circuit should run back to the main panel; unless you are an expert, have an electrician make the connection at the panel. Follow the same course for a moderate load that might overtax an already much-used circuit and for devices that need 240-volt current rather than the standard 120-volt, such as an electric kiln or a clothes dryer. If you are moving an existing clothes dryer to a new place, however, it is not always necessary to install a new circuit; sometimes you can simply move the existing 240-volt receptacle to a new location and extend that circuit to reach it.

Whatever approach you choose, make sure your plans for any new circuit meet local code requirements. For most such installations, you will probably be permitted to use flexible plastic-sheathed cable containing two insulated copper wires and one bare ground wire. The wire size will be dictated by the current the circuit will carry—No. 14 wire for 15-ampere capacity, No. 12 wire for 20-ampere, No. 10 wire for 30-ampere, No. 8 wire for 50-ampere. If the new line extends an existing circuit, the wire size should match the ampere rating printed on the circuit breaker or fuse at the main panel. On a 240-volt breaker, the amperage may appear twice; do not add the numbers to determine the breaker rating.

To minimize cutting into finished walls and ceilings, route new cable through attic or basement access holes drilled into the wall cavities where the new and existing outlet boxes are located. Feed one end of the new cable into the cavity to be occupied by the new box, pulling it out of the wall through a hole drilled next to the stud at the site of the new

box. Feed the other end of the new cable into the cavity occupied by the existing box, enlarging the opening at that box just enough so that you can reach in to clamp the cable into the box.

After the circuit is wired, you can patch the hole or hide it by covering the box with an oversized faceplate. Wherever the new cable runs along an exposed stud or beam, anchor it with cable staples at 4-foot intervals; if possible, anchor the cable within 1 foot of each outlet box.

Extending a 120-Volt Circuit

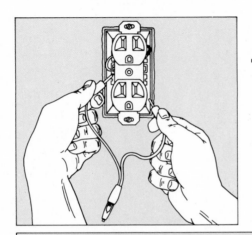

1 **Cutting off the power.** Shut off the circuit leading to the outlet you intend to tap, either by removing the fuse for that circuit from the main panel or by switching its circuit breaker to OFF. To verify that the power is off, remove the outlet cover and touch the probes of a neon-bulb voltage tester to all possible combinations of wires, terminals and metal parts of the outlet box. If the tester bulb does not glow, the current is off and it is safe to continue.

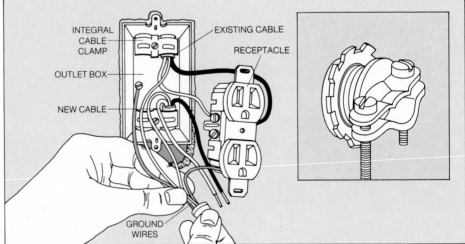

INTEGRAL CABLE CLAMP

EXISTING CABLE

OUTLET BOX

RECEPTACLE

NEW CABLE

GROUND WIRES

2 **Connecting the new cable.** Remove the receptacle from the outlet box, and thread about 8 inches of new cable into the box through a knockout hole, fastening the cable in place with the integral cable clamp inside. Or use a separate ½-inch cable clamp (*inset*), attaching it to the cable, then to the box. Strip the sheathing from the cable in the box, and strip ¾ inch of insulation from the black and white wires. Connect the bare ground wire to the wire cap containing the existing bare and green ground

wires; if there is no cap, attach the new ground wire to the box with a self-tapping screw.

Fasten the new white wire to an unused silver terminal on the receptacle, the new black wire to an unused brass terminal. If all the terminals on the receptacle are already in use, substitute a receptacle like the one shown in Step 3, and attach the new black and white wires to the appropriately marked push terminals located on the back of the receptacle.

3 **Adding a new outlet.** Thread the new cable inside the finished wall and bring it out through a hole made next to a stud where you intend to install a new outlet box. Clamp 8 inches of cable inside the box as in Step 2, then nail the box to the stud. Strip the sheathing from the 8 inches of cable and use a wire cap to fasten the bare ground wire to two green jumper wires at the new outlet, one attached to a screw on the box, the second to a green screw on the receptacle. (In Canada, loop the bare ground wire around a screw, leaving a 5-inch end, and fasten the screw to the box; then attach the end of the wire to the green grounding screw on the receptacle.)

Strip insulation from the white and black wires, using the stripping gauge on the back of a push-terminal-type receptacle as a guide to the amount required. Slip the white wire into the push-terminal opening marked "white" and the black wire into the unmarked terminal.

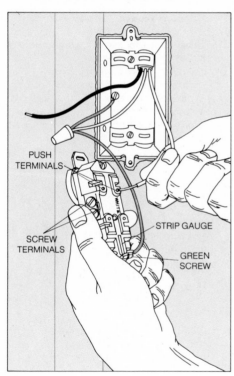

PUSH TERMINALS

SCREW TERMINALS

STRIP GAUGE

GREEN SCREW

Installing a 240-Volt Circuit

1 **Moving an existing receptacle.** Turn off the power to the receptacle that you want to move, testing it as in Step 1, opposite, to make sure that it is off; remove the receptacle from its outlet box. Disconnect all of its wires. Fasten the new cable to the outlet box with a ¾-inch cable clamp. Using a wire cap, join the bare ground wires of the new and old cables to each other and to a green jumper wire screwed to the box. (In Canada, simply screw each bare ground wire directly to the box.) Join the white wires to each other with a wire cap, marking both of them with black tape or paint to indicate that these wires are current-carrying and not neutral. Then join the two black

wires together in the same way. Cover the box with a blank faceplate.

If the existing receptacle is a plastic-bodied surface-mounted unit, replace it with an outlet box that has knockouts large enough for ¾-inch cable clamps. Clamp the new and old cables into the box, and connect the wires as for a recessed box. If the old cable has four conductors, use four-wire cable for the extension and make the ground-wire connections as described. Then connect the white, black and red wires of the old cable to the like-colored wires of the new, but do not mark the white wires with black, since they remain neutral.

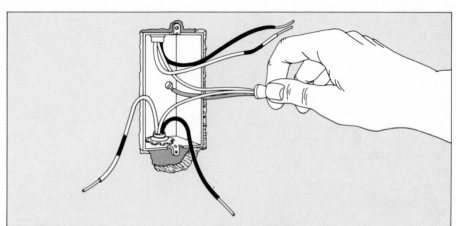

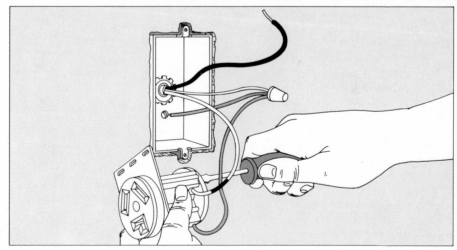

2 **Reconnecting the receptacle.** Route the new cable from the old outlet box or from the main panel, as described opposite. Attach the cable to a new outlet box with large knock-outs, installed in or on the wall; or, if desired, use a plastic-bodied surface-mounted receptacle. Connect the bare ground wire of the cable to two green ground wires, one screwed to the box, the other to a terminal on the receptacle marked "green" or "ground" or colored silver. (In Canada, loop the ground wire

around a screw on the box, and connect the end of the wire to the appropriate receptacle terminal.) Attach the two remaining wires to the brass-colored terminals, and mark the white wire with black tape or paint.

If the new cable has four wires, attach the bare wire directly to the box, and the white wire—unmarked—to the silver terminal of the receptacle. Then fasten the remaining red and black wires to the two brass-colored terminals.

Adding to the Artificial Light

Carefully planned artificial lighting is essential to many special purpose rooms, either for close work or for shadow-free overall illumination where natural lighting is insufficient. For broad, uniform light, energy-efficient overhead fluorescent fixtures are ideal—a single 4-foot fluorescent fixture with two 40-watt bulbs will generally light an area of 8 by 10 feet. For focused light, incandescent bulbs in track fixtures can be aimed to provide more direct illumination of a particular area.

The steps involved in installing any new fixture depend largely on the existing wiring. Most houses built before the mid-1950s already have an overhead fixture in each room. You can replace this fixture with a more appropriate one. Or you can replace it with several fixtures by running lengths of surface wiring, called raceway, from the ceiling box to new fixture locations.

In houses built after the 1950s, ceiling fixtures are rare. The light switch near the door of each room generally controls a lamp plugged into a wall receptacle. To install ceiling fixtures in such rooms, you can run raceway up the wall from the receptacle to one or more surface-mounted fixtures.

Most electrical stores carry all hardware you will need to mount fluorescent and track fixtures as well as to adapt existing ceiling and wall boxes for raceway. Before going to the store, determine exactly what hardware a specific installation may require. And before starting any wiring job, cut off the power to the circuits involved, as described on page 130.

Replacing an Existing Ceiling Fixture

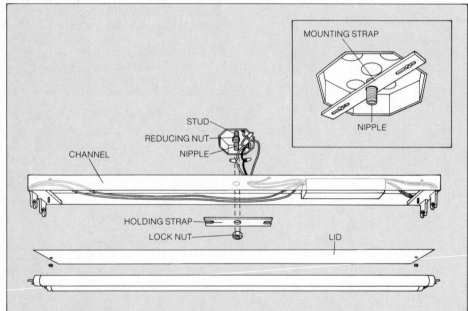

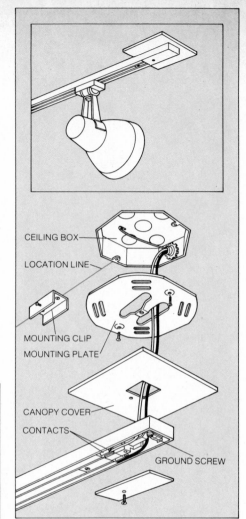

Installing a track light. After turning off the power to the circuit and exposing the ceiling box, install a prewired channel for track lighting in the sequence, from top to bottom, shown above. Pass the house wires through the mounting plate, and screw the plate to the tabs of the ceiling box. Snap a chalkline from the plate's center hole to mark the channel location, and screw mounting clips along this line at 3-foot intervals.

Remove the top and bottom covers from the live end of the channel—the end with the wiring contacts—and replace the top cover with the canopy cover, screwing it over the live end. Push the black and white house wires through the openings in the live end, and snap the channel onto its mounting clips. Tighten the ground screw in the live end into the center hole of the mounting plate. Then tighten the side screws in the mounting clips against the channel sides.

Strip the ends of the house wires to form leads, and fit each into its labeled contact. Finally, replace the bottom cover over the live end of the channel, and snap light fixtures into the channel *(inset)*, positioning them as desired.

Installing a fluorescent fixture. After shutting off the power to the circuit, remove the existing fixture and examine the ceiling box. If it contains a threaded metal stud, as here, add a 2-inch-long threaded extension, called a nipple, and join the two with a reducing nut. Remove the lid of the new fixture, to expose the channel. Screw a copper ground wire to the channel, then pull it and the fixture's black and white wires through one of the center cutouts on the back of the channel. Use wire caps to join each wire to one of the same color in the ceiling box. Finally, ground the ceiling box with a jumper ground wire from it to the other ground wires. Position the channel under the ceiling box so that the nipple protrudes through another center cutout. Slip a holding strap over the nipple and tighten a lock nut against it. To secure the fixture further, drive a toggle bolt into the ceiling through a mounting hole at each end of the channel. If the ceiling box does not have a metal stud *(inset)*, attach a special mounting strap with a threaded center hole, driving screws through the ends of the strap into tabs on the edge of the box. Then screw a nipple into the center hole of the strap, and mount the fixture.

Attaching Many Fixtures to a Single Box

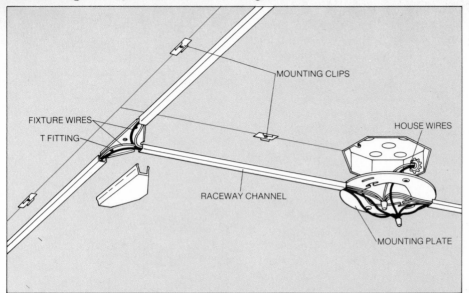

MOUNTING CLIPS

FIXTURE WIRES

T FITTING

HOUSE WIRES

RACEWAY CHANNEL

MOUNTING PLATE

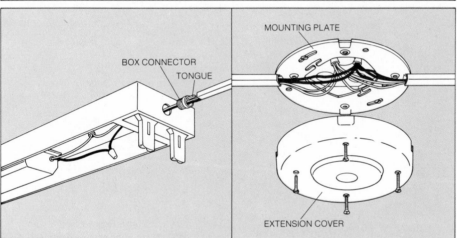

MOUNTING PLATE

BOX CONNECTOR

TONGUE

EXTENSION COVER

Extending a Wall Receptacle to Power Ceiling Fixtures

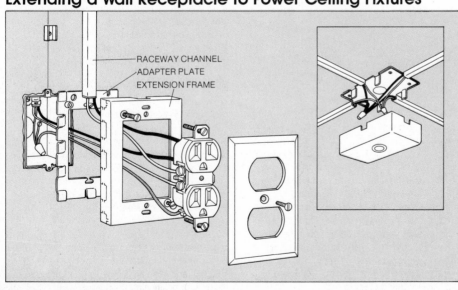

RACEWAY CHANNEL
ADAPTER PLATE
EXTENSION FRAME

1 Running raceway from a ceiling box. After turning off the power to the circuit and removing the existing ceiling fixture, install raceway in the sequence shown in this exploded view. Screw a mounting plate for a raceway ceiling extension over the existing box, and bring the house wires through the center hole in the plate. Cut lengths of No. 14 black and white TW wires, 2 feet longer than the raceway run, for each new fixture you plan to install. Using the tongues on the mounting plate as starting points, map out paths for the raceway to each new fixture location. Attach raceway mounting clips to the ceiling at 4-foot intervals along each path, adding the bases for any T or elbow fittings required for turns or intersections in the paths. Cut sections of raceway channel to fit each run, and thread wires through them. Slide each channel over a tongue on the mounting plate and into its mounting clips. Then snap the T cover and the elbow cover over their bases.

2 Installing fixtures and the box cover. Mount a fluorescent channel at each new fixture location, positioning the channel so that the end meets the end of the raceway run *(far left)*. Push a box connector into the knockout hole of each channel, add a lock nut, and bring the raceway wires through the connector into the channel, sliding the raceway onto the tongue of the connector. Connect the raceway wires to the fixture wires—black to black and white to white. At the ceiling box, connect the appropriate raceway wires to the house wires.

When all the fixtures are installed, use pliers to twist out knockouts in the extension cover so that the cover will fit over the ceiling box, with the raceway radiating from it *(near left)*. Screw the extension cover over the mounting plate.

Making raceway connections. In a room without a ceiling box, run raceway wiring from the new ceiling fixtures to a wall receptacle, routing it down the wall as described in Step 1, above. Turn off power to the receptacle, remove the cover and pull the receptacle out of its box. Slip a raceway adapter plate for a wall box over the receptacle and its wires. Then slip the raceway channel onto a tongue on the adapter plate. Remove the matching knockout on the adapter's extension frame, and slip the frame over the adapter plate. Screw both to the wall box.

Connect the black wire on the raceway to the brass terminal on the receptacle and the white wire to the silver terminal. Screw the receptacle to the extension frame, adapter plate and wall box. When only one fixture is being installed, connect the raceway at the fixture. If several fixtures are being installed, connect the raceways at a junction box *(inset)* on the ceiling.

Picture Credits

The sources for the illustrations in this book are shown below. The drawings were created by Jack Arthur, Laszlo Bodrogi, Roger Essley, Charles Forsythe, Dick Lee, John Martinez, Joan McGurren and W. F. McWilliam. Credits for the illustrations from left to right are separated by semicolons, from top to bottom by dashes.

Cover: Fil Hunter. 6: Fil Hunter. 8-15: Frederic F. Bigio from B-C Graphics. 17: James Anderson. 18, 19: Jody Ann Brown. 20, 21: Frederic F. Bigio from B-C Graphics. 23-27: Elsie J. Hennig. 28-33: William J. Hennessy. 35-41: Walter Hilmers Jr. from HJ Commercial Art. 42: Fil Hunter. 44-49: Walter Hilmers Jr. from HJ Commercial Art. 50-55: Eduino J. Pereira. 57-63: John Massey. 64-71: Frederic F. Bigio from B-C Graphics. 72-75: Snowden Associates, Inc. 76-79: Elsie J. Hennig. 80: James T. Tkatch, courtesy Thomas Jefferson Memorial Foundation. 82, 83: Armen Kachaturian, designed by Bruce Bierman; Elliot Fine, designed by Robert D. Martin, Donghia/Martin Associates—Robert Lautman, designed by Charles Turgeon. 84: Robert Lautman, designed by Elizabeth Stevens—Mark Ross, designed by Kevin Walz. 85: Mark Ross, designed by Thomas L. Foerderer. 86: Norman McGrath, John M. Johansen, Johansen & Bhavnani Architects—Michael Boys, courtesy Susan Griggs Agency, London, England, Eduardo Longo, architect. 87: Carla de Benedetti, Milan, Italy, I. Phillips, architect. 88: Fil Hunter. 90-93: Forte, Inc. 94-101: John Massey. 102-109: Frederic F. Bigio from B-C Graphics. 110: Fil Hunter. 112-117: Gerry Gallagher. 118-123: William J. Hennessy. 124-131: Walter Hilmers Jr. from HJ Commercial Art. 132, 133: Frederic F. Bigio from B-C Graphics.

Acknowledgments

The index/glossary for this book was prepared by Louise Hedberg. The editors also wish to thank the following: Henry Barrow, Glen Echo Park, Glen Echo, Md.; Linda Beeman, Washington, D.C.; Els Benjamin, Brookside Gardens, Wheaton, Md.; Guido Bini, Milan, Italy; Emmett Bright, Rome, Italy; Jerry Butcher, Arlington Career Center, Arlington, Va.; Steve Butcher, Springfield, Va.; Charles Campbell, Virginia Roofing Corp., Alexandria, Va.; Charles Crocker, Fairfax, Va.; Ronald V. Croy, Bethesda, Md.; Lawrence R. England Jr., L. R. England and Son, Winchester, Mass.; Bob Fisher, Projectapix Ltd., New York, N.Y.; Philip Gibson, Arlington, Va.; Lucia Goodwin, Charles L. Granquist, Thomas Jefferson Memorial Foundation, Charlottesville, Va.; Jo Dee Gonzales, Reginald Wolfe Interiors, Inc., Washington, D.C.; Guy L. Gray, Nancy Herndon, Guy Gray Manufacturing Co., Inc., Paducah, Ky.; Gregory Green, Alpha Construction & Maintenance, Inc., Vienna, Va.; Indoor Light Gardening Society of America, Inc., New York, N.Y.; Betsey Johnson, New York, N.Y.; William Kerins, Kerins Photographic, Temple Hills, Md.; Juan Montoya, New York, N.Y.; National Aquarium, Washington, D.C.; Frank and Fern Perka, Alexandria, Va.; Ilse Pfahl, Schöner Wohnen, Gruner & Jahr, Hamburg, West Germany; Kathi Radford, Marlene Radford, National Petland, Alexandria, Va.; Hank Savelberg, Heinrich Savelberg, Inc., Woodstock, Vt.; Francis Simmons, Bethesda, Md.; Danny J. Smith, Arlington Career Center, Arlington, Va.; David Thompson, Thompson-Eiden Construction Company, Inc., Oakton, Va.; Joe Weatherly, Falls Church, Va. The editors also wish to express their appreciation to Rachel Cox and Susan Perry, writers, for their assistance with the preparation of this book.

Index/Glossary